Unearthing
Forgotten Values

Unearthing Forgotten Values

Toward a Meaningful Archaeological Practice

SEAN P. CONNAUGHTON

© 2025 Purich Books, an imprint of UBC Press

All rights reserved. No part of this publication may be reproduced, stored in a retrieval system, or transmitted, in any form or by any means, without prior written permission of the publisher, or, in Canada, in the case of photocopying or other reprographic copying, a licence from Access Copyright, www.accesscopyright.ca.

Printed in Canada on FSC-certified ancient-forest-free paper (100% post-consumer recycled) that is processed chlorine- and acid-free.

UBC Press is a Benetech Global Certified Accessible™ publisher. The epub version of this book meets stringent accessibility standards, ensuring it is available to people with diverse needs.

Library and Archives Canada Cataloguing in Publication

Title: Unearthing forgotten values : toward a meaningful archaeological practice / Sean P. Connaughton.
Names: Connaughton, Sean P., author
Description: Includes bibliographical references and index.
Identifiers: Canadiana (print) 20250111438 | Canadiana (ebook) 20250111489
  | ISBN 9780774881043 (hardcover) | ISBN 9780774881050 (softcover)
  | ISBN 9780774881067 (PDF) | ISBN 9780774881074 (EPUB)
Subjects: LCSH: Archaeology—Moral and ethical aspects—British Columbia.
  | LCSH: Indigenous peoples—British Columbia—Antiquities. | LCSH: Cultural property—British Columbia. | LCSH: Cultural property—Protection—British Columbia. | LCSH: Salvage archaeology—British Columbia. | LCSH: Community archaeology—British Columbia.
Classification: LCC E78.B9 C66 2025 | DDC 971.1004/97009009—dc23

UBC Press gratefully acknowledges the financial support for our publishing program of the Government of Canada, the Canada Council for the Arts, and the British Columbia Arts Council.

UBC Press is situated on the traditional, ancestral, and unceded territory of the xʷməθkʷəy̓əm (Musqueam) people. This land has always been a place of learning for the xʷməθkʷəy̓əm, who have passed on their culture, history, and traditions for millennia, from one generation to the next.

Purich Books, an imprint of UBC Press
The University of British Columbia
www.purichbooks.ca

For Braedy and Johnny – may you experience kindness along your respective paths, may hope endure in your hearts, and may you contribute to a gentler world long after I am gone.

The real truth about it is, we're all supposed to try
– Songs: Ohia, "Farewell Transmission"

Contents

List of Illustrations / viii
Preface / ix
Acknowledgments / xiii
Introduction / 3

1 Birth of an Anthropologist / 17
2 Working in CRM, a Cautionary Tale / 35
3 Industrial Archaeology / 61
4 Indigenous Rights / 89
5 A Matter of Values / 115
6 Reimagining Archaeology / 141

Conclusion / 179
Notes / 189
References / 200
Index / 218

Illustrations

1.1 Map of towns and archaeological site in the southeastern United States / 19
1.2 Map of Fiji and Tonga / 22
1.3 Author holding an ugavule, also known as a coconut crab, alongside Sepeti Matararaba on Aiwa Levu, 2002 / 30
2.1 Map of Papua New Guinea and villages central to archaeology for the PNG LNG Project / 37
2.2 At the archaeological site Tanamu 1 in December 2009 / 43
2.3 Tedy Tolana, the author, Lahui Morea, Menson Menson, and Iava Homoka at the archaeological site Tanamu 1, March 2010 / 49
3.1 Current system of CRM in British Columbia, encapsulated within colonial and capitalistic frameworks and values / 68
3.2 The archaeological self and entities that influence CRM in British Columbia / 77
5.1 Map of British Columbia / 129
5.2 Harold Glendale Jr. and the author in Glendale Cove, Knight Inlet, British Columbia, August 2020 / 133
6.1 A framework for centring Indigenous heritage within CRM / 176

Preface

Sometimes, when the opportunity presents itself, I teach nights in the Department of Anthropology at a small university in British Columbia. The rest of my time is spent as an archaeological consultant working in cultural resource management (CRM). CRM is an industry built on managing and supposedly protecting Indigenous heritage through a process in which archaeologists and (ideally) Indigenous community members assess an area for archaeological potential ahead of any ground-disturbing activity – residential and commercial construction, municipal infrastructure projects, and development-driven energy projects, for example. For me, consulting on CRM projects isn't easy. Working in a context that prioritizes "getting the job done" over solid research and meaningful results challenges my sense of professional self-worth. The constraints imposed by tight schedules and the desire to minimize costs leave me little room to draw on my knowledge and skills, which begin to seem almost irrelevant to the work. This is frustrating: I didn't spend years in school learning how to do a shoddy job. But, perhaps more than that, I struggle with the ethical implications of what I do.

In British Columbia, most of which was never subject to historical treaties, proposed development projects typically involve unceded Indigenous land. In this province, as elsewhere in the world, Indigenous peoples are actively fighting for the right to self-determination and, in particular, for control over what happens on their traditional lands. But colonization is an ongoing process, and it did not, as Patrick Wolfe (2016) states, "impress its will on a blank slate" (20). From my perspective, a proponent of development routinely views Indigenous communities as unequal partners when it comes to projects within their own territories and seldom adequately consults them regarding the design and implementation of projects that will impact cultural heritage – even when the heritage in question is their own. In such cases, Indigenous heritage is still principally controlled by non-Indigenous people, including consulting archaeologists, government agents, and corporate executives.

I worked for a corporate CRM firm for five years. I spent much of my time trying to understand why the people involved were content to conduct archaeology in the manner they did. Explanations were in short supply. "It's the world we live in," I was told. "You just don't understand." It was true: I didn't.

Yet working within the corporate sector also gave me an opportunity to observe how archaeologists are taught to practise archaeology on the job, at least in British Columbia – how they are, in effect, miseducated (Connaughton, Leon, and Herbert 2014; Connaughton and Herbert 2017). Days filled with mundane fieldwork created space for honest discussions with colleagues, some Indigenous and some non-Indigenous, about what it was we were actually doing – about the circumstances in which archaeological work is typically conducted and about the values and assumptions underlying this practice. These conversations enabled us to contemplate, both collectively and individually, what we wanted archaeology to be and do and what would need to change in order for it to be so.

From the time I first set foot in an excavation unit, fieldwork has connected me to people, and it continues to do. These connections have multiplied and strengthened over time, and they have helped me grasp what Shawn Wilson (2008) means by "relationality" – a web of shared understandings and personal relationships that bind us together in a community from which an individual life derives meaning. They have helped me understand that I exist only in relation to others.

Living in and working with Indigenous communities have taught me much about what I do and how it should be done. These experiences have also shown me that fieldwork is never wholly apolitical: it has consequences. As a commercial enterprise, conducted on behalf of clients whose interests generally begin and end with economic development, CRM is necessarily situated within a capitalist framework that places little, if any, value on a culture's archaeological heritage – or, indeed, on that culture itself, except insofar as it can contribute to the project at hand. In this book, I argue that Indigenous communities should hold complete sovereignty over all decisions regarding their heritage within their territory (see Lyons, Leon, et al. 2022) – and that, when archaeologists and Indigenous community members are allowed to operate outside capitalist frameworks, archaeology can be a tool for social, political, and environmental justice (see Laluk et al. 2022). Archaeologists can foster this reframing by intersecting their practices with local Indigenous values and community-backed knowledge, practice, ethics, needs, desires, and sensibilities. Archaeologists can also step aside, to be facilitators rather than experts on Indigenous heritage.

The anthropologist in me cannot turn a blind eye to the inequities and inconsistencies in the corporate management of Indigenous heritage. I don't believe the "customer is always right." I don't believe that all projects should go forward. I side with Indigenous communities when they oppose development on their lands. Most of all, I rarely agree with the corporate client's goals, methods, and choices. I am, in other words, deeply troubled by the way that archaeology is practised in the context of development and its regulation. In the hands of corporate consultants, the profession has greatly distanced itself not only from any meaningful relationship with Indigenous communities but also from its original purpose – to contribute to our knowledge and understanding of the past without causing harm (Tax 1975). Heritage has become something to be "managed." Yet those who manage it virtually never consider this archaeological heritage from the perspective of Indigenous communities, whose identities and histories are, like those of any community, inextricably bound up with what survives of their past. Cultural heritage is alive, and it requires care, protection, and thoughtful stewardship. Descendant communities should be deciding what kind of archaeology they find meaningful and useful.

In what follows, I explore my notion of "miseducated" archaeologists more fully, offering, along the way, my thoughts on how the daily practice of archaeology could be changed. These thoughts are informed by my lived experience of archaeology as carried out on the ground, with and within communities, and I hope that sharing some of my own stories will start a conversation.

Who is this book intended for? Anyone with an interest in archaeology, especially archaeology as practised in the private sector. More particularly, it will be of interest to third- and fourth-year university students, graduate students, junior professionals working in archaeology, and those who have been in the CRM field for many years, as well as to Indigenous peoples, whose cultural heritage CRM routinely places at risk. Regardless of one's level of experience, this book offers an opportunity to rethink the practice of archaeology and to embrace meaningful change.

Above all, I wish to share what I have learned from my Indigenous colleagues, because it has helped me envisage another kind of archaeology. This archaeology recognizes and draws on traditional, place-based knowledge, both historical and environmental, rather than ignoring it. This archaeology respects and incorporates alternative ways of knowing the world and honours other ways of existing in relation to it and defining its value. This archaeology serves and is guided by the community; it does not exist to answer the needs of outsiders.

My goal in this book is to challenge myself, readers, and the profession as a whole to find ways to reorient the practice of archaeology so that it fosters connections, rather than divisions.

Acknowledgments

This book is a product of kindness shown to me throughout my career, written during a period of personal upheaval. The ideas presented here reflect the relationships I hold (and have held) with friends and colleagues worldwide. Acknowledging discussions, meals, fieldwork, phone calls, emails, and texts, the words on the following pages are my attempt to show gratitude for these relationships, which have filled me with joy. To be energized by the work we all do is to know that transformation is happening. In moving forward in our work together, with humility and openness, I often make mistakes, but I always try to listen to those around me in order to grow and learn. This book may present ideas you do not agree with, and likely contains mistakes, but please do not think the worst of me. I have tried to reflect upon my engagement and interactions with many of you, and to learn from your words and experiences, in an effort to challenge our industry and discipline. As no academic work is produced in isolation, I have not done my own learning alone. I am grateful to all who have been a part of my life. Below, I will try to honour all of you.

To begin, I want to acknowledge all of my friends and colleagues who have allowed me to work alongside them within their unceded Indigenous lands in British Columbia. I feel extremely privileged to have spent time working with you. In particular, I thank Darrell Guss (səlilwətaɬ), Karen Rose Thomas (səlilwətaɬ), Tia Williams (scəẃaθən məsteyəxʷ), Mike Leon (Katzie), Joey Anthone (səy̓em̓ qwantlen), Terry Point (xʷməθkʷəy̓əm), Wayne Point (xʷməθkʷəy̓əm), Jordan Wilson (xʷməθkʷəy̓əm), Richard Campbell (xʷməθkʷəy̓əm), AJ Speck (xʷməθkʷəy̓əm), Cooper Gunanoot (Gitxsan), Eileen Thomas (səlilwətaɬ), Mike Cook (Semiahmoo), Leonard Wells (Semiahmoo), Harold Glendale, Jr (Da'naxda'xw/Awaetlala), Cory Frank, Krissy Brown, and Candace Newman (K'ómoks), Chief John Powell, Jake Smith, Chip Mountain (Mamalilikulla), Gina Thomas (Tlowitsis), Christine Roberts (Wei Wai Kum), and scores of others who have shared not only meals and time with me, but also thoughts surrounding their heritage.

In March 2017, on the last day of the Society for American Archaeology conference in Vancouver, I had lunch with my old mentor, Prof. Ken Sassaman. Toward the end of our meal at the Elephant and Castle pub, I mentioned with embarrassment the idea for this book, which I had been writing off and on for a couple of years. Ken told me to write what is in my heart. And to write each day, even if it's gibberish. Some of this is likely gibberish, but it is from my heart.

My life as an anthropologist began in the South Pacific. I want to acknowledge Prof. Sharyn Jones, Dr. Patrick O'Day, and Dr. David Steadman, who gave me an opportunity to work and live in the Lau Group of Fiji between 2002 and 2003. I also thank the late Na Gone Turaga Na Tui Lau, Tui Nayau Ka Sau ni Vanua ko Lau, The Right Honorable Ratu Sir Kamisese Mara, for allowing me and my friends the opportunity to work in Lau. I greatly appreciate the hospitality offered by the people of Lau, especially the people of Nayau and Lakeba, for welcoming me into their homes and providing me with a wonderful research environment as well as local knowledge. The opportunity to meet and develop relationships with Sepeti Matararaba and Ratu Jone Balenaivalu (both of the Fiji Museum), Rusila and Caloti and their family, Cakacaka, and many others enhanced my experience living in Lau and shaped my understanding of what anthropology is and isn't, and what it could be. *Vinaka vakalevu* to Tui Liku, Tui Naro, Jack, Sera, and Lusi. My thinking was heavily influenced by those around me as I wrestled with theoretical texts and the anthropological canon while a young graduate student.

Prof. David V. Burley provided further opportunities to learn while in the field in the Kingdom of Tonga and Republic of Fiji between 2004 and 2008. In Vava'u, I was able to live and work in Neiafu, Vuna, Ofu, Otea, and Falevai. I enjoyed every minute there. I thank Peau Halanigano, Peni Latu, Mele Mapa Schmeiser, and, of course, Tenisi Tuinukuafe for logistics, good humour, and friendship. On Tongatapu, in Nukuleka, the crew I shared time with made for tons of fun in the sun, *malo 'aupito 'aupito pea 'ikai ilifia* to Sosaieti Tuiniuvala, Teleni Lolohea, Kaiefe Tali'ia, 'Uepi Finau and Steveni Feao, and Tevita Feao.

I am grateful to the friendships and fellowships built in Papua New Guinea with Prof. Ian J. McNiven, Prof. Bryce Barker, Prof. Bruno David, Tedy Tolana, Iava Hamoka, Lahui Morea, Dr. Nick Araho, Vincent Kewibu, Evanee Kove, Kim Sambua, Mick Bonner, Dr. Chris Jennings, Dr. Ben Shaw, Dr. Emma St. Pierre, Dr. Greg Morrissey, Dr. Jesse Morin, Dr. Ceri Shipton, Liam Mannix, Prof. Matt Leavesley, and many others.

I want to express my appreciation to many individuals who have been influential in my thinking and who have contributed to this book. These people have continued an ongoing dialogue with me on various subjects related to CRM and archaeology throughout the years. They include Dr. Michael Klassen, James Herbert, Ian Sellers, Walter Homewood, Kody Huard, Aviva Rathbone, Devin Forbes, Ailidh Hathway, Karen Rose Thomas, Tia Williams, Cameron Robertson, Dr. Genevieve Hill, Heather Kendall, Achinie Wijesinghe, Dr. Bill Angelbeck, Darrell Guss, Evan Hardy, Ginevra Toniello, Dr. Alice Storey, Dr. Greg Morrissey, Ryan Sagarbarria, Scott Harris, Dr. Jesse Morin, Prof. Chelsey Armstrong, Dr. Morgan Ritchie, Elroy White, Angela Buttress, and Vange Kesteven. I also want to thank Dr. Patrick Connell and Dr. Matt Hernandez with whom I timidly shared this idea for a book at Samer and Nadine's wedding. I also thank Whitney S. Boan for her steadfast support.

I thank Walter Homewood for helping draw the figures in this book from my sketches and taking the time to clearly illustrate my ideas.

I want to thank the following individuals who read earlier drafts of my chapters and provided thoughtful commentary, but I first need to single out Pamela Holway from Athabasca University Press. Pamela initially took in an interest in this rough manuscript and provided meaningful feedback on structure and organization. Her comments and guidance gave me the confidence to put in the time to rework the material. Although I didn't publish with her press, I wish to acknowledge her influence. To those who read drafts of earlier chapters, you made me feel that this book was needed, and you encouraged me to keep at it even when it felt completely silly to do so. For reading early chapters and providing comments, I thank Prof. Lynette Russell, Cameron Robertson, James Herbert, Prof. Sharyn Jones, Dr. Chris Jennings, Walter Homewood, Prof. Ian McNiven, Aviva Rathbone, Prof. Chelsey Armstrong, Evanee Kove, Dr. Ben Shaw, Kody Huard, Whitney S. Boan, and Dr. Michael Klassen.

My colleagues and friends at Inlailawatash have been instrumental in both challenging and supporting me as I navigate the issues associated with CRM and Indigenous sovereignty. I appreciate all of you: Mariko Adams, Lyndsay Cooper, Anisa Côté, Devin Forbes, Ailidh Hathway, Walter Homewood, Emma Lowther, Ian Sellers, Sarah Shaver, and Karen Rose Thomas.

First Nations Guardian programs are the eyes and ears for nations within their territories. Every nation should be supported by both the province and federal government to develop and cultivate such programs, so the programs are sustainable. Through Nanwakolas Council, I have been privileged to work alongside some passionate, caring, and dedicated people who love their history and ancestral lands. Without them opening up to me, I'd never have been able to build friendships with them that I truly enjoy. From Da'naxda'xw Guardians, I thank Harold Glendale Jr., Nolan Glendale, Steven Glendale, Stephen Glendale, Stanley Beans, and Angela Davidson; from K'ómoks Guardians, Cory Frank, Krissy Brown, Randy Frank, Caelan McLean, Cedar Frank, and Jessie Everson; from Mamalilikulla Guardians, Jake Smith, Chip Mountain, Wamish Roberts, Andy Puglas, Darren Puglas, Marvin Puglas, Caitlyn Puglas, Josiah Puglas, and Dave Puglas; from Tlowitsis Guardians, Gina Thomas, Mike Stadnyk, Alex Thomas, and Andy Stadnyk; from Wei Wai Kum: Christine Roberts and Anthony Roberts; from We Wai Kai: Shane Pollard, Anthony Seville, and Scotty Assu. From Nanwakolas Council,

I thank Scott Harris, Barb Dinning, Dr. Jordan Benner, and Diana Brown, with special thanks to James Hogan.

I am grateful to the professionalism and superbness of the UBC Press editorial team – Darcy Cullen, Karen Green, Meagan Dyer, and Barbara Tessman. Thank you for believing in me and this book.

In addition, I thank the press's three anonymous reviewers, whose encouraging feedback and constructive comments improved this book.

I thank Jessi Marie not only for our two sons, but also for encouraging me to take a job on a CRM project at səẃq̓ʷeqsən, which I initially did not want to do. She is as deeply missed as she was loved by those who knew her.

At səẃq̓ʷeqsən, I was privileged to work with community members from seven different First Nations. Although it was in CRM, it has created life-long friends who are now in positions of influence within their nations, tackling challenging projects and issues. It makes me feel joy to see you all out there doing the work, and to share laughs we when are together.

To Lara Herzer, whose creativity know no bounds as she conjured up book title ideas over coffee at Floriole Café & Bakery on Webster Avenue in Chicago. Again, your idea, and spirit, shone through. I am forever grateful for your kindness.

I thank my family for always loving me and supporting me in my endeavours to challenge the status quo, even when they may not completely understand what I do. Thank you Mom and Dad, Dr. Kelly Mansour, Dr. David Mansour, Megan Reichley, and Jimmy Reichley.

I'd also like to thank Indigenous scholars and authors whose words, insights, familiarities, and ideas that I have read while in the field and at home have greatly helped me in challenging the colonial world. To honour their voices and ideas, I've cited many in the following pages. I've tried to engage with you all the best that I can. I also encourage everyone to read Billy-Ray Belcourt, Alecia Elliot, Linda Hogan, Sterling HolyWhiteMountain, Stephen Graham Jones, Helen Knott, Therese Marie Mailhot, Tommy Orange, Joshua Whitehead, and many others I have yet to read.

This book was written over years, sometimes a single paragraph, other times with more concentrated effort, but always on my own time after work and family were cared for. The first draft was completed during some challenging times in my life – maybe as an escape from pain. It's taken me some time to do it, but it's done. And, in many ways, this book has been built by all of you who I acknowledge here. So, thank you, to all of you, for helping me along the way, and for being kind to me.

Unearthing
Forgotten Values

Introduction

In August 2015, I found myself field directing a project on Digby Island in Prince Rupert Harbour in northern British Columbia. Our crew had run through the safety briefing at Seal Cove prior to boarding our helicopter transport to the field. We had to wait. One of the client senior managers wanted to talk with me and the field crew about our objectives for the next few days. He was a typical oil and gas manager: overconfident, white, and mustached. He wanted to know why the field crew couldn't sort out whether seismic testing could take place atop a 6,000-year-old ancestral Tsimshian village. He wanted permission to drive seismic spikes into the cultural shell deposits for subsurface testing of the buried sediments to assess their integrity for supporting large-scale infrastructure.

"It's a recorded site." I said. "We'll need to discuss this with the nations first. Avoidance is best."

He proceeded to explain to me how the seismic testing works, and that the disturbance would be minimal.

"Fuck sakes, you'll do more damage tramping around on it than the seismic testing."

"That's debatable," I said, "but any impact on a recorded archaeological site warrants a permit under the Heritage Conservation Act."

"Bullshit." He then proceeded to indulge in a fifty-year-old-man snit in front of the field crew comprising local First Nations community members.[1] He screamed. He stomped. He sprayed spittle.

"It's ancient trash!" he ranted. "But, if you find a golden pyramid jutting through the midden, then, *then* you have something to talk about."

There it was: the golden pyramid. In an instant, the whole of Indigenous history spread out across North America was erased – their cultural identity dismissed – based on his own imaginings of what constitutes valuable, meaningful cultural heritage, as he derided local Indigenous archaeological sites as trash heaps. His limited understanding of archaeological village sites (their creation, use, and value) and indifference toward the heritage of descendant communities underscore a major chasm in contemporary cultural resource management (CRM) between "progress" and industrial development, which are the priority, and "trash heaps," which do not matter.

This is a book about the issues besetting the practice of archaeology in the context of cultural resource management and how to begin solving these issues. *CRM* is an initialism, used predominantly in the United States, referring to the laws, practices, and compliance surrounding the management of archaeological sites. It is also used in Canada, along with terms such as *heritage resource management* (HRM), *commercial archaeology, consulting archaeology, contract archaeology,* and *corporate archaeology*. All of these terms mean the same thing – that is, archaeology performed as a business – and refer to assessing heritage ahead of any subsurface impacts to the ground.

CRM is, at least aspiringly, focused on protecting and conserving tangible cultural heritage. In British Columbia, this heritage is overwhelmingly Indigenous. Archaeological sites in British Columbia that predate AD 1846 are protected under the provincial Heritage Conservation Act (HCA). The year 1846 was chosen because it represents the assertion of sovereignty by the British Crown over what would become British Columbia. Simply put, according to the act, Indigenous peoples who occupied a place in 1846 hold Aboriginal Title to that place, if they can prove historical use and occupancy.[2] The protection of pre-1846 archaeological heritage is provided only for tangible archaeological materials. The Crown, through the BC government, has appointed itself as the authority to oversee this protection, despite the fact that Indigenous Nations never relinquished control of their lands: they never surrendered their land through war; they never signed it away in treaties. In other words, British Columbia is largely unceded Indigenous land.[3] But in this province, as in Canada as a whole, Indigenous communities – whether First Nations, Inuit, or Métis – have no legislated protection over *either* tangible or intangible cultural heritage. I maintain, along with Indigenous peoples, that sovereignty over Indigenous heritage should reside with descendant communities. Instead, the colonialist system functions to repress Indigenous sovereignty with respect to managing their heritage. As a settler archaeologist, I benefit from this repression.

THE DISCOURSE OF MANAGEMENT
Archaeologists have several main career options: teaching at a college or university; working for the government (at the provincial or federal level); working in a museum as a curator, collections manager, museum designer, educator, or technician; or working in CRM, whether at a heritage firm or a large environmental/engineering firm, or directly for First Nations. The first requires a PhD; the others often require a master's degree or, in some cases, a professional certificate in archaeology. In an era of cutbacks in public funding, archaeologists are most likely to end up working for a CRM firm or a First Nation rather than the academy or public institutions like museums.

CRM firms exist to provide professional services to landowners, developers, government agencies, and First Nations, who pay to satisfy legal requirements and have their needs addressed. The early days of commercial archaeology in British Columbia were born out of the environmental and conservation movements of the 1960s and 1970s and sought to protect or mitigate archaeological sites prior to development. This work was done largely by university professors and students trying to protect sites despite limited time and provincial budgets. As the regulations increased, along with the demand for "salvage" archaeology, the universities didn't have the capacity to do the work. Besides, what academic wants to go dig thousands of shovel tests in a farmer's field when they can go somewhere else that is much more "interesting," excavating a site like Charlie Lake Cave near Fort St. John, for example?

The province adopted a "proponent pays" model for CRM, and many small "ma and pa" consulting outfits established themselves to handle residential and commercial development projects in order to manage cultural heritage under the HCA (Apland 1993; Klassen et al. 2009, 205; Spurling 1986). That legislation was initially designed to protect Indigenous heritage, often referred to as a "resource." The legislative regulations today, ostensibly created to safeguard these "resources," serve little purpose other than to require proponents to follow certain requirements prior to development. The goal for proponents is to satisfy these legal requirements as quickly and cheaply as possible so as to be in compliance with the HCA. As the term indicates, the field of cultural resource management assumes that archaeological materials are "resources" that require "management," much as "natural resources" (formerly known as nature) also require management. This ideological framework is bound up with the history of Western conservation ideals, which originated with concerns about the wanton consumption of nature's bounty. The idea was that natural resources should be consumed with due attention to their regeneration or preservation for the future. Natural resources come in two types, however: renewable and non-renewable. The former can be regenerated; the latter can't. And, within this "management" model, the rate of use of renewable resources often far outstrips their ability to regenerate.

In British Columbia, CRM began largely during the early 1980s, following the enactment of the HCA in 1977. By the mid-to-late 1990s and early 2000s, it had emerged as a "proper" business. Early on, people realized that archaeology could be a business outside of the academy.[4] That is, money could be made by commodifying cultural heritage and framing it as a "cultural or heritage resource." Yet "cultural resources" are non-renewable: they can either be preserved or destroyed. The question then becomes whether cultural materials are important enough to warrant preservation, and, if so, whether it will suffice to preserve only some of them – an approach known as *mitigation*. Mitigation allows for the preservation of what is often assumed to be a "representative sample" of the whole for study to produce knowledge from an altered (read: impacted) archaeological site. This assumption is generally unwarranted, given that, in the absence of the whole against which to judge the sample, it is impossible to know whether a sample is representative. In practice, then, mitigation simply amounts to preserving a sample, typically without a clear sense of the larger archaeological context, which could be determined only by the full excavation of a particular site. Sampling archaeological sites through excavation is not unusual in academic research. It provides an opportunity to learn about a site and place while preserving the rest of the site, since such sites are not typically under immediate threat. When sites are within a development footprint, is it enough to sample a small portion while the rest is destroyed for the development-driven project?

In British Columbia, mitigation entails applying for a permit – a Section 12.4 Site Alteration Permit (SAP) – and conducting an archaeological program to excavate cultural "resources" from the site. Despite SAPs' potential for destruction, applicants don't necessarily have to be a "provincially recognized" archaeologist.[5] A primary problem with site mitigations is that the process was built by settlers to help achieve settler goals, and, importantly, consent from descendant communities is not required in the HCA.[6]

Michael Klassen and his colleagues provide a rich and detailed history of the rise of CRM in British Columbia as it relates to First Nations' proactive participation and sovereignty (Klassen et al. 2009). It's a must-read for any consultant. As the authors explain, small firms of the 1980s and 1990s – some of which had established relationships with Indigenous communities – were eventually bought up by larger consulting firms (i.e., transnational corporations) that generally focused on architecture, design, construction, and engineering. These corporations figured it was easier and more cost-effective to house, rather than contract, a complete environmental services team that included archaeologists but also geologists, hydrologists, hydrogeologists, geochemists, biodiversity specialists, social consultants, and biologists. Prior to large development projects, regulators had to approve archaeological assessments, which, in some cases, were conducted as part of larger environmental assessments.

Corporations bet on the fact that archaeology could make them money, if their clients were required to conduct archaeological assessments prior to development and the corporation itself could offer that service as part of a package. Thus, the rise of large consulting firms, mega-projects, and what I call corporate archaeologists.[7]

The inclusion of CRM within these large-scale corporations has made for new challenges for corporate archaeologists, challenges not experienced by retired academics and CRM practitioners from the 1980s and 1990s. This new role finds archaeologists situated "in the middle," negotiating the space between proponents (i.e., the clients who hired the archaeologists), who want approval of their project, and Indigenous communities, who typically prioritize protection and conservation. When archaeologists made the conscious transition from academia to working for a commercial venture, archaeology became incorporated into a capitalist framework, its values and goals according with those of capitalism.[8]

It costs money to extract artifacts from the ground. Indeed, every aspect of commercial archaeology cost money. From pre-field evaluations to shovel tests to recording and analysing artifacts to final reports – all these activities have a cost, which is sometimes quite substantial. Commercial archaeology has commodified tangible heritage (Burley 1994; Colwell-Chanthaphonh and Ferguson 2008a; Hamilakis 2007; Shanks and McGuire 1996; Zorzin 2015), and, for any given development project, a commercial archaeologist can charge a client for deliverable archaeological products. Relinquishing control of this process means relinquishing control of these costs. Instead, by hiring archaeological professionals themselves, corporations can ensure that they remain firmly in control of these costs. The company may make decisions to keep costs down, and may clip hours from certain areas in the budget for "efficiency." My corporate managers used to say to me, "Does the client really need this?" "This" usually referred to any research design – and also including Indigenous communities in the research design and decision-making process – innovative methods, or informative analysis, or even taking the time to craft a narrative to tell a story about past lifeways. Typically, developers are unwilling to fund archaeological research of the sort that university-based archaeologists conduct – that is, research in the service of knowledge accumulation or data gathering directed by Indigenous communities.[9]

CRM AND THE LIMITS OF PROTECTIVE LEGISLATION

Protective legislation, embodied, in British Columbia, in the HCA, is obviously worthwhile, but it raises the question of who should be responsible for deciding whether cultural materials are worth preserving. Presumably, the answer is the people whose cultural history these materials represent – that is, descendant communities. But, in practice, control of the archaeology (the tangible heritage) is in the hands of non-Indigenous archaeologists who, as a profession, survey, assess, record, and document the archaeology, or the potential for archaeology to exist, in an area. They then make decisions about the relative value of archaeological materials, collect the materials, and take them away for analysis (or, rather, description, which really isn't analysis) and storage. In theory, archaeologists are meant to support the interests of those whose culture is at issue. Yet, properly conducted, archaeological work is expensive, which is why it's been built into a capitalist framework in which proponents can canvass consultants for bids, with the lowest bidder typically doing the work.

Who, then, is responsible for paying for the archaeological work? One possibility is the government, or, more specifically, the people who elect that government and whose interests it serves. The assumption here is that those who live in a country should have an interest in what came before – the history, both natural and human, of the land they now occupy (though I recognize that this can be a contentious issue for settlers). And, of course, by no means do all taxpayers recognize the value of preserving evidence of past lifeways. But even when they do acknowledge the value of insight into the past, they are unlikely to be willing to provide financial support for archaeological work that is conducted not for the purpose of accumulating knowledge but rather on behalf of developers whose goal is to accumulate capital.

The other logical option for paying for archaeological assessments is to place responsibility on the developers themselves. In theory, a truly independent archaeological assessment – one that conducts archaeology on unceded Indigenous lands with, by, and for descendant communities – would require any developer to obtain free, prior, and informed consent from the First Nations whose territories are within the project footprint. The developer would need to obtain the necessary permits from both the provincial regulatory agency (in British Columbia, the Archaeology Branch) and First Nations (if applicable). Then an archaeological team composed of professional archaeologists and representatives from the First Nations would assess, survey, test, and excavate an archaeological site (if identified) on their own timeline, with the understanding that the archaeologists and the descendant community would function autonomously from the developer: they would determine what needs to be done and would decide when the site has been adequately excavated, and the developer would be obliged to pay the bill, *whatever it may be*.

This is where CRM firms come in: a service industry has developed in association with legislated requirements, in which developers become paying customers. They hire a CRM firm to do the legwork of satisfying the law, and they expect the work to be done as quickly and cheaply as possible and to consist of the bare minimum needed to obtain a permit from the Archaeology Branch. This is the reality of state-run, bureaucratic archaeology, which is part of CRM today: to get into an area, assess it, test if need be, get out, and ship the artifacts, if any, to a museum repository (so they do not sit on the shelves in company offices). The CRM consultant helps the client get through the regulatory hoops, maximize profits, and keep analyses and reporting costs low. Just get the artifacts out of the ground and into a box. Besides, as one of my former managers told me, you can always get some graduate student to analyse the collections. The result: overconsuming and underdigesting of the archaeological record (Welch and Ferris 2014, 101).

Thus, as will be discussed in greater detail in Chapter 3, laws designed to protect archaeological heritage enable a situation in which decisions about archaeological value are made by firms that survive by keeping their customers happy, and their customers are people whose interests lie with the destruction of archaeological heritage, not with its protection. One begins to see the problem.

ARCHAEOLOGY AND THE SETTLER-COLONIAL STATE

In a settler-colonial country such as Canada, the problem with commodification- and profit-driven CRM has another, critically important, dimension. As in settler-colonial countries elsewhere, where settlers attempted to replace the Indigenous population (e.g., Canada, the United States, Australia, New Zealand, countries in Africa), archaeological materials overwhelmingly represent the cultural history of Indigenous peoples, not of the settlers who now "control" the land. Moreover, most settler Canadians continue to view Indigenous people as "other." Regardless of their attitudes toward Indigenous people, developers are most often seeking permission to destroy a cultural heritage that is not theirs, despite the fact that descendant communities exist today on the same land their ancestors lived on, often for millennia or since time immemorial.

British Columbia is one of the most linguistically and culturally diverse Indigenous regions in North America. More than thirty Indigenous languages are spoken in the province, with each language spoken by a distinct nation (Klassen et al. 2009; McMillan and Yellowhorn 2004). Prior to Confederation and into the early part of the twentieth century, Indigenous peoples in British Columbia were involuntary organized into nearly 200 bands. Aboriginal affairs and Aboriginal rights became a federal responsibility, regulated by the Indian Act (1876). That act, however, does not cover Indigenous cultural heritage. Rather, under the British North America Act, provincial governments became responsible for lands and resources, including, eventually, Indigenous cultural heritage (Burley 1994). In British Columbia, outside of a few colonial-era treaties on Vancouver Island, Treaty 8 in the northeastern part of the province, and some modern treaties (e.g., Nisga'a, Maa-nulth, Tla'amin, Tsawwassen), most First Nations never signed treaties with the federal government. Therefore, the province of British Columbia exists on unceded Indigenous lands. Given the lack of treaties, questions of Aboriginal Rights and Title (the legal term) have been brought before the courts by politically organized Indigenous communities that argue for their unextinguished rights. For many Indigenous communities, these rights already exist through local protocols, customs, and governance. Indigenous law is asserted not through the colonial courts, but on the land, through relationships and activities like fishing, hunting, plant collecting, cultivating, tree harvesting, and defending the land from commercial extraction (Martindale and Armstrong 2019; Napoleon 2013; Spice 2016, 2018). In this context of situating Indigenous practices and ideologies ahead of colonial laws and treaties, one could argue that all of Canada is unceded Indigenous land, with local, Indigenous laws and protocols having existed since time out of mind.

Heritage stewardship and questions of jurisdiction have become a sticking point within the larger battle over Aboriginal Rights and Title, and have led to a gap in protection that First Nations have tried to fill themselves. Development proponents fail to understand that Indigenous lands were never conquered, sold, or relinquished, and that title was never extinguished, and so Indigenous people have the right to manage their cultural heritage. Throughout the province, descendant communities are asserting their identity in the face of dispossession. Along the Northwest Coast, this assertion of identity and stewardship for heritage is exemplified through programs like the Guardian Watchmen. Guardian Watchmen programs increase the level of archaeological and cultural protection by being the eyes and ears of their nation. They proactively conduct field assessments, assess vulnerable sites, and record data that improve their nation's inventory database for archaeological sites and cultural heritage areas.[10]

Archaeological sites are not isolated entities; they are tied to a larger landscape in which they were made and are imbued with meaning, knowledge, and identity. Indigenous peoples view cultural landscapes as a local constellation of people, places, and natural resources. Indigenous communities' notion of placemaking by living, teaching, and being on the land is often not understood by proponents pushing for development projects that could affect these communities' lifeways and impact their health, happiness, and well-being.

Archaeological research, especially in the service of development, is thus bound up with Indigenous land rights. These rights constitute a huge and highly contested issue, one for which the solution preferred by the settler-colonial state has been consultation – another huge and highly contested topic (Hanson 2018).[11] As presently practised, consultation aims at various forms of compromise, in which Indigenous Nations are, if nothing else, placated or – better yet, from the perspective of the state – co-opted, drawn into the capitalist structures that undergird the settler-colonial state. The state has thus far firmly rejected the prospect of Indigenous sovereignty, in which autonomy – the right to political, economic, and cultural self-determination – is fully restored to Indigenous Nations (see L. Simpson 2017).

Examples of continued dispossession have been explored by Audra Simpson in *Mohawk Interruptus* (2014) and Glen Sean Coulthard in *Red Skin, White Masks* (2014), which focus on the violent transformation of Indigenous social structures and economies prior to colonization into capitalist forms today. Both Simpson and Coulthard discuss legislation, policy, development-driven projects, and legal cases, which continually fail to address structural inequality in Canada (see also L. Simpson 2017). Heritage regulation is another arm of the colonial government that secures access to Indigenous lands (and their natural resources) on behalf of proponents, thus keeping Indigenous owners and stewards of their land at bay and, in effect, supporting continued dispossession.

Coulthard (2014, 30–31) cynically questions why any Indigenous community would ask for "recognition" to self-govern from the dominant entity (i.e., the federal government) when that government has failed to modify, or transcend, the current relationship between these two groups. Obtaining recognition from the government does not change the imbalance of power. When reconciliation is invoked, as the government often likes to do, it's "framed as the process of individuality and collectively overcoming the harmful 'legacy' left in the wake of this past abuse, while leaving the present structure of colonial rule largely unscathed" (Coulthard 2014, 22). The land is central in both Simpson's and Coulthard's arguments about how to transform the dominant political economy in Canada. Repatriation of land, which would enable engagement in sustainable local economies, would see Indigenous peoples reconnect with their ancestral lands (Coulthard 2014, 170–71). This would allow for multiple opportunities to use, learn from, and be on the land, but Coulthard (2014, 171) warns against economic dependency built on extractive capitalism, which is at odds with the central core of most Indigenous relationships with the land.

CRM is a continuation of accumulation by settler colonialism that has dispossessed, and continues to dispossess, Indigenous peoples. When Indigenous archaeologists talk of decolonizing archaeology, and the choir made up of many non-Indigenous archaeologists sings along with them (myself included), it cannot be as social justice warriors, it cannot be a "metonym for social justice," as Tuck and Yang (2012, 21) clearly stated. Such decolonization requires the repatriation of Indigenous land for Indigenous lifeways. I do think some archaeologists see that, and those who work for, or closely with, First Nations may be advocating and doing the work toward that goal, but, for the present moment, we are still actively engaged in the economy of contemporary settler colonialism (Wolfe 2006). Archaeologists are not in the position to directly dismantle the colonial system, but we can slowly degrade it from the inside, reimagining archaeological practice in a new form. And we can advocate for and support Indigenous peoples in obtaining positions within government and heritage firms to drive change in CRM from the ground up, both in practice and policy (the HCA and other legislation) to reflect Indigenous laws and values.

In *The Beneficiary*, which examines the idea that our fate is causally linked with the distant suffering of others through globalization and capitalism, Bruce Robbins (2017) stated: "You cannot see anything as wrong unless and until you can see or at least sense that it can be otherwise" (12). Archaeology as it is practised today within development capitalism is shaped largely by Euro-Canadian values tied to colonial beginnings. Acknowledging that archaeologists are the beneficiaries of inequalities in the archaeological system is a first step in addressing this issue. Recognizing the historical imbalance of power intersecting development, archaeology, heritage management, regulators, and Indigenous communities is critical, since no work that archaeologists do is apolitical (Berreman 1968; McGuire 2008). There are other ways of knowing and doing archaeology, and archaeologists can help facilitate meaningful and relevant archaeological stories for, with, and by Indigenous communities (Nicholas 1997). A shift in control of power, ownership, equity, and process must occur if we are to transform archaeological practice into an inclusive and safe space where compassion and Indigenous values drive archaeological work.[12] Social responsibility is an important component of the work archaeologists do, as archaeology is not done in isolation from current events, politics, or economics, and there are larger, international political narratives that tie into what CRM archaeologists are doing locally each day on the ground. Those who practise archaeology can look to each other for support, but, also, we have to be cognizant of how we in British Columbia learn to practise archaeology, who teaches us, and how we are conditioned to practise the craft. There are no easy answers, but human values can be recentred within archaeological practice by asking ourselves, why do we do archaeology, for whom do we do it, and how best can it be done (Nicholas 2014, 137)? A lot of good can come from compassionate, human values being reinserted into archaeological practice, but is it enough?

This book touches on a number of highly complex topics, among them the meaning of decolonization, Indigenous land rights and sovereignty, capitalism, and the continuing support of the state for projects that will contribute to climate change. A full exploration of such topics is the work of an entire library, not a single book; thus, the intention here is to consider these topics within the context of an exploration of the role of archaeology in contributing to a maintenance of the status quo. By acknowledging and critiquing that role, this book doesn't merely argue that the situation needs to change; it also discusses ways in which we, as archaeologists, can contribute to that change. Such a discussion is critical because, until we understand that change is possible, we will not likely work toward it.

I acknowledge that I am not an Indigenous person: I am a settler archaeologist who works for an Indigenous-owned heritage management firm. I am not writing this book from any other perspective than that of a practising archaeologist who is profoundly dissatisfied with the degree to which archaeology is used to undermine the interests of those whose material culture it allegedly seeks to preserve and interpret. My experience both with university-based archaeological fieldwork and with

CRM archaeology has led me to conclude that the current situation is deeply disrespectful and ultimately unethical and oppressive.

But I also believe that errors, once recognized, can be corrected, and my hope is that this book may help to chart a new course for professional archaeology.

1
Birth of an Anthropologist

I was conceived, as an anthropologist, in the Lau Group of Fiji. Moored off the tiny island of Vanua Vatu, the *Tai Kabara* was finally still. Still was good. Still was calm. For twenty hours, this ship had lurched and plunged its way through the South Pacific. I had not been able to stand and had resigned myself to the stern of the boat, lying atop cargo and holding onto the railing along the starboard side. My stomach ached from all the dry heaving, and my breath reeked. But here I was, in Fiji, en route to the more traditional islands of the Lau Group, which are separated from the eastern side of Fiji by the artificial boundary between Melanesia and Polynesia.

Earlier, prior to departure, I had eaten a late breakfast of fried eggs, toast, and mango juice. Once we were removed from the safety of Suva Harbour and into the open ocean, my stomach turned, and I began convulsing. The little ship soared atop the crest of waves and back down again. I tried to make it to the head on the ship, but I quickly realized others had beaten me to it. I bolted to the back deck, threw myself up against the railing, and heaved.

A bit of runny egg hit a Fijian. "*Neu!*" he shouted.

I attempted to put my hand up in an apology, but I had only one goal: cast everything out of my body. Lying in the fetal position atop a crate, looking out along the starboard side, the ocean spray misting me now and again, I tilted my head to see the stars. Blazing stars by the billions, oh, so clear, as if I could look deep into time, seeing the beginning of the universe, or perhaps the ancient light, just hitting me now, from when Fijian ancestors first sailed to Lau. The stars looked like a dome across the sky, its edges absorbed into the horizon. The Southern Cross shone brightly. I mustered my remaining strength and turned to gaze at the moon, which was bouncing, zigging, and zagging across the sky, sliding violently back and forth behind the ship's mast, and I began to hurl nothingness once more into the deep, cerulean sea.

I should provide some personal context. I'm male, "white" (i.e., of various ethnicities), arguably middle class, born and raised in Florida. I'm third-generation American. My father was a dentist and instructor at a small community college turned university. In his later years, he served as a lieutenant colonel in the U.S. Air Force Reserve in Tampa. He has since retired from both positions. My mother raised me and my two younger sisters while my father was in private practice. When he left his dental practice to teach, she went back to school and ultimately earned a master's in education. She was a Kindergarten teacher for over twenty years and retired in 2021 during the pandemic. My own family now includes two sons, whom I love dearly.

I grew up in the small, racially divided town of Starke. Witnessing racism and experiencing prejudice impacted my thinking as young person. A sense of social justice was instilled in me at an early age, and I did act on it at times, despite the consequences for me among my white "peers." In 1993, when I was fourteen, my family moved to Melbourne, Florida, and I went to high school near what had been Zora Neale Hurston's home, where she wrote *Mules and Men* (1935), an influential ethnography for me in my university years. But I didn't know that back then.

The prologue that I am weaving in this chapter combines my personal history and formative experiences and my understanding of anthropology and archaeology. I consider myself an anthropological

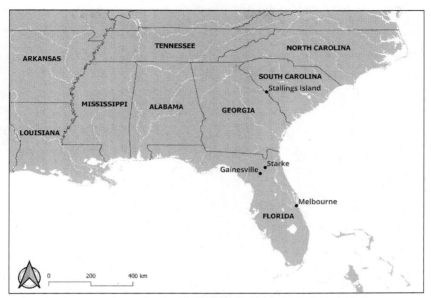

FIGURE 1.1 Towns and archaeological site in the southeastern United States mentioned in the text. | Created by Walter Homewood via Natural Earth.

archaeologist, and I will often flip between calling myself an archaeologist or an anthropologist. Anthropology adopts a comparative approach to better understand societies and cultures by examining differences and similarities in how cultures are structured and how people construct meaning in their everyday lives. When anthropologists talk about *culture*, they are referring to symbol-based learned behaviour.[1] In other words, there is meaning behind tangible materials made in a community and intangibles ways of being (normalized social behaviours) learned as children. Children are enculturated into the community in which they are born, as they examine, challenge, and develop an understanding of themselves and their community.[2]

Archaeology is the study of such communities through material culture. I use archaeological methods, combined with both anthropological and archaeological theory, to understand the past lifeways of humans. Within the context of methodological trends, both anthropology and archaeology were "scientized," and once archaeology and anthropology were assimilated into science in the late 1950s and early 1960s, its human roots begin to erode, with the researcher cast in the role of distant and "objective" observer. The processual approach – a positivist, scientific approach to explaining factors that promote cultural change viewed in the archaeological record – dominated archaeology for decades, especially in North America (Trigger 2000, 298–303). Processualists, practitioners of the "New Archaeology," dismissed the notion that living members of descendant cultures might have anything to contribute to the discipline of archaeology (Trigger 1980, 667; Trigger 2000, 408–11). These positivist approaches ultimately came into question – among anthropologists somewhat earlier than among archaeologists – and the disciplines' claim to "scientific" status was the main target of early Indigenous critiques, most notably by Vine Deloria Jr. (1969). Beginning in the 1970s, post-processual critiques challenged archaeologists through a variety of specific interpretive frameworks that continually developed between the 1980s and the early 2000s. When I use the term *anthropological archaeologist*, I am arguing for the restoration of the anthropological into the archaeological. This theme – the need to rehumanize, or re-anthropologize, archaeology – is woven throughout the book (see Tax 1975).

In recent years, anthropology has striven to be more inclusive and more relevant to and useful in everyday life.[3] Today, anthropologists represent many nationalities, numerous ethnicities, and various genders and sexual orientations. Anthropology is much more diverse today, and is better for it: the discipline reflects multiple voices of its practitioners, who have varied backgrounds and distinct experiences. That said, equity remains an issue in positions of power and influence (Hodgetts et al. 2020).[4] Still, the work anthropologists do, in partnership with the communities they work within and with, provides access to alternative realities, which are brought forth through their scholarship, as well as a space for marginalized voices. I believe that compassion may be generated through this process, and that this may, in turn, engender deeper or more empathetic feelings for the lives of our fellow humans, allowing us to better understand their experiences. This insight and understanding can contribute to the creation of a more caring society, one in which ignorance of others can be erased through connection and compassion. Anthropologists can shine a spotlight on lived lives in hopes of illuminating socially underrepresented communities and can advocate on their behalf (or alongside them) to inform the broader society – and the "experts" within it – about the complex issues at play.

All of my archaeological experience has been working with heritage that is not my own; rather, it is the heritage of Indigenous descendant communities with whom I am privileged to work and live. I work closely with living communities who have deep ties to the spaces and places where we conduct archaeology and learn more about their ancestors. In doing so, I think about those who came out of largely processual archaeological programs and were the early forerunners of cultural resource management. They have strongly influenced the historical development of CRM archaeological practice, one that has been, and continues to be, dominated by processual assumptions long after they have been supplanted in academic archaeology. Indeed, even now, my experience is that CRM centres methods and results on the tangible and on client-driven needs, while not acknowledging either the sociocultural world we inhabit when we perform archaeology or the value of Indigenous knowledge from descendant communities. These practitioners seem to have little awareness of how their work may be viewed by others (e.g., media, governments, Indigenous communities) and insufficient concern about making sure no harm comes to the Indigenous communities who privilege them as guests in their territories.

Possessing self-awareness is critical for anthropologists and archaeologists. We need to recognize that we are not influenced solely by kin, but also by others in our lives – friends, colleagues, lovers, teachers. Through our recursive interactions, they all inform us about our world, our surroundings, how we think, speak, eat, laugh, and play. This was true for me, both as I pursued my undergraduate degree and a master's in anthropology at the University of Florida (UF), and when I undertook a PhD at Simon Fraser University. It was at UF where I first received an opportunity to live and work with people culturally different from me. I was given an opportunity to be a research assistant and travel to the Lau Group in Fiji. Working closely with Sharyn Jones (a PhD student at the time), I contributed to her ethnoarchaeological investigations on the social relationships surrounding food, women, and fishing that make up the subsistence economy of a small Fijian village (Jones 2009; O'Day

2004). This experience, and the stories from my time there, helped me develop personally and understand archaeology more fully and how to better perform it.

ASHORE IN THE LAU GROUP, FIJI

Once on shore in the small but important village of Tubou on Lakeba Island, I was a new person. It was early morning, and we found our accommodations at "Jack's Guest House" with our host family, Jack, Sera, and their daughter, Lusi. We organized our belongings in the *vale* (house). Soon after our arrival, we were served fresh fruits, curry mangrove crab in a bisque-like broth, tea, and Nescafé instant coffee, which I eventually learned to enjoy.[5] Once full, I took in the sights and sounds of village life in Tubou. I always remember how clean and manicured the village paths were – a sign of respect from the people toward their chief (and toward the king of Lau). I was greeted with *"bula"* everywhere I turned. I was a curiosity. A ghost. A *palagi* (foreigner). People wanted to know why I was there, my purpose.[6] I easily spoke with them.

Sharyn, Patrick O'Day (also a PhD student, and at the time, Sharyn's husband), and Fiji Museum archaeologist Sepeti Matararaba (known

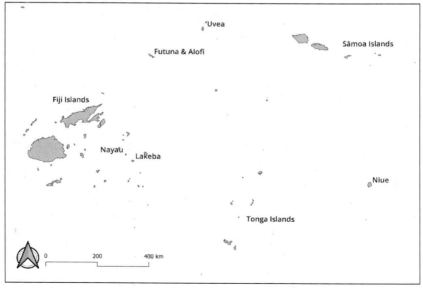

FIGURE 1.2 Fiji and Tonga. | Created by Walter Homewood via Natural Earth.

as Mata) had arranged for us to meet with kin of Ratu Mara, the local high-ranking chief, for a *sevusevu* to seek permission to conduct research on the nearby islands of Aiwa Lailai, Aiwa Levu, and Nayau and to discuss our being there. A *sevusevu* is typically performed when guests arrive in a Fijian village, and it includes a ritual presentation of kava (*Piper methysticum*) to the local hereditary chief (*Ratu* or *Tu'i*). Kava (*yaqona* in Fijian) is a popular crop cultivated across most of Polynesia as well as in some areas of Melanesia and Micronesia.[7] It's a mild narcotic that can numb one's mouth and cause temporary loss of feeling in the extremities. *Yaqona* can be consumed formally, as during *sevusevu*, or, more commonly, informally in the evenings. It is drunk mostly by men, but I have been in informal kava circles where women drank alongside us. In more conservative villages, the women in the *vale* might sit behind a *tapa* (bark) cloth curtain in the kitchen, and we would slide the *bilo* (coconut cup) of *yaqona* to them.

I like kava. I enjoy drinking it. Holding the *bilo*, feeling its smooth coconut base, which has been sanded and fitted to my hand, I ask for "high tide" (a full bowl). Sure, it tastes like liquid wood, but I enjoy the peppery tang and the comradery and stories that take place around the kava bowl. It's an opportunity to bond and laugh and show your personality after a long day of work. This work may have been in the garden, mending nets, doing household chores, or doing archaeology.

In Fijian culture, the *sevusevu* is part of local protocols, and it is required when individuals arrive in a village that is not their father's (Shaver and Sosis 2014). For the stranger to gain acceptance, a *sevusevu* is conducted to discuss the reasons for their presence in the village and ultimately to gain approval by the host chief. Acceptance during the *sevusevu* symbolizes that the host chief and his village will offer hospitality and protection during one's stay.

Mata prepared us. He said we would not talk in the beginning. He would introduce us once we were seated in front of the host chief. We should not make eye contact with *Ratu*, adverting our gaze until the *sevusevu* is done and he specifically addresses us. When we enter the *vale*, we should humbly approach the chief, carrying our bodies low to ground, practically crawling in to greet him, and then sit cross-legged, heads down, eyes on our feet. Those were all our instructions. I entered head down, hands clasped together tightly, and navigated myself to my spot on the side. The *tanoa* (kava serving bowl) was across from me, and some very large Fijian men were in front of me. We were in a circle, and all discussion clipped by me quickly in Fijian, specifically the local Lauan dialect.

Within the conversation, I picked up pieces of Fijian: an *io* (yes) here, a *vinaka* (good) there, a *vanua* (land) or *kuro* (pottery) peppered about. Sentences were bookended by "hmms," "aahs," and such. Finally, the chief spoke to Sharyn and Pat. He mentioned how he liked the flagging tape from the last visit, that it marked where we had been and how to navigate in the island forests. We all laughed. We drank kava and he welcomed us into Tubou, and he opened up the entire Lau Group to us. We were free to move about the village, the island, and beyond. If we were to seek accommodation in another village, another *sevusevu* would be performed with the local ranking chief.

Our reason for staying in Fiji was academic. Sharyn was conducting research for her PhD in ethnoarchaeology, and my own cultural education began immediately. The research program we were conducting centred on questions steeped in archaeology and Western science. But simply by being present, I started to understand other ways of knowing and being in the world. The *sevusevu* was the first introduction to this learning, which included the impact of my presence and behaviour in a community. It was after the *sevusevu* that I understood the necessity of adopting local customs, learning the language, and following protocols when working as a guest in another's backyard. I was so ignorant and had so much to learn, and I knew that I would never understand more than a fraction of life there. I'd spend about six months over the next two years working and living in the Lau Islands. It fundamentally shaped me as an individual.

ARCHAEOLOGY IN THE AMERICAN SOUTHEAST: WHERE ARE THE PEOPLE?

I didn't start out as a Pacific archaeologist. The seed was actually planted September 11, 2001, around 8:00 a.m., in the basement of Marsden Library at the University of Florida. I was happily searching for ethnographic texts for my hunter-gatherer-fisher class taught by Ken Sassaman.

Soon, I would be pulled into my supervisor's office to watch the dreadful events of that day. Prior to that, unaware of the historical importance of that day, I soaked up the musky scent of old books, clambering among the stacks, searching for and thumbing through ethnographies. Before most students had eaten breakfast, I had come across the Lau Islands of Fiji through two ethnographies, by Laura Thompson (1940) and A.M. Hocart (1929). These two books opened a world unknown to me. I didn't realize at the time that my friends, Sharyn and Pat, both PhD students, were conducting an ethnoarchaeological research program there; all I knew was that they were in Fiji for the semester. I had always been interested in the history and lifeways in the South Pacific. Intrigued by these texts, I checked them out for my term paper. Little did I know that, less than a year later, I too would be in Fiji.

I began my archaeological training in the southeastern United States. When I was nineteen, I volunteered in the laboratory of Ken Sassaman, who had recently been hired by the university. Although an undergraduate, I didn't want just to read textbooks; I wanted to get hands-on experience. Ken gave me the opportunity to sort bags of cultural shell deposits from archaeological sites he had excavated in Georgia and South Carolina. I kept showing up. I would volunteer three days a week. Ken was somewhat surprised by this effort. My free labour in the lab turned into an opportunity to do field research on the Savannah River, working on a site where the first pottery was produced in the southeastern United States, about 4,500 years old ago (Sassaman 1993, 2006). This was on Stallings Island (Site 9CB1), on the Savannah River, which marked the border between Georgia and South Carolina. It was a wonderful experience: my first archaeological dig, with precise research objectives and archaeological methods to be learned on the job. It was fun. I learned tons. Ken was (and still is) an excellent teacher and mentor. Because of him, I met interesting archaeologists such as Dan Elliot, Al Goodyear, and Dennis Stanford, among others. I ate outstanding South Carolina barbecue and drank gallons of sweet tea. An important moment during that fieldwork was when we uncovered ancestral (human) remains in an excavation unit. The remains had been previously disturbed by looters, digging into graves in search of burial goods. We could determine the nature of the disturbance by the jumbled condition of the graves: dirt and artifacts were tossed aside as the looters hastily dug for "valuable" belongings. Desecration of the site was also evinced by looter pits. One pit that we excavated contained a snack wrapper coming out of a hole near the zygomatic arch of a skull: a light snack for the grave robbers.

My first experience with Indigenous North Americans was at Stallings Island. This was in the very late 1990s, and the Native American Graves Protection and Repatriation Act (NAGPRA) was a relatively new piece of legislation.[8] Being only a second-year university student, I wasn't a part of the discussion between Ken and a tribal representative who appeared on behalf of the local Georgia Council on American Indian Concerns. The state of Georgia does not have any "federally recognized tribes" within its borders.[9] My memory is faint, but I recall a representative from this council coming to the site to examine the ancestral remains we had uncovered. She came, saw them, had a discussion with Ken, and left. As quickly as she appeared, she was gone. The ancestral remains were reburied on site.

That moment was the only engagement or interaction I ever had with any Indigenous peoples of the southeastern United States. I found that odd, given that we were on the cusp of the twenty-first century, a time when archaeologists were increasingly recognizing the importance of engagement with local Indigenous peoples. That said, I was well aware of the horrid history of Indigenous-settler relations in the area, including legislation under President Andrew Jackson that had led to the violent removal of Native Americans from their homes, setting them on a forced migration along the Trail of Tears, and decimating Indigenous populations throughout the South.[10] Still, I continued to question the situation in my head: Why weren't we doing more? Why aren't Indigenous people involved? With the hubris of a privileged university student, I questioned the lack of engagement of local Indigenous people. I wanted the Indigenous representative (and her community) to be part of what we were doing. I wanted to know more about Indigenous communities in the South, and my own deep ignorance frustrated me. I didn't even know what I *needed* to know to contribute to different practices and outcomes in archaeology. I was a sophomore at the University of Florida trying to learn the ropes of field methods and techniques. I was concerned with recording sediment correctly, identifying a cultural occupation layer, or drawing a detailed profile. Hell, I was just learning how to use a trowel properly.

Looking back, I understand that this was the beginning of my dismay with the way archaeological practice closes the door to other ways of knowledge and other understandings. Although I didn't fully understand it, that moment has never left me – that feeling of ignorance and not fully realizing why archaeology was the way it was. All I knew was that I didn't want to dig alone. I wanted my archaeology to be anthropology, or I too would consider it nothing (see Willey and Phillips 1958, 2). I wanted to be surrounded by people and learn from them about their history, if they would have me.

I had to experience archaeological practice that way so I could begin to awaken to principles of community-based archaeology. Community-based archaeology is community-driven research that produces results relevant for the communities involved (Atalay 2012, 10). It uses methods (and theory) from archaeology but also Indigenous knowledge to drive research questions – or, perhaps more accurately, it centres Indigenous epistemologies within archaeological project goals that Indigenous communities will find of interest. It does not necessarily reject Western ways of knowing (see L. Smith 2012, 41); rather, it creates the space for multiple ways of knowing and being (Nicholas 2018a). It's an approach that brings knowledge holders together – whether they be archaeologists, anthropologists, or local community knowledge holders – to solve problems, answer questions, and/or deal with potential impacts to cultural heritage. It seemed – and seems – to me self-evident that white settler archaeologists were doing themselves, and everyone else, a disservice by barring entry by others into the secret club of archaeologists.

FIRST LESSONS FROM FIJI
During my graduate training, I lived and worked in communities across the South Pacific, largely in Fiji and Tonga, with other experiences in Sāmoa and Papua New Guinea. That was the life. Digging, swimming, fishing, gardening, drinking grog, and living in the village among the local people. Those experiences shaped my thinking, and they moulded

my being as an anthropological archaeologist. I made mistakes. I cried. I laughed and smiled. I sang and danced. It was in the South Pacific that I learned my craft. But, more importantly, I learned how to be socialized into a Polynesian community (Morton 1996): to be present and listen. I learned how to explain ideas, teach in another language (as best I could), and find meaning in the work I was doing. I also saw very clearly how, as an outsider, I had an impact in a community – both good and bad. When you're working in a Polynesian community like Lau or Tonga, it's invasive. You're in their backyards. Literally. You're in their gardens, their *'api*, conducting archaeological excavations. Being so close together generates new ways of knowing and teaching. Working side by side with descendant communities, not only conducting archaeological investigations but also going fishing, planting taro, taking care of the children, and playing in their village as a guest, was profound for me. It made me feel alive. It made the archaeology feel true.

Working and living within an Indigenous community affects the archaeological work. On Nayau Island, in the Southern Lau Group of Fiji, Sharyn Jones's PhD research was both archaeological and ethnographic: a direct historical approach was employed to understand the contemporary practices of local Lauan people and those of their ancestors, by studying archaeological materials, specifically zooarchaeological remains. Local people were involved in the research, as archaeological assistants conducting excavations in old village sites, and as interlocutors, knowledge keepers, and participants, sharing their insights into subsistence practices, hierarchy, and identity in contemporary times through interviews. Many households even kept their food remains for a week so that their rubbish (i.e., the faunal remains) could be recorded by Sharyn. She then made comparisons between zooarchaeological samples from archaeological sites and contemporary collections of food waste in multiple households. Insights into the past could be drawn from contemporary practices that help illuminate the more muddled social aspects of the archaeological record.

Because of our presence, conversations were constantly had in the village revolving around the research we were doing and what it was we were trying to learn. This led to engaging discussions on local Lauan history, food, fishing, gardening, family relationships, Lauan language and culture, rugby, and archaeology. A wonderful consequence of doing archaeology within the community was that we had curious children come by and work with us. Lauan children would come by the site at Namasimasi on Nayau Island and help me excavate. Working with children and young people let them see first-hand what we were doing. They would then go home in the evenings and share this knowledge, their interests, and questions with their family. In this way, archaeological information and conversations crossed inter-generational lines.

My closest family of friends included Sepesa Caloti, his wife, Rusila, and their sons, Toro and Lagi. The boys would often bring their friends from school to the site, where I would teach them, and they would teach me. My field time was open to them. Children between six and thirteen years old would show up and want to participate. A few of the older ones even skipped school to hang out and work with us. I'd involve them by showing them what we were looking for in the screens. I'd show them how we excavated, gave them trowels, showed them how and why we were doing this and that. Sharyn and Pat, too, were always welcoming of the children, and we eventually went to the school on Nayau and gave a little talk about why we were there, what our research goals were, and why we were interested in their history and daily life. We donated books to the school library and learned about what the teachers needed.

I was amazed that, after just a couple of days in the field, the kids seemed to quickly master excavation techniques. I've taught field schools to university-age students, and it's taken me four to six weeks to get them to harness the skills Lauan children learned quickly. The children demonstrated such a remarkable aptitude. But they also taught me. I learned vocabulary in the local language, games, daily village gossip, and stories. While I was working alongside the children, I kept wondering, if they're so interested and like doing this kind of work, what opportunities were going to be available to them when they grew older. Was this going to be a one-time shot where some foreigner shows up, has an exchange, and then goes away, never to be heard from or seen again? For my part, the latter was a distinct possibility. I understood that, as a graduate student, I might not be able to access funding that would give me the

FIGURE 1.3 Author holding an ugavule, also known as a coconut crab, alongside Sepeti Matararaba on Aiwa Levu, 2002. | Photo courtesy of author.

opportunity to go back, since grants are both competitive and political. So, I did what I could, focused on each day and on spending each moment with them.

Living and working in Lau, I learned that local Lauans possessed a sense of community connection to their heritage. Through archaeology, combined with oral traditions and knowledge, stories unfolded about past lifeways reflected in the archaeological record. Conversations took place around the kava bowl, in homes, or around the *lovo* (earth oven). I recall butchering a *puaka* (pig) with other men, which was to be cooked with other foodstuffs such as *dalo* (taro), *tavioka* (cassava), *kumala* (sweet potato), and *uto* (breadfruit). During the meal preparation, conversations turned to pigs in the past, how to see their arrival archaeologically and use through time. Stratigraphy within an archaeological site is a great way to document events, the passing of time. Often an archaeological feature like a *lovo* can be seen in the wall of an excavation unit. This method of cooking is used today, much as it was nearly 3,000 years ago when the community's ancestors first sailed into Lau.

The opportunity to discuss past lifeways was always there within the community. But more than that, the effort to show that Lauan heritage and identity exist today as they once did in the past was demonstrated to me by people in the community encouraging me to use the language, participate in fishing, and share in local humour. As a guest in the host community, I wanted to act with courtesy, learn the language, and be observant of custom and protocol. Doing so was important, because it allowed me to share in people's lives as they opened their doors to me. I had to learn how to sit, how to dress, when to eat, who eats when, where people stand, how to talk to women, how to talk to men, how to talk to elders, how to talk to youths. These are all things that you learn when you're a guest in another community.

This "being in a place" provided a cultural context for the archaeological materials excavated, not only from the information people shared during interviews but also through the practical knowledge they demonstrated through their daily routines of food production and participation in village life. Combining archaeological practice with ethnography and ethnohistory, researchers are able to more fully realize and enhance the understanding of past lifeways, including social issues related to local Lauan foodways, hierarchy, and identity (Jones 2009). For example, fish are classified and understood collectively by their specific names, behaviour, and value. On Nayau, certain fish are highly prized for their "sweetness" (Jones 2009, 145). Such an insight helps archaeologists provide alternative interpretations about archaeological fish remains, as size may not be the only variable for selecting and targeting certain fish. Rather, taste or sweetness plays an important role. So, while fish remains can be counted, weighted, and identified by species, understanding personal preference and taste, and how it might by reflected in the archaeological record, can be gleaned only by working with communities. Along with questions of taste, other aspects of food consumption may not make it into the archaeological record. Women in Lau are excellent fishers and hold deep knowledge about both intertidal and pelagic species. When they collect and eat invertebrates as snacks while fishing, this behaviour is not reflected in the archaeological record because the by-products of snacking (i.e., the shells) rarely make it back to the village to be deposited in the shell midden (cultural shell deposits). The preparation of a *lovo* is typically men's work, and they are used for feasts (typically once a week, perhaps on a Sunday, but for other occasions as well). We learned that reef fish are hardly ever prepared in a *lovo*, and this knowledge meant that we could interpret the remains of small reef fish associated with an archaeological *lovo* as the remnants of snacks eaten during *lovo* preparation (Jones 2009, 146). Thus, faunal remains identified in the archaeological record that prove difficult to interpret may be better understood when researchers apply knowledge obtained from living with and learning from descendant communities whose daily activities provide rich insight into past lifeways.

FULL-BODIED ANTHROPOLOGY

The opportunity to travel with Sharyn Jones and Pat O'Day as a research assistant in Fiji exposed me to another world – one I had only read about. My training at the University of Florida was in an integrative four-field approach to anthropology. I was able to draw on this holistic approach, which comprised archaeology, linguistics, physical anthropology, and ethnography (cultural/social anthropology), to more deeply understand the past, while living and working in the present with descendant communities. During my second field excursion to Lau, I was reading *Hawaiki, Ancestral Polynesia* (2001) by Patrick Kirch and Roger Green, which is a rich, textured history drawing from archaeology, comparative ethnography, and reconstructions of ancestral Polynesian languages to create the social world of past Polynesian lifeways. I was literally in Hawaiki, the ancestral Polynesian homeland of Polynesian peoples and cultures, which Lau was initially a part of, along with Tonga, when the first Lapita ancestors showed up on the shores (Connaughton 2015). Working there, I was able to live in the culture myself and compare my experiences to those of other anthropologists (e.g., Hocart 1929; Thompson 1940).

While in the field, I was learning Fijian, learning the history, learning how to communicate with those I worked alongside as we excavated their heritage. I was learning how to do archaeology with and within descendant communities. Although I didn't realize it at the time, I was being trained as a community archaeologist – that is, on projects where descendant communities participate and contribute to the archaeological program. I was learning first-hand from those who accepted us as guests in Lau. This was the type of archaeology I wanted: a full-bodied anthropology with relevance and meaning for local communities. I was using a four-field approach with guidance and teachings from the community of people around me.

This experience would translate well when I was back at university. I was shy in the classroom during my first year in graduate school. I felt that the other students, who had come from all over the world, some from pre-eminent universities, understood better than me the theoretical texts and literature we were reading. They were intelligent. It was not until I stepped foot on the islands in Fiji that my learning began to take a deeply meaningful turn. I could now challenge the anthropological discourse and bring my own lived experiences into the discussions in class. Living and working in Fiji expanded my classroom so I could draw on the knowledge shared with me in the field and engage with my peers and with the literature we were learning in the academy.

In Lau, I was fishing each day with my friends, helping in the garden, feeding pigs, and playing rugby on the beach. I helped in the kitchen when the women would allow me. I was a novelty and was often made fun of (in good humour) as I tried to do simple things, like butcher a chicken. Rusila would tease me and make Sharyn and the other women laugh. While sitting outside on pandanus mats in the village, cutting pandanus with bivalves for future weavings, we'd watch Sepesa, Pat, and the other men come ashore to unload their fishing gear and nets. I'd get up to help, but Rusila would tell me to stay and sit, saying that I was "soft, like a jellyfish," making Sharyn and the women cry with laughter. "Sit. Sit down. You are like a limpet."

I remember one evening on the beach near Salia that, for me, encapsulates full-bodied anthropology. It was a Sunday. We had participated in the service that morning, which was done in both Fijian and English, since we were guests. We then took part in the Sunday feast, which was typical Lauan fare cooked in the *lovo*. There were the staples like taro, cassava, and sweet potato but also a variety of inshore fish, shellfish, and seaweed. *Palusmai, rourou*, and various fruits were also set before us. Food was plentiful, and the communal aspect of eating together crossed many social and cultural boundaries reflecting status and one's identity in the village (Jones 2009, 2015). Afterwards we went on a hike to Narocivo with Sepesa. Upon our return, Sepesa and Rusila wanted us to take pictures of them with our fancy cameras in their formal Fijian attire. So, we obliged and later mailed them the photographs. That night on the beach, the skies were crystal clear, and the moon was out. The fire provided warmth as the soft, cool breeze came off the ocean. We were all stretched out on the beach sharing stories. We had spent the day together like family. We would be back to excavating tomorrow, but the peacefulness of that memory of sitting beside the fire with everyone is something that can't be captured in an anthropological text. It can't be analysed, deconstructed, or interpreted in the classroom. It has to be lived and felt.

2
Working in CRM, a Cautionary Tale

My first experience in cultural resource management was in Florida after I graduated from college. I was offered a summer stint with a small CRM firm run by Lucy B. Wayne and Martin F. Dickinson. Martin, who was my boss, had a lineage: his family name adorns Dickinson Hall, the old location of the Florida Museum of Natural History on the campus of the University of Florida in Gainesville. Martin's kingdom was in cultural resource management. It was not like anything I was taught while an undergraduate. I spent one hot, sticky summer doing CRM. I couldn't stand it. I wasn't very good at it – so much so that I earned the moniker "carrot-hole kid" due to shape of my shovel test holes.[1]

On transects as long as the panhandle coastline, I trudged my way through saw palmetto and pine. I was paid seven dollars an hour while working across the state from Ebro to Ocala. My piddly per diem barely covered supper. Martin would set up the field crew for the day and often leave us alone in the morning. We would run our transects under the Florida sun, banging out shovel tests, the humidity helping the soil stick to our faces and arms.

I was never really sure what we were doing or why we were doing it. I don't recall who the clients were on any of the projects, what the proposed developments were. Maybe I didn't care. Maybe I have forgotten. I had graduated and was waiting to start my master's, so why not shovel bum it for a summer? I naively believed that it would be the last time I would have to think about archaeology as a business. Archaeology as a business: what a concept, I had thought. No research design, no analysis, no meaningful interpretation. I'll never do this as a career. At twenty-two, I possessed a summer of shovel testing under my belt and the arrogance of a new graduate student, and I had concluded that I loathed CRM. Didn't want to be near it. It was nothing like my university experience and training. I vowed never to work in it again.

Yet within a few years, in 2009, I ended up in Papua New Guinea working on a CRM project directed by Monash University in Melbourne, Australia. This project was far more complicated than my summer digging holes in Florida. It opened my eyes to true on-the-ground inequities and power imbalances inherent in CRM. It forced me to think through this question: Where do you search for purpose in your fieldwork when so much seems to be out of your control?

CORPORATE ARCHAEOLOGY IN PAPUA NEW GUINEA

Between November 2009 and March 2010, while I was wrapping up my PhD, I took a job as an excavation director for Monash University on the Caution Bay archaeological program in Papua New Guinea (PNG). The program focused on the mitigative excavation of newly identified archaeological sites that would be destroyed by international capitalistic enterprises to extract liquid natural gas (LNG) from the southern Highlands and process it along the Central Province coast for export. The project came to be known as the PNG LNG Project.[2] Monash was subcontracted by Coffey Natural Systems to undertake an intense archaeological field program focused on Portion 2456 within the footprint of the project area. Coffey, the lead environmental contractor, was subcontracted by Esso Highlands Limited (EHL), a subsidiary of ExxonMobil, which led on-the-ground operations. The PNG LNG Project was a co-venture between EHL, Oil Search, and ExxonMobil. ExxonMobil is the world's largest publicly traded international oil and gas company, with revenues of $290 billion and profits of $21.8 billion in 2018.[3] It has the ability, granted by its size and position of economic power, to traverse nation-state boundaries and employ tens of thousands of people. It functions as its own mobile nation, and, in Papua New Guinea, it was ultimately funding the archaeological program for the PNG LNG Project.

The archaeological component of the project was directed by Professor Bruno David, Professor Ian McNiven, and Tom Richards from Monash University. Monash had acquired a contract with Coffey Natural Systems to design and implement an archaeological assessment (David, McNiven, Richards 2009), and the university hired an international team of archaeologists who worked alongside villagers from Boera, Kido, Lea Lea, Papa, and Porebada; faculty and students from the University of Papua New Guinea (UPNG); and staff from the Papua New Guinea National Museum and Art Gallery.

Papua New Guinea is home to 8.2 million people. It is as culturally rich as it is diverse. Over 850 languages are spoken, with Tok Pisin serving as a bridge language across the country. For over a hundred years, anthropologists have spent time here learning about cultural diversity and

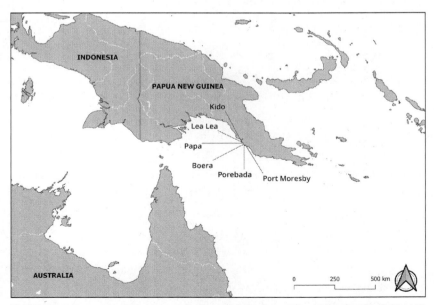

FIGURE 2.1 Papua New Guinea and villages central to archaeology for the PNG LNG Project. | Created by Walter Homewood via Natural Earth.

Indigenous interactions with Western ideas and projects. In PNG, 85 percent of the population live in rural villages, with 83 percent of food energy coming from subsistence practices in agriculture (farming crops), livestock, fishing, and hunting.[4] Jobs and wages are not easily come by: there are varied reasons for this, but the complexity of a country with such cultural diversity cannot be simply explained in global economics (such as GDP), especially during a time of such profound social, economic, and environmental transition (West 2016, 66–86). Although not a fair indication of economic wealth relative to revenue and profits, the GDP of Papua New Guinea in 2018 was $24.11 billion and has been on the rise due to oil and gas exploration and extraction (World Bank 2024).

Doing archaeology in Papua New Guinea under the umbrella of ExxonMobil was surreal and very challenging. It illuminated the inequities in the political and power structures of corporate archaeology and how transnational corporations control and frame Indigenous representation through rhetoric, wages, and safety culture rather than through consultation with the communities themselves (West 2016). The challenges of conducting archaeology within development-driven capitalism raised, and continue to raise, moral, philosophical, ethical, and political issues.[5]

MITIGATIONS AND POWER

Essentially, in PNG, ExxonMobil was paying the "cost" to damage Indigenous heritage in order to extract and export a commodity, a development that would have physical, social, economic, cultural, and environmental impacts. In the world of resource development, this process is most commonly referred to as "mitigation," as if the destruction of a landscape and loss of a culture can be mitigated. As the hired archaeologists on site, we were indoctrinated in ExxonMobil culture, policies, safety procedures, and other practices. My time in Papua New Guinea was marked by pressures and stressors that were forced on the field from high above and that illustrated the discrepancy in power and values between ExxonMobil and the entire archaeological field crew. The archaeological fieldwork was closely monitored and observed by ExxonMobil and its subcontractor, Coffey. For example, daily reports from the field focused on the volume of soil excavated each day by the field crew.

But such monitoring was mild, compared to corporate practices affecting members of the local communities. My understanding of the relationships between local communities and ExxonMobil and their subcontractors was obtained through what I observed and lived, day to day, on the ground, in the field with a crew who were from the local villages. My observations from the field were not the sort of thing one would read about in an annual environmental and social report, yet the interactions, relationships, and behaviours espoused by ExxonMobil employees mirror the thoughts and beliefs of those at corporate headquarters.

It was obvious that ExxonMobil, Coffey, Oil Search, and Curtain Brothers Group (construction contractors) valued their expat employees far more than they did local villagers. This inequality was evident not only in wages, but in differences in the food and transportation provided to fieldworkers. For example, large trucks with cages were used to transport Indigenous workers from villages to the work site, while most expats had cars or vans with hired drivers. Indigenous field crews were going without breakfast, due to their early morning commute from village to muster site. To stave off hunger, they chewed *buai* (betel nut) in the field, which was against ExxonMobil policy.[6]

Both the actions and commentary of Coffey and ExxonMobil employees in relation to local Indigenous communities in Papua New Guinea created a tension observable from the field. (Unsurprisingly, parallel issues plague archaeology and heritage in British Columbia today, but I was introduced to them doing archaeology on behalf of a corporate giant in a foreign land.) To overcome this tension, as if I could thwart the oppressive structure of operations, I centred the community I was working within and developed personal initiatives to lift up and celebrate my field crew and colleagues. And, admittedly, despite the capitalistic pressures and espousal of corporate values, the archaeological program provided an opportunity to build on the work of local archaeologists in Papua New Guinea. Due to the scale of the project, it afforded opportunities for many UPNG students and local communities to carry out archaeological research and practice that could foster future archaeologies in Papua New Guinea.⁷

This is all complicated stuff: to find myself working on Indigenous lands with Indigenous customs secondary, and now "illegal," as determined by a transnational corporate culture and their policies. Existing in such a world challenged me as an individual, as I struggled with how an oil giant's economic values could take precedence over local protocols and lifeways. I wondered where to search for purpose in our fieldwork when so much seemed to be out of our control? In the end, this experience taught me how to focus on what I could control within a project that was encapsulated within an insatiably racialist and dominant corporate structure that, from the outset, "othered" the Indigenous communities we worked alongside. The archaeology and my relationships to the field crew were things I could own, cultivate, nourish.

"THEY DON'T WANT TO BE MODERN"

Land is an integral part of Papua New Guinea communities: they have meaningful relationships with it and the features and creatures on it (Kewibu 2010; Knauft 1996; P. West 2016). Oil and liquid natural gas resources are an integral commodity for ExxonMobil, as they, currently and historically, drive the global economy. Many Indigenous lands house natural resources. Commodifying such resources through extraction continues the colonial legacy of exploitation, fallacies of "race," and misrepresentations of local life and culture, because to access a natural resource, corporations need to remove the rightful owners, both physically and figuratively, from the land. Papua New Guinea is often referred to by Western corporate employees as "raw," "untamed," "untouched," "natural," or "pristine," a characterization in which the people are secondary or even become a part of the physical landscape.⁸ This framework casts places like Papua New Guinea as precapitalist societies that do not live in the present and are incapable of "modern science" or "technology" (West 2016, 79–80).

Rhetoric enables action such as dispossession. A common comment from ExxonMobil and Coffey was that the people of Papua New Guinea "don't want to be modern." I was gobsmacked when I first heard this on the telephone during my PNG LNG Project induction teleconference call one evening in Vancouver. This insensitive and uninformed comment, which came from one of the safety managers, draws on what Jeffrey Sissons (2005) calls *eco-indigenism*, in which "the indigenous community is portrayed as having an overriding moral responsibility to care for the threatened environment and to defend it against the destructive forces of western progress and global capitalism" (23). The implication is that local Indigenous communities protect nature because they are one with it and defined by it; that their technology, social structure, religion, and lifeways are not of the twenty-first century; that they exist in the past. Something more "primitive," they exist as an earlier reflection of ourselves; they are of another era.[9] They are not modern. The erasure of Indigenous knowledge and epistemologies through such rhetoric is deliberate. Yet, in Papua New Guinea, nothing could be further from the truth. The diverse peoples there are not "part of nature"; they are not the fauna of a "pristine," rugged, and raw landscape in which they refuse to be "modern." They have held agency over the land for tens of thousands of years. Their ancestors innovated and adapted through time. Descendant communities today have concerns and raise issues over treatment of the environment, particularly when the economic development of their ancestral lands via an international corporation threatens cultural survival and when their individual voices are not heard. They do not refuse to be modern – they resist being forced to change into something they do not want to be.

Local communities acquire knowledge from the land and the sea, and, for some, in the classroom too. Many households in Papua New Guinea depend on subsistence farming, hunting, and fishing. Poverty, in a Western sense, is known, but people garden, hunt, and fish for sustenance. Moreover, many own cellphones and have access to social media. Culture is always evolving. Many of the students I worked with were being trained in university classrooms, but their natal homes were deep in the mountains, or situated on the coast, or along major river systems such as the Sepik.

What does it mean to be "modern" anyhow? Doesn't living in the world today, as you read this, make you modern? Are we all not of the current time and place? Isn't anyone who is alive at this moment modern? For project personnel to say these people "don't want to be modern" completely disregards Papua New Guineans as humans with agency, and it reflects a very profound misunderstanding of life in PNG. Such a mantra helps rationalize the behaviour of those working for ExxonMobil, and their subsidiaries, to take the natural resources from the land of Indigenous peoples while claiming that the local people could not, or cannot, fathom the value of such work or do not possess the capability, knowledge, or education to accrue capital, develop a corporation, and extract the natural resources themselves. Such a misrepresentation is then used to justify dispossession (P. West 2016). In her anthropological research in Papua New Guinea for the past twenty years, Paige West has observed, critiqued, and documented how development, tourism, and nongovernmental organizations (NGOs) construct narratives about Papua New Guineans. Her research illustrates how outsiders, whether surfers or transnational corporations, devalue Indigenous knowledge and practice, further reinforcing inequalities for one-sided economic gain. With respect to large-scale extraction in general, but with a spotlight on the PNG LNG Project in detail, the question of whether unlocking "value" from "stranded" gas resources on Indigenous land *should* be undertaken rarely seems to enter the picture for such companies.

Yet, if transnational corporations are going to impose their Western economic system and structures on Indigenous communities, forever changing the dynamics of the landscape and of those communities, I would argue that these corporations have a social – and moral – responsibility to engage not only with the national government but also with the local people in a meaningful way, centring Indigenous heritage ahead of a project's goals. To do so, they must be in tune with the local cultural norms, practices, and protocols and understand the vast diversity across different cultural groups and languages.

Was such an approach reflected in the PNG LNG Project? It is true that land holders, elders, and community leaders were "consulted" for this project under the ExxonMobil umbrella, which includes local Papua New Guinea community stakeholders and investors. But, of course, "consultation" has various levels of meaning and engagement. At its core, if all parties agree on methods and outcomes, consultation works well (this is why the United Nations Declaration on the Rights of Indigenous Peoples (UNDRIP) emphasizes free prior, and informed

FIGURE 2.2 At the archaeological site Tanamu 1 in December 2009. The young men from the village of Papa are en route to traditional fishing grounds. They no longer not have access to certain portions of these grounds. | Photo courtesy of author.

consent).[10] When there are disagreements with respect to wants, values, or needs, consultation is much trickier. The development of an LNG plant with a massive footprint was going to have consequences for those in many communities, from the Highlands to the coast. The proponent's formation of a Community Affairs Committee, made up of certain high-ranking people from five villages (Boera, Kido, Lea Lea, Papa, and Porebada) as well as an expat, was an attempt at dialogue with the chiefs and stakeholders. The pitfalls of such an approach are discussed in a slightly different context by Bruce Knauft (1996, 95–104), who studied a large Chevron oil and gas project (Hides Gas Project) in Papua New Guinea in his book *Genealogies for the Present in Cultural Anthropology*. He discussed how the efforts of the corporation to construct an underground pipeline met with resistance from local communities whose land would be impacted. Large-scale projects are notoriously complex, with different levels of government involved, monies to be allocated by the corporation to national and provincial governments and local villages, and funds set aside for infrastructure such as roads, schools, and clinics, as well as for environmental stewardship. These efforts frame the oil company as appearing to be protective of or concerned for the well-being of local peoples but, at the same time, they enable the corporation to ignore local social and political realities, opinions, and impacts (Knauft 1996, 97; Weiner 1991, 72). Knauft (1996) makes the point that local details matter, and "if Chevron had been more in touch with local people, more direct in their compensation, and more sensitive to the social impact of changes, the difficulties could have been greatly ameliorated" (99). Instead, colonial mindsets were being enacted in the neo-colonial present, when Chevron, which spent a huge amount of money to secure safe conduct around its massive project, gave very little of it to the local people whose lands had been dramatically impacted (Knauft 1996, 97).

The disconnect is not limited to that between corporations and local communities. Commenting on mining in Papua New Guinea, Professor Alex Golub (known as Rex on the anthropology blog Savage Minds (now Anthro[dendum]) accurately noted: "the big picture is that Papua New Guinea is torn – between politicians in [Port] Moresby who are want [sic] to use mining revenue to enrich and develop the nation, and grassroots Papua New Guineans who don't see why they should suffer so others can gain the benefits of mining revenue" (Rex 2010).

Today, the PNG LNG Project employs many local Papuan New Guineans, somewhere between 3,000 and 9,000 people (ExxonMobil 2018b). ExxonMobil runs training and educational programs for these employees. There are multiple environmental studies from the Highlands to the coast. ExxonMobil (2018b) boasts of community investment and environmental stewardship. Yet, I am left wondering whether the dispossession of land, resources, and cultural practices (Main 2017) truly makes life better for those villagers along the coast with whom I worked.

I don't know.

What I do know is the experiences I had on the ground trying to do archaeology with communities who were being forced to deal with the construction of a massive LNG plant along their coast.

NOGAT MAN BAI KISIM BAGARAP (NOBODY GETS HURT)

The Safety Vision on the PNG LNG Project was "Nobody Gets Hurt." In Tok Pisin, this is *"Nogat man bai kisim bagarap."* Safety is part of ExxonMobil's corporate citizenship model. By cultivating a culture of safety, based on perceptions, personal attitudes, capabilities, and behaviour, ExxonMobil has centred safety as a core value integral to each project. Yet, this doesn't mean cultural or spiritual safety or safety from racism or sexism. Instead, health and safety management teams draft policies, handbooks, and hazard assessments, and employ safety officers (also called compliance officers), to ensure safety conditions are met on the job site. No matter where ExxonMobil is operating in the world, it is "committed to doing the right thing, the right way, every time so that every employee and contractor comes home from work safe and healthy each day" (ExxonMobil 2015, 19).

In the past twenty to twenty-five years, safety culture has emerged in CRM across the world. Corporations have created whole departments that focus on safety. An entire industry has been built around safety culture. I am not against working safely. One of my former colleagues died on a CRM job site in British Columbia in 2017. I have worked with excellent safety officers both in Papua New Guinea and in British Columbia. These individuals are usually skilled in their trade and have an ability to solve problems when they arise and not focus the blame on individuals. They engage in discussions to co-develop solutions to potential hazards. But how safety is implemented, discussed, enforced, and dealt with in the field and cross-culturally varies from company to company and in place to place, and it can be a reflection of how a company "sees" the local culture (MacEachern 2010).

ExxonMobil and Esso Highland claim that they are personally committed to "a workplace where people can freely express their concerns and will willingly listen to better ways of working safe (ExxonMobil 2009, 11)."[11] ExxonMobil also claims to respect local and national cultures, and it has pledged its commitment to "maintain the highest ethical standards, comply with all applicable laws and regulations, and respect local and national cultures" (David, Duncan, et al. 2009; ExxonMobil 2002). Yet these statements are problematic in their references to listening and to respecting local and national cultures. In the PNG LNG Project, those conducting the multiple inductions (both prior to coming to Papua New Guinea and while in country) made it clear that we would be working in a country with "low levels of literacy" and a subsistence lifestyle; that the partial reliance on a cash economy would equate to locals not understanding the concept of "loss of jobs"; that local workers would require "extra" supervision, given their limited industrial experience; and that these workers were "slow paced" and possessed a limited concept of punctuality.[12] In addition, we were warned that the local peoples were violent – a belief apparently derived largely from stories of "revenge killings" in the Highlands and kidnappings. These condescending and misleading messages seemed to be bound up in corporate concerns for how best to ensure the safety of its foreign employees. ExxonMobil's induction teams were telling us that the collective goal of expatriates was "to have minimal impact, minimal intervention in the ongoing daily lives of these indigenes" (ExxonMobil 2009, 55). They seemed to be utterly unaware of the absurdity of issuing a directive about "minimal impact" when the goal of the project was to build a large-scale LNG facility from the Highlands to the coast.

During inductions, the us/them divide was made explicit: "their [referring to the *other*, the local people of Papua New Guinea] values, agendas and behaviours reflect a different culture – our agreement, acceptance or assessment of these values are not solicited and should not be expressed" (ExxonMobil 2009, 55). And "it is not our agenda to 'make them like us' – but to appreciate in what the difference consists of, and to allow them to make informed choices." The message was clear: for your own safety, do the work but do not engage with the locals. Do not share any information; do not lend knives, axes, or sharp instruments (I always bring knives as gifts – they're tools); do not make promises on behalf of the project; do not approach local women; do not engage in sexual conduct (for HIV is an epidemic, they said). And there was a whole set of rules around behaviour toward and with women. At the same time, we were to act as "guests," even though none of the guidelines seemed like those followed by a good guest.

After the initial inductions, additional health and safety documents and material were sent to all future workers who would be on site in the coming weeks. I combed through the material and the appendices. In Appendix O, a safety recommendation caught my eye and left me shaken. A rule dictated by ExxonMobil and its subcontractors said, "If involved in a vehicle collision, do not stop. Do not attempt to render assistance, even if you have struck a person or child" (Coffey Natural Systems 2009, 24). If you strike a child, you do not stop the vehicle or seek to help. You immediately flee the scene. Such a directive would be unthinkable in a manual for an American or Australian project. It likely reflects, to some extent, apprehension about the "eye for an eye" approach to justice in some parts of PNG, but how can one be a considerate guest and respect local customs when the corporation tells you that the local people are to be ignored – even if you strike one with your car?[13]

A bigger question is inherent in these concerns for the safety of expat employees: If a corporation can't figure out a way to develop a project without requiring these kinds of rules, should the project be going forward, and should foreigners even be on the ground? If an employee cannot stop and help a child whom they have hit with a car without fearing retaliation, maybe the transnational corporation shouldn't be putting their employees in that position.

Without question, ethics are part of the discourse, training, and practice within archaeology (Meskell and Pels 2005; Silliman 2008; Wylie 2003; Zimmerman 1989; Zimmerman et al. 2003). From that perspective, it is disturbing to see which rules ExxonMobil enforces based on Western law, or corporate values, and which local laws and customs it deems are not to be followed while in a country. Clearly, ExxonMobil believed that its rules were needed to keep its employees safe. But that's not the point. The safest mitigation is always avoidance, and this company failed to work within the culture in a way that would have ensured the safety of all. Instead, it imposed these rules in order to protect its staff from the locals, an approach that was easier – and cheaper – for the company.

A key issue here is the apparent belief that, simply because a large transnational corporation has capital and resources and is footing the bill, it is able to treat Indigenous heritage (and people) however it chooses. My interactions with those on the proponent side proved this sentiment true: the purpose of expats was to ensure project success, through whatever means necessary. Re-evaluation of such ideas is long overdue in the field of CRM. I would argue that, despite the perspectives of most proponents and regulators, managing archaeological heritage is not simply a box to be checked. Moreover, notions that wealth endows greater rights or power, or gives greater value to a human life, do not justify a transnational corporation treating Indigenous heritage as they please. Large-scale engagements to extract natural resources are complicated ventures, but that does not mean that Indigenous being, identity, and heritage should be undervalued or considered inconsequential. Rather Indigenous concerns need to be put first, and Indigenous peoples need to be at the table and be able to participate in decision making, at a minimum, when it comes to their lands, heritage, and lifeways.

WAGES

In Papua New Guinea, my wonderful field team of Tedy (Teto) Tolana, Iava Homoka, and Lahui Morea spent countless hours talking, thinking, laughing, and enjoying each other's company while we excavated at our site, Tanamu 1. At the same time, the three of them were becoming pros at archaeology. They were learning the importance of provenience, vertical control in excavation, material culture, and how to recognize archaeological features and interpret them.

One day, I was feeling unwell on site and tried to hide it from the safety officers. I felt overheated, worn out, and tired from long days of fieldwork. I could barely work when I reached our site. I was exhausted and likely dehydrated. The 35°–40° Celsius heat was draining me. After chugging two bottles of water, I asked the crew if they would mind if I napped on the wooden stairs that lead down to our unit, where it was shady and relatively cool, leaving them to run the show. I asked them to wake me if the safety officers showed up on site for an audit. They let me sleep. I awoke near lunch time, feeling refreshed. The crew laughed at me as I came to. I checked their notes, the labels on the bags with sediments and artifacts and their provenience. Teto, Iava, and Lahui had carried on excavating, recording, and trowelling like seasoned veterans. They had collected radiocarbon samples and noted significant artifacts.

Working with people in close quarters, day in and day out, you get to know them – their family, thoughts, perspectives, fears, and aspirations. Iava, for example, told me stories of trying to go to technical school and being harassed by the Raskols (local PNG gangs). Perhaps it was inevitable that, eventually, our conversation would land on wages for the PNG LNG Project. How was I to handle this one? According to the inductions, I was to share nothing with my crew. No project information. No details about wages. The latter is common – disparity in wages

FIGURE 2.3 Tedy Tolana, the author, Lahui Morea, Menson Menson, and Iava Homoka at the archaeological site Tanamu 1, March 2010. | Photo courtesy of author.

can cause rancor among employees and toward the employer.[14] But the guys told me their wages – 4.85 *kina* per hour. That equated to roughly AU$2.00, which was slightly better than ExxonMobil was paying other crews around that time period.[15] For an eight-hour day, they were making about 38.80 *kina*, or AU$16. I was making AU$400. I didn't understand this rationale – why such an enormous discrepancy in pay between expatriates and local villagers? Yes, I had a young family at home in North America whose expenses required North American wages. But the rationale for this gross discrepancy was clear from the rhetoric of the induction, which revealed how ExxonMobil understands local villagers' worth, their literacy, their untrustworthiness with knives, their human value, and their skill (or presumed lack thereof). Sure, degrees and publishing refereed papers are something, but were my skills and training twenty-five times more valuable than local Papua New Guinean skills and labour? An inherent problem with imposing capitalist values on a community is that doing so privileges the skills deemed important by the corporation doing the imposition, and not necessarily those held, or held important, by the community. People might say "well then no one would come work here if ExxonMobil had to pay United States-level living wages to local peoples, or if you paid Indigenous workers American wages, you'd destroy their economic balance," and so forth. To that, I restate: if a corporation cannot build something on Indigenous lands without causing physical, mental, economic, or emotional harm, then why is it doing so? The only answer is because it values profits more than it cares about hurting people.

It was impossible to justify the crew's wages, particularly considering how proficient and skilled they had become. We were a well-oiled machine, floating around each other, anticipating what each other needed, taking meticulous notes, excavating with care, thinking and discussing as we worked. At the same time, though, we were laughing and enjoying each other's company. We shared meals. I shared pictures of my wife and children, and they told me details of their lives. We knew something about each other, and we loved one another, in a way that is common across South Pacific cultures. These emotions help build relationships in the field, and local Indigenous communities were fiercely protective of us. The friendships forged between local villagers and non-Indigenous archaeologists led to capacity building on both sides. Non-Indigenous archaeologists developed deep listening skills and grew to value other forms of knowledge and an appreciation of other cultural values and lifeways. For local villagers and UPNG students, most increased their technical/archaeological skill sets, delved deeper into anthropological thinking, and better understood the goals and methods of research and what can be learned and shared in that process, in spite of the corporate conditions – one potentially positive outcome among all the negative impacts on the project.

BUILDING AN ARCHAEOLOGICAL COMMUNITY IN PAPUA NEW GUINEA

Vincent Kewibu, a PNG archaeologist, has identified the need for collaborative archaeological research in his country, "with visiting international scholars and local Indigenous archaeologists, based on both the Indigenous knowledge of the past and archaeology" (2010, 162). He argues that, in an undertaking like the PNG LNG project, "the engagement of relevant national institutions, provincial and local authorities, and local communities within the country should be a priority." The archaeological component of this project constituted the first necessary step in laying a foundation upon which to build such engagement. Collaboration between international archaeologists and staff from the PNG National Museum and Art Gallery, faculty and students from the University of Papua New Guinea, and Motu- and Koita-speaking communities created a relationship in which Western and Indigenous individuals could begin to exchange knowledge, learn from each other, and develop trust.

Peter Schmidt (2010) rightly criticizes the use of the rhetoric of collaboration when archaeologists are actually talking about participation. *Participation* is working together, with goals developed independently; *collaboration* means that goals are developed jointly (Colwell-Chanthaphonh and Ferguson 2008b Nicholas et al. 2008). True collaboration won't "arise, like a fog from ground" (Schmidt 2010, 269). In a project like the one in PNG, international archaeologists can take the opportunity to begin to develop partnerships that may ultimately lead to true collaboration with local communities and those who practise Indigenous archaeology.

These partnerships can begin in the area of education. Monash University's archaeological excavation as part of the PNG LNG Project was an opportunity from which some of Papua New Guinea's archaeological and educational needs could be met (Kewibu 2010, 157–58). Having Monash archaeologists, such as Professor Ian McNiven, assembling a team of professional archaeologists from around the world (Richards et al. 2016, 183–84) – including local practising PNG archaeologists such as Dr. Nick Araho, Vincent Kewibu, and Herman Mandui, and UPNG faculty such as Professor Matthew Leavesley – exposed UPNG students and local communities members to multiple ways of learning, thinking about, and doing archaeology. International researchers, many of whom had hands-on teaching experience, drew on their own backgrounds when discussing with their Papua New Guinean field crews and students issues associated with the project, which helped elucidate the archaeological potential in PNG. Yet, an essential quality to being a good teacher is listening, something essential to collaboration. Elders and knowledge holders too possess deep knowledge (Leavesley et al.

2005). In Papua New Guinea, archaeological interest centres on ancestral sites, burial sites, and terraformed landscapes constructed by the ancestors, places that contribute to common identities and shared cultural teachings and protocols among local Indigenous communities. It is important, then, for Indigenous knowledge, protocols, and teachings to be part of any archaeological plan.

Education and training programs are needed in PNG, and the results of archaeological research need to be disseminated in many languages so all Papua New Guineans can understand them (Kewibu 2010, 159). The extraction of LNG from the southern Highlands provided the monetary resources to enable such a bold archaeological plan. UPNG students and local villagers, who have gained archaeological experience to complement their own cultural knowledge, have the capacity to be involved in future archaeologies.

My small role, as I envisioned it, was to be a catalyst and motivator for the next generation of Papua New Guinea scholars with whom I had the privilege to work in the field. The archaeological program, in the end, provided new and exciting knowledge about western Pacific history and culture. Through our collective efforts, we expanded the known geographic distribution of the Lapita Peoples, to include, for the first time, mainland Papua New Guinea (David et al. 2011; David et al. 2022; McNiven, David, Richards, Aplin, et al. 2011; McNiven, David, Richards, Rowe, et al. 2012; Richards et al. 2016).

Working side by side, international archaeologists, UPNG students, and local villagers developed deep, meaningful friendships, predicated on open dialogue, honesty, and trust. Such relationships enabled a range of discussions, not only of issues pertaining to archaeology, origins, and history, but contemporary issues as well. These relationships represent one of the intangibles that come from Indigenous archaeological practice – that is, things you can't physically see or touch but serve to embrace aspirations and propel a new generation into the discipline. Dr. Nick Araho, a professional Papuan New Guinean archaeologist, mentioned to me one day while we were working at archaeological site Tanamu 1 that "you don't realize how much it means to these people [i.e., the field crew] that you people [foreigners] are here teaching and working alongside them, day after day. They are soaking everything up." To hear this felt good. I was not trying to teach my crew simply descriptive recording, which is important, but also analysis and interpretation. In many instances, the site history, stratigraphy, material culture, and oral traditions seemed to collide, providing stimulating conversation and allowing for Tedy, Iava, Lahui to engage in interpretation. This process gave meaning to the field methods carried out each day, and it made archaeology *fun*. Interpretation and analysis were conducted not only in the field but also in the field laboratory, where artifacts were processed, inventoried, and analysed. This work was led by Dr. Cassandra Rowe (Monash), who did an excellent job under challenging circumstances.

In time, I hope, this archaeological event will give way to community-driven, local archaeology, as determined by Papua New Guineans. Ideally, students and community members, stakeholders of their own cultural heritage, will have the means to operate independently, asking questions that are important to them. They also have the option to call on the assistance or guidance of international archaeologists to jointly construct a research design that meets the historical, cultural, and economic needs of their community.

The villagers and students we worked alongside each day were not just digging; they were engaging with archaeological theory, method, and practice. They were one with us and were treated with the respect and kindness by most of those in the field. An ultimate goal for the archaeologists on the project was to develop and build capacity and to create enduring relationships, and to do it with integrity and honour, the way our hosts treated us on their lands.

TRAGEDY ALONG THE COAST

On Sunday January 31, 2010, the phone rang in my apartment on Motukea Island. It was Higo and Goro (local members of our field team), reporting that violence had erupted between the villages of Porebada and Boera.[16] Regardless of the reasons – whether they were cultural, historical, and/or arising from the PNG LNG Project – four young men from Porebada were dead and two were wounded. They had been killed by shotgun and then mutilated, an uncommon event among the Central Province coast. We passed a sleepless night as we worried for our friends. We had heard that the village of Boera, where many of our field crew lived, was relatively empty, as many fled with their families to the bush, to Port Moresby, or to other villages, fearing retribution.

The archaeological team had been contacted by our friends from the field. We knew what happened before ExxonMobil or Coffey staff acquired the information and presented it to us.[17] Once ExxonMobil became aware of the incident, its spokesman in Port Moresby said that a police investigation would provide more information about the "tragic event." "The safety and security of our workforce and the communities in which we operate are of the utmost importance and we are monitoring the situation closely," he continued. "The project has temporarily suspended work in the area out of respect for the victims and their families."

The day after the killings, we did not go into the field out of respect for the lost lives. Would there be retaliation? Would more bloodshed occur? We were not sure. We didn't leave Motukea Island for a few days. I went down to the containers where some of the Papua New Guinea staff were housed and spoke with some of our drivers, and I was able to get the names of friends who had made it away and were safe. One of the cleaning staff had lost her brother-in-law, yet she showed up to clean the accommodations of the oil and gas expats.

The company officially suspended work for four days out of respect. After that, it was up to the archaeologists to determine when work should resume. Peter Leahy, head of Community Affairs for the PNG LNG Project, came to speak to the archaeologists, providing an adequate synopsis of the situation and answering our questions regarding the event and our friends.[18] Peter's visit was the first time information was truly shared. After he spoke, other ExxonMobil staff discussed our safety in the field and encouraged the archaeological team to get back to work. I decided, along with five other archaeologists, not to go into the field for one more day. My reasoning was respect – for the dead, but also for members of our crew who were pained by the events. Moreover, many of our crew were among those who had gone into hiding for several days. I felt that one more day was needed for ExxonMobil and Coffey staff to figure out logistics and for Community Affairs to have one more meeting with the two villages to see how the agreement would shape up.

I returned to Tanamu 1 on February 6th with Tedy and Lahui. Iava, who is from Boera, was not present. My friend Pune Vagi, from Porebada, came to the site but was asked by ExxonMobil/Coffey staff, along with others from that village, to go to the muster site, where the field lab was located. It was decided by ExxonMobil/Coffey later in the day that their safety was a concern, so they could not be in the field with us. Our crew discussed this in a very serious tone when Pune left. Because Iava was absent, Dr. Nick Araho came to our site to work alongside us. On February 11th, twelve days after the violence, Iava returned to the site. The crew was together again, with new additions Nick and Pune. Around lunchtime, Higo took a break from his excavation unit and stopped by our site to chat. Higo, who was older and had travelled out of the country, had an intense conversation with Nick, which focused on leadership, elders, and young people. They discussed grassroot ideas around organization, communication, and how to build up communities. No one in our crew talked. We all listened to these elders, these two knowledge holders, think and discuss issues important to them and to their people's future. Their values, ideals, needs, and wants shone through their discussion, as did ideas on how to move their community forward. Higo also discussed, in some detail, the events of the 31st. The violence, the fires, the tension and frustration, the people fleeing, families scrambling across the mudflats to avoid the roads, children scared and clinging to elders as they made their way to Papa or Lea Lea or to Buria Mountain. His retelling of the events brought to light the deep pain and loss regarding what had happened, the violence people witnessed.

That day in the field was not all about sadness, but included reunion, healing, connection, and laughter. At one point mid-afternoon, Iava farted really loudly in the excavation unit and blamed Tedy. Tedy shouted up to us outside the unit, "Iava's back!"

On the morning of February 23rd, the funerals were held. Many of us felt it was our responsibility, given our relationship with our crew, not to go into the field that day. Previously, I had discussed with members of my Indigenous field team the good and bad points of working or not working on the day of the funerals. My inclination was not to work, partly in response to the worry I saw in Iava's eyes. In many cultures across Oceania, when the dead are buried, those in the community resign from labour other than the work necessary to care for the dead and their family. People offer their respects and mourn and celebrate the dead. We were still at Motukea Island that morning discussing what we, as archaeologists, should do. One of the head safety officers for ExxonMobil came out and reported that we were safe to work and that she wouldn't let anything happen to us. The archaeological team, led by the head field director, Professor Ian McNiven, responded that our professional ethics dictated that we shouldn't work on funeral days of people from the communities of team members: it is not simply about safety but also respect. The safety officer told us that, if we did not go back to the field, we would be viewed (by whom, she didn't specify) as supporters of "martyrdom" while the dead bodies were "paraded about." "It's not our job to be involved," she claimed, and observed that we could be seen as "terrorist sympathizers." The message was that, if we stood down during the funeral, we were bowing to those who were killed, implying that their deaths were righteous ones. During our discussion, the safety officer turned to Ian and said, "you don't know how it works here," and then reinforced her claim that we would be seen as siding with the slain villagers. Ian McNiven possessed more than twenty years of working with and developing partnerships with Indigenous communities in Australia and Torres Strait. He was well aware of the situation. She wrapped up by telling us that "seventy-five workers were willing to work and were waiting on us." If we did not work, any delays would be our responsibility.

The members of the archaeological team had many discussions that morning, with various opinions, comments, and insights expressed. In the end, we decided to go to our friends in the field, as the days leading up to the funerals had been tense. Only about half of the seventy-five workers the safety officer claimed we'd be inconveniencing were there. A few archaeologists – Ian McNiven, New Zealanders Ben Shaw and Chris Jennings and myself – called a meeting in the carpenter's shed so we could speak with the field crews, as they wondered why we were late to the muster station. We explained the issue, told them about our feelings, and asked them how they would like to proceed for the day. With no ExxonMobil or Coffey staff present, the villagers opened up to us, as they always have done. Some of them did not want to be there. Others – about twenty or so individuals – preferred to stay and work. We, as the archaeological team, supported all their decisions. We did not go out to the field to excavate that day: we worked in the lab with those who chose to stay. We didn't work too hard, either. The day was more about talking and joking and being together as we processed, catalogued, and analysed the belongings we had been excavating for months.

After we returned to our accommodations on Motukea Island for the evening, ExxonMobil held another meeting, with McNiven, Jennings, Shaw, and corporate staff. ExxonMobil wasn't happy that our archaeological team didn't trust Community Affairs when it said it was safe to work in the field that day. Ian said that Community Affairs didn't know what it was doing, as we had been informed by the local community that most people did not want to work because it was a funeral day. ExxonMobil representatives turned to Coffey staff and said that the archaeological team needed to be more professional about their work. McNiven responded that we were being professional, citing our professional ethics as archaeologists.

That night, I lay in bed thinking about the day and the discussions. I was struck by the disingenuousness of Exxon and Coffey in never discussing the possibility that their presence might be tied to the violence. And I was thoroughly offended on behalf of my colleagues by the lack of professionalism on the part of the safety officer in accusing the archaeological team of supporting martyrdom, and even terrorism, in its decision not to work on the day of the funerals. The reason why the inductions preached detachment from the local people became apparent. Just digging holes, as ExxonMobil put it, while actively charting our progress each day, kept us focused on the technical chore and not the people. It allowed us to not be aware of the social-cultural context in which we were situated. Yet, my own code and my own archaeology do not take place in a vacuum. The events of that month were hard for all of us. But, of course, our experience pales in comparison to the turmoil of our colleagues in the villages who had to bear witness to such violence.

RETURNING HOME, TAKING STOCK
I left for Jackson International Airport in Port Moresby in the early hours of March 7, 2010. The night before, over thirty villagers had come to see

me off and imbibe and sing and laugh for one more night with the Monash archaeological team at a pub in downtown Port Moresby. We had never held this type of joint celebration before.[19] As I got into the company car, I was a bit groggy, due to the early flight time and perhaps a few too many SP Browns and Tradewinds (PNG's local beer and rum). Yet, I was sober enough to take in a conversation between our driver, whom I knew from the field, and the same ExxonMobil safety officer. That conversation served as a microcosm of the relationship between ExxonMobil and the local Motu and Koita communities. The safety officer constantly chastised the driving, dictated how to turn and at which speed to proceed, and then applauded him, condescendingly from my perspective, on how he downshifted to ascend a steep incline. This may not matter much to the casual viewer, but words, language, and tone matter. People are not immune to the meanings and subtext behind language – in this case, language with a clear a colonial undertone, as if the driver should respond "Yes, Masta." Of course, our driver was polite and said yes and nodded accordingly. As we pulled into the terminal, the safety officer quickly grabbed her bags and left, not saying goodbye to either of us. Our driver came to me as I unloaded my gear, helped me organize my things, and said good words to me. He commented on my time in PNG, my openness, my laughter. We shook hands and hugged. I picked up my things and walked into the terminal.

My time in Papua New Guinea was not without consequence, and the stories in this chapter capture only small snapshots of what life was like there. Each day was a grind in the hot tropical sun. Up in the early morning, well before first light, we were drenched in sweat before we even set foot on site. And we worked late into the evening in front of a computer, downloading data-driven results. I wrestled with what I was doing and how I was doing it. I didn't realize how much of a pressure cooker CRM archaeology would be. When I entered the project, my good-nature and humour helped me easily make friends and build relationships with fellow archaeologists, students, and our crew. In contrast, I found it very difficult to respect, much less befriend, those on the consulting or business side of the project, particularly those associated with Coffey and ExxonMobil. The misinformation, deceit, and lack of transparency made it hard to trust them. That experience taught me to deal cautiously with proponents in the business world. It galvanized me to advocate for conservation and protection and education, and on behalf of marginalized voices whose heritage was to be impacted by the harvesting of resources that would be used elsewhere. And it highlighted the importance of asking questions about who benefits from any given project – in this case, what benefits came to those communities in Boera, Kido, Lea Lea, Papa, and Porebada?

My experiences in Fiji and Papua New Guinea were distinct: the first was of an archaeology with and within an Indigenous community, one that embodied compassionate archaeology; the second, an archaeology that revealed the challenges of trying to work with Indigenous communities within a corporate structure. In both examples, though, on-the-ground engagement illuminated that archaeology is truly about humanity, about closeness and interrelationships. Such an approach seems necessary in a situation in which one handles another person's heritage, that from which they draw their identity. In this sense, archaeology is very personal, and there is a beauty in being in a place and practising within a community alongside local people, in learning from one another. In the physical space where archaeology is performed, archaeologists can have the most impact by taking their acquired knowledge of archaeology (and the world), and the overlying structural parameters in which archaeology is conducted, and incorporating it with the needs, wants, and values of the local community. Archaeologists can play a vital role in producing an archaeology that is compassionate, generates new knowledge, and is meaningful to a local Indigenous community. Archaeologists and Indigenous peoples are not mutually exclusive categories – more and more, they are mutually inclusive.

Archaeology is a science used to understand the past, yet it takes place very much in the present, with all the social, political, economic, and cultural variables at play. Archaeology is not apolitical: it never has been and never will be. The world we all inhabit is socially constructed: people, in their everyday lives, live in, and sometimes question and remake, the social world inherited from their predecessors. In Papua New Guinea, responsibility for this inherited world, and the role of archaeology, was complicated by the values and interests of development capitalism, where resource extraction was the primary goal. Conducting archaeology as a business creates an uneasy tension, a notion supported by archaeologists such as Randall McGuire (2008), who advocate for archaeology as political action through praxis. *Praxis* refers to the "uniquely human ability to knowingly and creatively make change in the world" (McGuire et al. 2005, 356). McGuire (2008) asserts that "praxis becomes emancipatory when it advances the interests of those marginalized" (3), something that is possible when archaeology is informed by Indigenous values (80). Relaying Indigenous values and concerns while conducting archaeology under ExxonMobil was not going to change the corporation's goal of extracting LNG. The manner in which a corporation conducts itself in another world is steeped in power, control, and capitalist rules. The archaeological program in Papua New Guinea was only a part of the larger ExxonMobil work. Yet, how could anyone contribute to emancipatory action while conducting archaeology when encapsulated within ExxonMobil as part of resource extraction project? The dangers that lie within such a venture where archaeology is a simply a component to be ticked off are many and varied (MacEachern 2010).

These dangers are not limited to distant places like Papua New Guinea. In British Columbia, upwards of 90 percent of the archaeology performed is CRM. Where proposed development projects take place on unceded Indigenous lands, educating proponents on history, imperialism, and colonialism typically falls on the archaeologists. Consequently, archaeologists need to be knowledgeable about both provincial heritage legislation and local protocols within Indigenous communities. Archaeologists are facilitators on projects, making the space necessary for all voices – including those of Indigenous community members, who must play active roles in managing their heritage. Archaeologists are more than science technicians: they are educators and facilitators, helping create awareness of and clearly demonstrate the responsibilities clients have toward Indigenous heritage. Yet, power, control, and ownership over Indigenous heritage lie largely with non-Indigenous people, institutions, and governments. A dissection of industrial archaeology, which is presented in the next chapters, is thus necessary to understand the legislative context, regulatory system, and archaeology as management.

3
Industrial Archaeology

Cultural resource management has acted as the handmaiden for industry in British Columbia, a state of affairs both arising from and perpetuated by regulations grounded in legislation. Since the emergence of CRM in the mid-1970s, bureaucrats and archaeologists have appointed themselves "experts" and stewards of archaeological heritage ahead of Indigenous communities (Ferris 2003, 154–55; Klassen 2008, 10; Klassen 2013, 78, 106). The tension between "expert" archaeologists and "non-expert" Indigenous knowledge holders has been consistently challenged by many Indigenous communities, who have demanded greater participation, roles, ownership, and power in CRM and heritage policies. They have asked repeatedly for legislation that reflects their values, concerns, and beliefs (see, e.g., Apland 1993; Armstrong et al. 2023; Colwell-Chanthaphonh et al. 2010; Dent 2016, 2017; Klassen et al. 2009; Lippert 2006; Mohs 1994; Steeves 2015; Stryd and Eldridge 1993; Wickwire 1992). Scholars have also emphasized how the practice and politics of archaeology are deeply entangled with the larger battle over Indigenous Rights and Title, drawing from firsthand accounts within Indigenous communities (see, e.g., Angelbeck and Jones 2019; De Paoli 1999; Klassen

2013; Lilley 2000; Lyons 2013; Martindale and Armstrong 2019; McNiven and Russell 2005; Sabloff 2008). Indigenous peoples themselves have raised these issues with governments, proponents, and the media, and directly with archaeologists in the field.[1]

Are archaeologists going to listen?

How CRM is practised today certainly causes introspective archaeologists to pause and consider the current situation. Modern-day CRM is encapsulated within a larger legislative, regulatory, and management domain steeped in capitalism. As it exists, CRM exploits and consumes Indigenous heritage, which is "owned" by the government (Klassen 2013). Archaeologists who recognize the inequities in power, ownership, and control inherent in the current system are more likely to explore how to contribute to meaningful and transformative structural changes that elevate Indigenous needs, wants, and values.

THE LEGISLATIVE CONTEXT

In British Columbia, the Heritage Conservation Act (HCA) (2019) authorizes the province to manage heritage resources. The stated purpose of the HCA is to encourage and facilitate the protection and conservation of heritage property in British Columbia. The act includes thirty-two sections that cover the management of tangible Indigenous heritage that predates 1846, both on provincial Crown and private land. An additional twenty-eight bulletins include information on how to manage Indigenous heritage, the necessary qualifications for those who can manage it, and other bureaucratic guidelines like reporting and site forms. The HCA automatically protects archaeological sites from damage, desecration, alteration, or excavation, but it also has the power to impact sites through a permit system. Although the HCA ensures that people, including archaeologists, cannot alter sites without a permit, there is very little reference to archaeology in the act. In this sense, it's less about knowledge production and the discipline of archaeology and, historically, more concerned with prescriptive archaeological studies on behalf of development.

As mentioned in the introduction, Canada has no federal heritage legislation that addresses the rights of descendant communities with respect to the treatment, repatriation, and disposition of cultural belongings such as utilitarian artifacts, spiritual artifacts, or ancestral remains. (By contrast, the United States does have federal legislation, the Native American Graves Protection and Repatriation Act (1990), but it addresses only part of the material cultural record.) In Canada, each province and territory provides its own heritage framework, with implications for the kind of archaeology that may be performed.

In Yukon, sites are managed by the Yukon Historic Resources Act (2002), which was written within the framework of the Umbrella Final Agreement on land claims, according to which Yukon First Nations and the territorial government must be involved equitably in the management of heritage resources.[2] The act established an advisory board, known as the Yukon Heritage Resources Board, half of which must be chosen from people nominated by governing bodies of Yukon First Nations. In theory, the board facilitates respectful decision making, because the values and culture of Yukon First Nations peoples are brought forward when advising federal and territorial ministers responsible for heritage, heritage resources, and heritage policies (Jansen 2010). A similar board was established in British Columbia, under the Archaeological and Historic Sites Protection Act in 1960, which was written primarily for the protection of precontact archaeological property (as opposed to structures) (Weil 1978, 52). The Archaeological Sites Advisory Board (ASAB) was made up largely of academics, bureaucrats, and representatives from the public, to advise the BC government on heritage (Apland 1993). ASAB's jurisdiction and enforcement were limited, and it was eventually disbanded in the early 1990s (Apland 1993).

In Alberta, heritage legislation is governed by the Historical Resources Act (HRA) (2000). The act, which was first passed in 1973, has the power to control development and any actions affecting historic buildings, structures, and areas, and includes processes to document, survey, designate, and mitigate sites. In the late 1970s it was considered a strong piece of legislation with broad protection, penalties for contravention, compensation to affected property owners, and minimum standards for a permit holder (e.g., a master's degree) (Weil 1978). The HRA also offers some protection for a breadth of traditional use sites, such as historic cabins; cultural/historic camp sites; ceremonial and spiritual sites; ceremonial plant- or mineral-gathering sites; historic trail features; historic sites; sweat, thirst, and fasting lodges; and oral history sites. Beyond the act, some archaeological sites in Alberta have received additional heritage designations. For example, Head-Smashed-In has been designated both a national historic site (1968) and a provincial historic site (1979), and in 1981 it received world heritage status from UNESCO. In 2019, Writing-on-Stone, or Áísínai'pi, also was granted world heritage status, which demonstrates, on some level, an acknowledgement of the importance of cultural sites and landscapes within Alberta. However, today, as in the 1970s, there is no mention of Indigenous communities in the HRA.

In British Columbia, Bill 14 (the Heritage Conservation Amendment Act) received royal assent on March 30, 2019. It had been over twenty years since the province had made any change to heritage law. The new changes purportedly strengthen the protection of archaeological and historic sites. The act forms part of the province's commitment to implement the United Nations Declaration on the Rights of Indigenous Peoples (UNDRIP), as legislated in the province's Declaration on the Rights of Indigenous Peoples Act (DRIPA) (2019). The changes to the HCA included a mandatory requirement to report the discovery of potential heritage sites or objects (Section 8.2); an expansion of the Archaeology Branch's ability to refuse, amend, suspend, or cancel permits (Sections 12.4 and 12.6); and the improvement of compliance and enforcement tools (Sections 15.1–15.3, 16.1, and 20.1). In addition, the amendments may require property owners to pay for archaeological assessments. Commenting on the amendments, the deputy minister of the Ministry of Forests, Lands, Natural Resource Operations and Rural Development (as it was known at that time), Doug Donaldson, said that "people who want to develop land where there is little knowledge of its history may be required to complete an archaeological study on the property" (CBC News 2019). To date, the Archaeology Branch cannot compel anyone to undertake an archaeological assessment if no recorded sites exist on the property. The claim by the province that the changes to the HCA recognize Indigenous calls for improved heritage protection in alignment with UNDRIP remains to be seen. Yet, it is already clear that the act does not address a critical issue for many Indigenous communities, which is that they, rather than the province, exercise authority and jurisdiction over archaeological heritage and CRM processes (Klassen 2008).

Michael Klassen (2013, 61–63) has noted that, at least on the surface, the HCA appears to be a strong piece of legislation. It possesses equal authority on both private and public land; allows for investigation of contraventions to the act; has the potential to designate heritage sites such as traditional use sites, sacred places, and cultural landscapes (under Section 9); and has incorporated provisions for agreements with First Nations communities (Section 4). Although, to date, no Section 4 of the HCA has been successfully completed, the Stó:lō Nation is working on one now.[3] Under the HCA, the minister possess discretionary powers, with approval, to create policies to protect heritage sites owned by the government, with the authority to issue a protection order for 120 days to prevent any impacts to land that may be deemed to possess heritage value (Section 16.1).

Yet, the HCA fails to resolve the question of ownership of heritage objects and ancestral remains. Moreover, the act doesn't even mention the duty to consult First Nations, nor does it provide First Nations with any co-management role over decisions affecting their own heritage.[4] Clients, archaeologists, or institutions carry the burden to consult, but that is largely voluntary. Thus, even the amended legislation fails to mandate a space for Indigenous role(s) and participation in the CRM process. Joanne Hammond (2009) stated the issue succinctly: "the Crown has been able to bypass issues of rights and title by offering First Nations the opportunity for involvement in heritage without ever specifying what it is about their relationship to the archaeological record [that] might justify such a privilege" (53). In short, the HCA serves to ensure that development projects, and the permit holders, are compliant with the regulations overseen by Archaeology Branch. With the province having the final word over heritage resources, the interests of non-Indigenous archaeologists, clients, and bureaucrats are privileged over those of Indigenous communities through a regulatory process that can either uphold the spirit of the law or serve to subvert it.

THE REGULATORY SYSTEM

Archaeological consultants must balance the needs of their clients with the regulatory requirements set by British Columbia through the Archaeology Branch. Until spring 2022, the Archaeology Branch was housed within the Ministry of Forests, Lands, Natural Resource Operations and Rural Development, but it is now under the Ministry of Forests (MoF), as part of the ministry's Integrated Resource Operations Division.[5] The placement of the Archaeology Branch within the structure of the government speaks volumes about its intended function. The MoF is responsible for the stewardship of both Crown land and natural resources, and it is significant that the archaeological and heritage materials that the ministry is charged with protecting are often referred to as resources. In addition, the ministry is responsible for developing policies and operational management by implementing and overseeing fifty-two statues and associated regulations.

The Archaeology Branch oversees a land base of nearly ninety-five million hectares, is responsible for nearly 65,000 archaeological sites, promotes sustainable management of these resources (i.e., archaeological sites and belongings), and supports industry development as well as public access to these lands for recreation and hunting and fishing. The branch employs nearly forty individuals in various roles: director, operations manager, managers of policy and engagement as well as consultation and negotiations, supervisors for permits and assessment, site inventory officers, heritage resource specialists (i.e., permit officers), compliance and enforcement staff, and various administrative support staff. The first provincial archaeologist was Bjorn Simonsen, appointed in 1971; his mandate centred on salvage fieldwork, some research, site inventory, and administrative tasks. The branch's workload has intensified since the transition to a business archaeology with clients focused on profits in the name of provincial compliance (the BC Energy Regulator is a whole other kettle of fish, with the ability to allow proponents to regulate themselves regarding Indigenous heritage – a complete conflict of interests).

The Archaeology Branch administers the Provincial Archaeological Inventory Database (also known as RAAD, Remote Access to Archaeological Data), which is the official record for all registered pre-1846 archaeological sites in British Columbia. RAAD is a basic resource for consulting archaeologists, as it provides inventory forms for each documented site. These usually consist of details about the type of site, the kind of archaeological assessment that was conducted there, and who conducted the assessment. Forms for each site include polygons encapsulating the site's boundary. Sometimes these forms are quite thorough and detailed; many other times they are completely blank. Archaeologists know all too well that the data in RAAD are incomplete and that the database is not a true record of archaeology in the province. Yes, there are dots on a map, showing where sites are located, but the data are, in many cases, preliminary and require further detailed assessments, preferably with a research design. Yet, proponents, especially logging/forestry companies, use these dots as gospel truth when laying out cut blocks, often impacting sites (Inlailawatash 2019b). Moreover, such incomplete data in effect restrict proponents from undertaking archaeological assessments, if their project footprint does not overlap with a known site boundary. Thus, costs are kept down, as proponents do not undertake any archaeological work to properly assess the extent of archaeological sites recorded in RAAD. Another issue is that site forms constantly need updating and new ones are being submitted. The Archaeology Branch is backlogged in processing site forms, largely due to underfunding and limited staff resources.

The Archaeology Branch oversees the Provincial Archaeological Resource Library (PARL), which houses reports from permitted fieldwork. All CRM reports in the province are held in this digital library, although sometimes they are not in the physical repository. Neither RAAD nor PARL are accessible to the public, including First Nations, unless the nation's infrastructure allows it to hire individuals who have approval to access this information.

The Archaeology Branch sets the tone for day-to-day archaeology by implementing, regulating, and enforcing the HCA. Figure 3.1 illustrates the current system and processes within CRM under the current structures. The Archaeology Branch manages and oversees the inventory of archaeological sites through permits, updating site records, notifying First Nations, and housing all the reports from permitted fieldwork. According to the *British Columbia Archaeological Resource Management Handbook* (Archaeology Branch 2018), "the role of the Archaeology

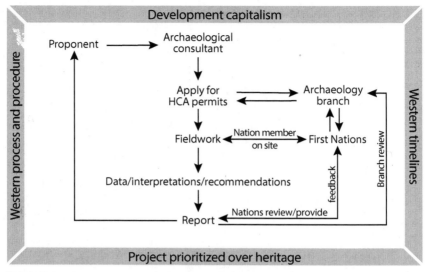

FIGURE 3.1 Current system of CRM in British Columbia, encapsulated within colonial and capitalistic frameworks and values. | Original conceived by author and drawn by Walter Homewood; redrawn by Julie Cochrane.

Branch is not to prohibit or impede land use and development, but rather to assist the development industry, the province, regional authorities, and municipalities in making decisions which will ensure rational land use and development." The HCA affords the Archaeology Branch considerable discretionary authority in determining under what conditions, and to whom, permits are granted. So, "when the benefits of a project are sufficient to outweigh the benefits of archaeological preservation, the Branch's primary concern is to work with the proponent in determining how the project may be implemented with minimal archaeological resource loss and minimal effect on the development" (Archaeology Branch 2018).

The Archaeology Branch's true power comes from its ability to appoint custodial caretakers to remove archaeological "resources." It regulates archaeologists through gatekeeping, vague policies (e.g., Bulletin 17), confidential "internal policies," and lack of transparency. Material culture at archaeological sites can be removed from the ground only with a permit granted to an approved archaeologist who meets the requirements set forth by the Archaeology Branch. Thus, only selected personnel can control and manage archaeological materials. As is often said in the dark recesses of dive bars where archaeologists quaff libations, the Archaeology Branch is more concerned about regulating archaeologists than about regulating archaeology. To gain permit-holder status, an archaeologist must first accumulate the required days under permitted archaeological projects and be vetted by the Archaeology Branch before they are conferred field-director status. The branch is not clear about what it is looking for in the field director application, and approval or rejection seems to depend largely on who reviews the applicant's field experience matrix (and what the reviewer wants to see in it, as this varies from officer to officer). Field-director status allows archaeologists to work under a permit-holder's permit to assess archaeological potential, test for archaeological materials, and excavate an archaeological site. The end game is to acquire permit-holder status, through which the archaeologist can hold provincial permits to conduct archaeological studies for proposed development projects on behalf of clients and oversee projects from beginning to end.

There are two types of permits archaeologists can apply for under the HCA. A Section 12.2 Heritage Inspection Permit allows for subsurface inspection in the form of an archaeological impact assessment (AIA).[6] AIAs are undertaken when proposed development projects may possibly disturb or alter the landscape, thereby potentially endangering archaeological sites. An AIA process has two results: identification of archaeological materials, and management recommendations. The identification of archaeological materials is typically concerned with the location of the site, its size, and complexity (e.g., the number of archaeological features, deposits, and materials). The management recommendations provide options regarding what to do with the archaeological "resources" relative to the footprint of the proposed development project. If the site can be avoided, and thus not impacted, protection is typically not an issue. However, if the site cannot be avoided during construction, then a Section 12.4 Site Alteration Permit (SAP) may be applied for, which authorizes the removal of archaeological deposits once the AIA is completed. These two permits, which are granted to archaeologists by the provincial government, confer the right to conserve, alter, or destroy any archaeological site these parties deem appropriate, with or without the consent of local Indigenous peoples (Klassen 2013).

WEAK SPOTS IN THE SYSTEM

Much like heritage legislation in other provinces, the HCA fails to define *heritage* in a way that is meaningful for Indigenous communities, at least partly because it privileges tangible heritage while ignoring *intangible* heritage (Connaughton and Herbert 2017; IPinCH 2014; Klassen et al. 2009; Lepofsky et al. 2020; Nicholas 2017a, 2017b). The province equates heritage with archaeology, thereby excluding intangible sites with cultural or spiritual significance. Yet, archaeological evidence is only one part of a much larger story of Indigenous identity and occupation, which can be found in origin stories, oral histories, place names, language, continued use of littoral and terrestrial resources, sacred spaces, and cultural practices. Safeguarding intangible and tangible heritage is part of the stewardship most Indigenous communities want, in order to protect their heritage for future generations.

The HCA primarily facilitates the management of tangible, pre-1846 "archaeological resources." A narrow definition of *archaeological resources* excludes most heritage sites that postdate 1846, even though Indigenous communities with connections to that site have continued to occupy villages, procure resources, and practise their customs after 1846.[7] This date has no relevance to Indigenous communities in relation to their material culture or archaeological sites. Additionally, this date means that the heritage of Chinese, Japanese, South Asian, and other immigrant communities is not protected.

While the purpose of the HCA is ostensibly to encourage and facilitate the protection and conservation of cultural heritage, the Archaeology Branch seems to focus more on supporting proponents as they navigate the requirement of the act. Archaeologists have to follow prescriptive permit applications, follow branch standards and guidelines (which clients often see as the minimum to meet their projects success), with no legislation to encourage co-produced field studies, peer-reviewed articles, or community reports within Indigenous communities whose heritage is at risk. In reality, in British Columbia, bureaucratic, state-sponsored archaeology exists not to prohibit or impede land use and development, but rather to assist the development industry within the province. The *British Columbia Archaeological Resource Management*

Handbook (Archaeology Branch 2018) states that "archaeological sites are valuable provincial resources, as are mineral deposits, arable land, forests, fish and wildlife ... The protection of significant archaeological sites so that their intrinsic values may be realized is important. However, the use of land for this purpose must often be compared with other viable uses the land base is capable of supporting."

The HCA, Section 2, states the purpose is to protect archaeological sites, but it does no such thing. In practice, it – or, rather, the Archaeology Branch – determines whether alterations and impacts to sites can or cannot occur. Despite amendments to the act, and the oversight of the Archaeology Branch and the Compliance and Enforcement Office – all housed within the MoF – archaeological sites are impacted, destroyed, and vandalized each year. Some impacts are reported, though most are not, and some sites have been affected so many times that the impacts can be described as cumulative (Inlailawatash 2020a). Even though the amendments were added to allow natural resource officers and officials to enter private land to enforce the act, the HCA provides a mechanism for archaeological conservation as opposed to archaeological protection and operates in the service of industry.

An example of the problem is the Grace Islet controversy, which arose in 2014 when the Archaeology Branch permitted a residential home to be built on a known burial island near Salt Spring Island (Nicholas, Egan, et al. 2015, 42–43). Despite the existence of sixteen previously recorded burial cairns, development was allowed to begin, under permit, until protests by local First Nations and residents halted the construction. The landowner asserted that he had met all heritage legislation requirements and that he was within his rights to develop the property, a position the province supported. However, the fact that the heritage process permitted a development to impact a burial island highlights major flaws in heritage policy and execution. The lack of protection for Indigenous burial sites, compared to non-Indigenous burial sites, illuminates the continuation of colonial policies implemented by the province. Ultimately, the property was purchased by the province in 2015 for $5.45 million. The province paid the landowner $840,000 for the property and $4.6 million for "losses suffered." (Nicholas, Egan, et al. 2015, 47). The province's stated rationale for purchasing the property was its unique ecological setting, not its ancestral remains. The whole event highlights the continued dispossession of Indigenous sites, resulting in a situation in which the province deemed that the private property owner was the one who had "suffered," not the First Nations who were struggling to protect the burial site of their ancestors. In this instance, as in so many others, the province viewed First Nations as nuisances, impediments to personal freedom and private development. In the end, through the Intellectual Property Issues in Cultural Heritage (IPinCH) project at Simon Fraser University, the Declaration on the Safeguarding of Indigenous Ancestral Burial Grounds as Sacred Places and Cultural Landscapes was created as a guide for provincial officials, local governments, First Nations, and archaeologists (Nicholas, Egan, et al. 2015). An interesting, if unanswerable, question is whether the Grace Islet landowner would have been granted a permit had the amended HCA been in place in 2014?

Among the Archaeology Branch's various responsibilities is ensuring that First Nations potentially affected by heritage decisions are given an opportunity to have their concerns considered prior to making decisions. Typically, the branch notifies a First Nations community about an impending archaeological project by providing them with the archaeological permit application already completed by an archaeological consultant. The community then has thirty days to comment on the methods described in the permit and send their response back to the Archaeology Branch. This process assumes that the First Nations community has the infrastructure and support to evaluate permit applications at all, let alone within thirty days. In any case, the HCA allows Indigenous communities no real power to decline archaeological projects, which are usually tied to a larger development project.

It is usually best if the proponent (not the archaeologist) engages First Nations through consultation – however that term is defined – prior to development, and prior to any HCA permit application, although doing so is not mandatory under the act. Proponents have a legal obligation to follow provincial heritage laws. This work is typically carried out by archaeological consultants who identify, record, and assess the value of the cultural heritage. Consultation also plays into the larger government to government consultation process, but that is separate from proponents engaging Indigenous communities. Any legislation or government decisions that enable destruction of or alteration to a heritage site (including permits issued through the Archaeology Branch to conduct archaeological assessments) are essentially infringements on Aboriginal Title and should trigger the duty to consult the affected community. Consultation creates the space for Indigenous roles, rights, and responsibilities in relation to their own stewardship within their ancestral places and among their belongings (i.e., artifacts).

If proponents were to genuinely embrace free, prior, and informed consent (FPIC) – that is, to follow Indigenous law and practices, and the interests of First Nations (as articulated in UNDRIP) – then meaningful consultation would be more likely to transpire (Hanson 2018). The approach to such consultation should be cautious and respectful, one where the proponent carefully accrues information at each step, while recognizing that it is a privilege to even propose a development project on unceded Indigenous lands. The proponent, in consultation with First Nations, would commit to conducting a thorough archaeological impact assessment. It is in the proponent's best interest to undertake an AIA, especially if they want to work with First Nations, but they are not legally obligated to do so if no archaeological sites appear in RAAD within the proposed project area. If an archaeological site is registered with the province and falls within the boundaries of the proposed development property, then the proponent has a legal duty to seek provincial permits. Unfortunately, as the Grace Islet travesty reveals, such permits do not guarantee an outcome that meaningfully reflects the concerns, values, or interests of the Indigenous communities involved. A proponent may undertake other (e.g., ecological, social, economic, health) studies in addition to archaeological ones to determine the immediate (and possibly cumulative) effects of the project. Even then, after the reports have been reviewed and vetted by all "stakeholders," including nations, if the local nations do not want the project to go forward on unceded Indigenous lands, then, under FPIC, it should not.

ARCHAEOLOGY AS MANAGEMENT

Most of the archaeology being performed in British Columbia is commercial archaeology where the proponent pays (La Salle and Hutchings

2012, 10). Within a commercial model, archaeological consultants conduct archaeological assessments prior to a development project in order to identify any physical evidence of cultural heritage (e.g., belongings/artifacts). Consultants typically perform assessments at the request of a client who wants to develop an area of land, whether for a grocery store, parking lot, road, pipeline, mine, dam, or liquid natural gas facility. In a few cases, projects are focused on habitat restoration or developing infrastructure on or near reserve land, often by the Indigenous community itself, but proposed development is usually focused on a commercial venture or municipal upgrades (e.g., water, sewer, power) on Crown or private lands. Archaeological consultants evaluate potential cultural heritage within a project area and identify the "risk" to clients through a series of evaluations and background research as well as field studies.

CRM is more than just archaeology, but let's focus on the nuts and bolts for a moment. Say a potential client wants to build a structure on a piece of property. The archaeologist could start with an archaeological overview assessment (AOA), which is essentially a background report on previously recorded archaeological sites within the project area. An AOA report analyses the potential of finding as yet unidentified archaeological sites. It uses a variety of data sets, which may include known archaeological sites near the project area, previous archaeological studies in and around the project area, ethnographic data (e.g., place names, oral histories, Indigenous trails), historical use and development, and geomorphological data (e.g., sea level, sediment development). The archaeologist might conduct a preliminary field reconnaissance (PFR), which is a non-intrusive way (i.e., no digging, no permit required) to conduct a pedestrian survey to identify any areas of archaeological potential that could be included in the AOA report. A PFR is a good thing, because the archaeologists walk the land with member First Nations. However, it does constitute another cost to the proponent, and sometimes the archaeologist will avoid one in order to save the client money (or they perform a "windshield" survey, which is simply driving around an area and not walking the land). In British Columbia, it is standard practice that First Nations representatives accompany field crews whenever they are conducting archaeological assessments within their traditional territories. So, prior to undertaking an AOA, the archaeologist pulls together the cost estimate, provides a scope of work (like described above), and submits it to the client for review prior to signing a contract to conduct an AOA.

The conclusion of the AOA report might be to recommend an archaeological impact assessment and to apply for a Section 12.2 Heritage Inspection Permit (HIP) from the Archaeology Branch, which will allow for subsurface inspection. An AIA will employ subsurface testing (e.g., shovel tests) to inspect landforms within the project area in order to identify any surface or subsurface archaeological deposits. If, during this process, a new site is found within the project area, the archaeologist may be able to suggest a way to avoid it, depending on the construction footprint. If not, they may recommend mitigation actions. This could entail applying for another permit, a Section 12.4 Site Alteration Permit (SAP), to conduct a mitigative program to excavate cultural "resources" from the site. Mitigation is a compromise between industry and knowledge: a small portion of the site is excavated to produce knowledge before the eventual destruction or "alteration" of an archaeological site.

All these individual projects (i.e., AOAs, AIAs, SAPs) might go out for referral or a request for proposal (RFP) by clients seeking archaeological consultants to perform the work. Consultants then determine how many hours are dedicated to field staff, GIS teams, administration (permits and meetings), analyses (more like recording descriptive metrics), reporting, and printing. From the outset, archaeological consultants decide where to cut costs and save time, because clients typically select the lowest bidder. As a result, projected hours are thin. All the client wants to know is if anything in the project area will preclude development. Budgets will often not cover a comprehensive field study or report, but they do provide enough hours to meet regulatory standards (which may differ from First Nations expectations).

Generally, consulting archaeologists are not interested in producing meaningful narratives about ancient lifeways or stories about the past. Perhaps that assessment is somewhat unfair: most archaeologists do archaeology because they want to contribute to a narrative, even if it is through a scientific lens. They produce quantifiable results in technical reports to comply with Archaeology Branch requirements and meet the needs of their clients. But in doing so, they transform the archaeological record into a commodity, one that is continually called a "resource" and is viewed as something that can "constrain" a project. In other words, Indigenous archaeological materials in a project area on unceded Indigenous land are viewed simply in terms of their "risk" to the project. The proponent can sometimes come up with strategies to avoid these risks, but, if this is not possible, then they have to mitigate constraints for the project to go ahead. Indigenous heritage, although the reason for archaeology, is never the first priority, and it is the interests of the client, not the affected Indigenous communities, that takes precedence.

I worked for a large transnational corporation in Vancouver for five years. Archaeology conducted within a corporation demands timely deliverables for clients. Making the space to include Indigenous insights, values, and voices, whether on the ground conducting fieldwork or in the final reports, was a constant challenge in such a setting.[8] A field director has limited discretion, as they report to a string of higher-ups – discipline leads, technical leads, assistant project managers, project managers, clients, and the Archaeology Branch. Compressed by the pressures and authorities that manage archaeologists, a consultant's autonomy is, at times, subverted by others. Any sense of the ability to set personal goals and make ad hoc adjustments to field projects is limited in the face of so much structural bureaucracy. This lack of autonomy/agency affects personal relationships in the field, which are key for any practising archaeologist who attempts to centre Indigenous voices. Archaeologists may push back at upper management to make the space for their Indigenous colleagues to contribute within this system, but it is often a lonely road.

THE MISEDUCATION OF ARCHAEOLOGISTS

As it currently operates, archaeology as heritage management under the HCA is enforced largely by non-Indigenous agencies such as the Archaeology Branch and the Compliance and Enforcement Office, both under provincial jurisdiction; is performed by largely non-Indigenous archaeologists; and is paid for by mostly non-Indigenous proponents. The regulatory system, legislative context, and companies that employ archaeologists all contribute to how an archaeologist fresh out of university learns to practise in this field. Three "teachers" – the Archaeology Branch, corporations (especially corporate culture), and clients – contribute to the miseducation of archaeologists in British Columbia, regardless of the values they have accrued through life and at university.[9] Consulting archaeologists are exposed to all three teachers, through interactions, relationships, and the regulatory requirements discussed above.

Corporate culture sets the tone in the way it indoctrinates its employees into the corporate system and teaches them to be corporate archaeologists (Connaughton and Herbert 2017). It teaches employees behaviours and ideology based on company practice. Archaeologists who are employed by transnational corporations are made aware of the behaviour

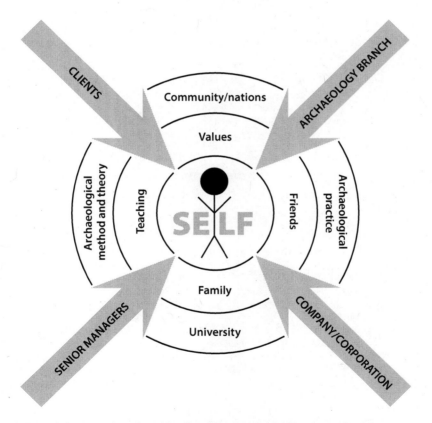

FIGURE 3.2 The archaeological self and entities that influence CRM in BC.
| Original conceived by author and drawn by Walter Homewood; redrawn by Julie Cochrane.

and attitudes expected by these companies and of the obligations to generate profits for the shareholders each financial quarter. The values within the corporate world dictate how archaeologists in CRM approach Indigenous communities, how they practise archaeology, and what they produce. Moreover, within this system, senior archaeologists teach and train the junior staff and show them how to navigate the many challenges of doing commercial archaeology.

For consulting archaeologists to exist, they must have clients, and clients must have proposed development projects that require archaeological assessments to be conducted as stipulated by provincial regulations under the auspices of the Archaeology Branch. The client chooses and employs the assessor; as a result, the assessor can be influenced by the goals of their client (see Wickwire 1992, 77). Archaeologists have to meet provincial standards, but they do so in tandem with their clients, with the additional goal of making their clients happy. After all, repeat business is key to sustaining an archaeological practice.

The idea of learning from knowledge holders within Indigenous communities is not part of the standard practice for consulting archaeologists. Corporations have no interest in prioritizing the heritage of descendant communities. The process of CRM relays a belief that Indigenous communities are incapable of managing their own heritage: this is part of the rationale for the province, though its legislation and regulatory offices, appointing itself as the owner of Indigenous heritage. It is also the reason non-Indigenous "experts" are formalized under provincial regulations and why CRM has remained the same for decades without making space for other knowledge holders, specifically those from descendant communities whose lands are being impacted for economic gain.

I do think some archaeologists sincerely look for that balance, that is, incorporating both Indigenous and western knowledge within field methods, recording and managing high-quality data, and producing clearly written reports on time. But the structure and goals of the corporation, the interests of the client, and the constraints of the regulatory system, make it nearly impossible to do good, meaningful work (Dent 2016, 316–17; Hutchings and Dent 2017; Zorzin 2014, 2015). To be sure, projects can be complex and involve many "stakeholders," not least of which are Indigenous communities. But, all too often, Indigenous communities or individual First Nations are not clients. They're certainly not the regulators. And they're rarely even field directors. So, where do they fit within this commercial world? What is the relationship between corporate archaeologists and local First Nations?

INDIGENOUS REPRESENTATION IN CRM
A management approach that is more consistent with how Indigenous peoples view heritage would be to acknowledge a larger cultural landscape where Indigenous heritage, both tangible and intangible, resides as a local constellation of people, places, and resources. Data on this heritage would be robust and not exist solely as isolated polygons; moreover, all spatial and recorded information would be accessible by nation members and not hidden away in a provincial database with limited access.

Because of the lack of inclusion in heritage legislation and policy, several First Nations have developed their own heritage policies and permitting systems in the Lower Mainland of Vancouver. Doing so is a proactive measure to assert their sovereignty into archaeological projects within their territories. Although the province does not recognize First Nations permits as legally binding, most archaeologists apply for them, if the nation they are working with has a permitting system, and try to live up to the spirit of these permits.

First Nations permits are generally issued with a set of cultural protocols or policies around the treatment of heritage resources, among which ancestral remains and spiritual places are particularly sensitive. These permits allow for First Nations to comment on and provide input into each archaeological assessment, including its methods, to request on-site representation in any fieldwork, and to review draft reports. Reviewing applications and issuing permits provide each nation with a proactive way to insert their voice into archaeological and heritage concerns. Proponents do not apply for nation permits; the archaeologists do, so they can work within a nation's territory. The approval of permits serves to regulate the archaeologist more than the proponent, and it builds on the relationships between archaeologists and First Nations. Although not perfect – permits cannot, in and of themselves, change imbalances that abound in CRM in relation to power, ownership, and control over

Indigenous heritage – First Nations permits enable a modicum of Indigenous oversight into the process of CRM (Schaepe 2018).

Consulting archaeologists typically notify First Nations communities of upcoming projects within their territories either through an email or through a nation's permit system. Archaeologists "hire" First Nations representatives (at a cost to the proponent) while conducting archaeological assessments (Budhwa 2005; Connaughton, Leon, and Herbert 2014; De Paoli 1999, 53). For the past thirty years in British Columbia, the CRM industry has employed member First Nations as "field technicians," "representatives," or "monitors" during field projects. This practice is even written into professional codes of ethics and conduct (see, e.g., Canadian Archaeological Association 2024; British Columbia Association of Professional Consulting Archaeologists 2005).[10] These codes are a step in the right direction because the industry has historically treated First Nations representatives as both allies and adversaries, depending on the project, the company, and the individual archaeologists. At times, assessors have allowed Indigenous representatives little involvement in the analysis, interpretation, or final reporting, treating them as tokens, labourers, even nuisances (Connaughton and Herbert 2017; Connaughton, Leon, and Herbert 2014; De Paoli 1999; Hanna 1997; Klassen 2013; Robinson 1996; Steeves 2015). In other situations, where projects have welcomed Indigenous engagement, local nations have contributed greatly to logistics, methods, and locating sites (Angelbeck and Grier 2014; Angelbeck and Jones 2019; Inlailawatash 2017, 2018, 2019a, 2020b, 2021; Klassen 2013; Lyons 2014; Lyons, Dawson, et al. 2010).

The role of First Nations has not always been clear to archaeologists or, sometimes, to the nations members who join them in the field. This lack of clarity can be improved through education and through discussions between archaeologists and Indigenous representatives prior to any fieldwork. For me, Indigenous representatives are part of the archaeological process: not only do they represent their nation, but, in the words of Mike Leon (Katzie First Nation), they "ensure that their ancestors have the representation and voice they deserve" (Connaughton, Leon, and Herbert 2014, 552). Indigenous representatives observe the archaeologists, ensuring that they do their job correctly and professionally, and they report back to the nation on the results of each field day.

Archaeologists working under permits from individual First Nations to conduct archaeological assessments within their unceded territories are required to have representatives on site. Yet, having First Nation representatives oversee archaeological work in this way isn't the same as meaningful government-to-government or industry-to-government engagement, and it highlights the need for meaningful consultation and engagement between proponents and First Nations (Connaughton and Herbert 2017). This consultation must be conducted separately, between the proponent and the nation, and not facilitated through an intermediary such as an archaeological consulting firm. Ideally, proponents would engage with Indigenous communities to obtain free, prior, and informed consent for any project that could potentially affect their lands, territories, or resources, and ultimately their right to control their own cultural heritage.

Nation representatives are on site to ensure that archaeologists make informed, appropriate, and respectful decisions regarding their heritage in consultation with them. In this sense, the archaeologists are being supervised, monitored, and challenged when working in the field with First Nations representatives. And they should be. They are visitors on unceded Indigenous lands. Archaeologists need to recognize their role as visitors and should seek meaningful approval and permission prior to any fieldwork and avoid the practice of "helicoptering" into communities (Atalay 2012, 111; Connaughton and Herbert 2017, 329; Herbert and Connaughton 2017). Indigenous communities are not passive stakeholders; rather, they own their heritage and have a legal, ethical, and moral right to fully control how research is conducted on it and any development that might affect it.

Indigenous representatives are present on the ground during most field-based projects, including the most common type of assessment: archaeological monitoring. Archaeological monitoring typically involves both an Indigenous representative and an archaeologist being on a construction site within an urban, built landscape to watch a backhoe, geotechnical drill, or excavator remove sediment. Such monitoring might occur when a city puts in a new watermain underneath a road through trenching. Although no archaeological site has been identified in the footprint of the watermain, monitoring allows both archaeologists and

Indigenous representatives an opportunity to be on site when construction is carried out and to ensure that previously unidentified archaeological materials are not impacted by the work. It's slow going. There's a lot of standing around. The importance of our existence as an archaeologist comes into question, as we wonder why we are watching an excavator remove road fill. The presence of representatives from First Nations offers opportunities to assess subsurface deposits, which is critically important, considering how much Indigenous heritage was impacted at the onset of colonization and industrial development. Even if archaeological materials are disturbed and not in primary context, they are still protected under the HCA. Ancestral remains buried under roadways are sometimes identified this way, which allows them to be cared for properly.

COVID-19 impacted Indigenous representation on archaeological fieldwork by removing these representatives from sites for most of 2020 and at least half of 2021. This is because Indigenous communities are vulnerable to pandemics, and protecting elders and knowledge holders is culturally important. Archaeologists have had to educate proponents so they could understand the reason why Indigenous communities were taking the pandemic seriously. Local First Nations in Vancouver asked archaeologists to discuss with each proponent whether a project was essential and determine if proceeding on any fieldwork during the pandemic was absolutely necessary. (Unsurprisingly, nearly every proponent felt their project was essential.) Since Indigenous representatives could not participate directly in fieldwork, a remote monitoring program was developed by First Nations and archaeologists, which allowed representatives to monitor projects from home via phone calls, texts, and a daily summary of fieldwork. Proponents loved this option, as it presented an opportunity to proceed with all work during the pandemic. But this program added another burden on already stressed Indigenous communities who were trying to focus their priorities on supporting their members on reserves amidst the pandemic. Indigenous priorities were not the proponents' priorities. Indigenous concerns didn't stop proponents from demanding that their projects go forward, and development did not slow during the global health crisis. In fact, workloads increased for both archaeologists and Indigenous communities.[11]

In "normal" times, archaeological monitoring also offers an opportunity for other interactions on the site, such as that between archaeologists and the construction crew. While on site, archaeological crews engage the construction crew and get to know the foreperson. Often, archaeological crews are part of the morning safety meetings and daily planning of the construction team. Such interactions provide an opportunity to learn new terminology, hear colourful language, and see first-hand how the contemporary world is built and maintained. They also present opportunities to educate the construction crew, or perhaps get them excited about the past and take an interest in local Indigenous heritage. Indigenous representatives contribute to the education process, teaching about their descendant communities and their heritage. Conversations between the construction crews and nation members help contribute to the breaking down of racist stereotypes through a process of engagement and education, enabling good things to come out of such monotonous work.

This discussion brings up a crucial question within the process of CRM: are Indigenous representatives archaeologists? In the eyes of the province, no. Most Indigenous representatives do not meet the standards for field director or permit holder status set by the Archaeology Branch. Most Indigenous representatives do not possess a university degree, nor have they been trained in archaeological method and theory. In British Columbia, not every archaeologist is allowed to conduct archaeological assessments for a client. A First Nation member who has participated in numerous field studies (as any junior non-Indigenous archaeologist would have) will find in hard to obtain field director status, especially without a university degree. But possessing a university degree, even a graduate degree, doesn't automatically earn an individual field director status – according to the Archaeology Branch, it has to be earned in the field. This position seems illogical: if the branch has determined that field experience matters more than formal education, why does it make it so difficult for Indigenous individuals with plenty of field experience but no degree to become field directors?

From the perspective of the descendant community, Indigenous representatives possess the knowledge, training, and experience to successfully manage cultural heritage resources in their territories. It is *their* heritage after all. Indigenous knowledge – knowledge that has been learned within the descendant community whose heritage is being assessed – is an invaluable part of any project. I may have postsecondary degrees that provide me with archaeological knowledge and the technical skills to identify, record, and manage cultural heritage, but they do not replace local community knowledge. I learn from community members: we are colleagues who possess different knowledge sets, and we can use each other's knowledge to co-conduct archaeological assessments. Therefore, I refer to the many Indigenous representatives I've been privileged to work with as archaeologists. Why do they need the colonial government to approve their right to manage their sites, a right they have inherited from their community? Many of my Indigenous colleagues are fluent in archaeological methods, possess a breadth of knowledge about the past, and understand cultural landscapes. Under CRM as currently regulated, there is no formal way to recognize Indigenous knowledge and knowledge gained in academia as equally valuable. But recognition of Indigenous knowledge occurs in the field and through ongoing relationships between Indigenous and non-Indigenous archaeologists.

Even though the expertise of Indigenous representatives contributes greatly to archaeological projects, this contribution is limited to fieldwork: representatives' access to other aspects of archaeological knowledge production, such as analysis, interpretation, and reporting, is significantly limited (Connaughton and Herbert 2017, 322–23; Mickel 2021, 67). These aspects of archaeological practice need to be opened up thorough engagement between archaeologists and Indigenous representatives.

LEARNING ON THE JOB

Local Indigenous representatives working with archaeologists are teachers in the field, if archaeologists learn to listen and pay attention to the lessons woven through stories tied to places across the cultural landscape. In cities and towns today, people from all different backgrounds live within the same area but experience it differently. Two people can grow up in the same city and live completely different lives, as ethnicity, socioeconomic status, religion, language, occupation, and culture impact their lived experiences.

I have a friend, colleague, teacher – DJG – who has lived most of his life in the Lower Mainland of Vancouver. He is an archaeologist for his First Nation. DJG grew up on the səlilwətaɬ reserve in North Vancouver (IR No. 3). In his youth, he played soccer until he left high school. He spent time with his cousins, listening to music, going to rock shows, drawing, painting, writing, and playing pool in bars across the city. DJG met all kinds of people through construction, odd jobs, art school, and archaeology. He represents his community on archaeological projects throughout Vancouver. His role is to monitor the archaeologists and to make sure the ancestors and their belongings are cared for. But DJG opens himself up at times to archaeologists so the crew can glean a sense of who they are working with. Such efforts are part of Indigenous people's never-ending fight to be recognized as they are, not as the settler gaze constructs them.

Dotted across Vancouver are stories of my friend's life, his experiences tied to places, events, people. His world view is shaped by his experiences lived on this land through time. His memories are imbued with the landscape. The morning ritual of picking up DJG for work offers a phenomenological experience. As we drive across town to perform archaeology, he shares his stories of past memories. I ask questions. He answers with more stories. I come to know the world inhabited by him, one very different from my own. Although we live in the same city, it offers us different opportunities: to know a different place, during a different time. To know my friend, a life he led, the experiences he accrued, how others related to him and treated him, is to hear his stories. These are his words:

> I have been here, there all over the city. Seen it at different stages of my life. As a child my parents would bring me into the city. Along with my brothers and sisters. One of my happiest memories going to see Santa at Woodward's. Then we'd go to the Save On Meats, have a burger and floats. While our parents would look for what we wished for. The area is all changed now, no more Woodward's store.
>
> As a youth running wild, roaming the city. Believing I knew more than I really did. Soon my eyes would be open to the world around

me. I learnt of the history from our side. Not the history we were taught in school. How we ended up here on Reserve #3. We lost the freedom we once had. Our numbers were cut down, almost vanished all together. Many other nations did vanish. If not for the strength of the generation before us, we'd be gone, after the ships came sailing into our waters.

In my years as a young adult, I tried to venture further. I wanted to go to places artists I looked up to came from. I wanted to walk the ground they once did. To see what they once seen. I worked whatever jobs came along. Never saved anything. All went to what I believed was fun. But in reality, I was holding myself back. The trauma I went through as a child never went away, I pushed it deep down. It wasn't until I realized it, got off my path of destruction, I found my true path, for now.

Now having been here, over 50 years, I'm doing what I love doing. It isn't always easy. At times I need to remember the words of elders I grew up listening to, learning from. I take a step back, try letting what weighs on me go. Remain on the path. I know there are things I want to save. Visiting places our ancestors walked. Doing what I can for them and my nation. Revisiting places I was in different times of my life. I have seen the city change. I have changed myself, grew, learnt, and survived. No longer lift those bottles. Sober, I try not to come across preachy. But I put it out there, I believe I'm in a better place. Believe I wouldn't be doing this work if I wasn't sober today. We all find our path, it isn't always easy. I know there are things I want to see through. Before my canoe is ready. I cross over to a new shore. Before the wind erases my foot prints. I start a new journey perhaps in a new form. Raised believing in the other side, we take care of our loved ones. "Raise my hands to all my relations"

As we drive down Hastings toward Main Street, we take in the mix of old and new buildings: a new brewery, a new library (with its name in hənq̓əmin̓əm̓), new apartments. The Astoria Hotel with its vintage neon sign and seven stars that hang off the old brick façade. A shadow economy begins to awaken on the sidewalk. A half-finished beer dangles in a person's hand. My friend wonders aloud what will happen to all the old places. Will they just be destroyed for newer business and housing? Who will be able to afford the rent? What will happen to the locals we're passing on the streets? Where will they go? Where can they go?

We slide into downtown Vancouver among the mixed built heritage of Art Deco, steel, and glass. The change on the street is pronounced. Suits, skirts, and dresses hustle along the sidewalk. Coffee cups and cell phones bob along the way. DJG cracks the window for air. We turn right onto Robson Street. My friend reveals another story, something about missed opportunities.

We pull into Stanley Park. Another story. We can see Kitsilano across the water. The Locarno Beach site. A story about Wayne Point (of xʷməθkʷəy̓əm) and Louise Williams (from Skwxwú7mesh Úxwumixw), teaching my friend about the importance of the work they do, why their presence matters. A commitment to the ancestors. Taking care of them. A reminder to me of why we are here. My friend does not need to be direct. He looks out across English Bay and narrates. The rings on his fingers reflect the early morning sun as he subtly gestures toward the ancient villages.

I won't ever be able to experience the city like my friend does. He slides through it, with his stories guiding his way. Places he knows and once knew. I won't ever understand what it is like to experience the city as an Indigenous person. To be local but to be ignored or, worse, heard only when convenient. My friend knows prejudice. He knows pain, loss, and suffering. He knows good times too: warmth, friendship, and laughter. I won't ever be able to experience his city, but, listening to his stories, I've come to map the city differently in my own head. Now when I am in locales once frequented by my friend, I try to imagine myself in his shoes, in his own time and place. I think of my friend now, as he is. DJG's unforced aura of cool, with his own stance and gait. The dark colours and fresh kicks he wears when not working. The new lime-green North Face bag he totes when working.

As an archaeologist, I can see the city before the city. How ancient places articulated with one another thousands of years ago. How they are still important, places where the spirits still reside. But I also see the more recent past. How my friend's experiences and memories are part of a never-ending story, a continuous layer of Indigenous occupation atop older stories that lie with their ancestors.

CRM is currently driven by the needs of clients whose interests lie with economic development, carried out within a capitalist framework that rests on the demand for ever-increasing productivity. In their eyes, archaeological materials and the laws designed to protect them are fundamentally obstacles that frustrate their objectives and stand in the way of "progress." This is evident in the language used by the province and proponents. Terms such as "resource," "constraint," "risk," frame heritage as a problem to be dealt with, a box to be checked so a project may succeed. From the proponent's perspective, the entire regulatory system is an impediment to their project.

Archaeology suffers because time and money are not afforded to the archaeological components of a project. Proponents focus on the project's path to completion, not on heritage. This leaves assessments superficial, rather than as an opportunity to explore meaningful information with and for descendant communities. Indigenous scholars have described how to work alongside Indigenous communities to shift the locus of power in CRM and develop more sustainable partnerships between Indigenous communities/governments and industry, colonial governments, and academia (Atalay 2006b, 2012; Atalay et al. 2014; Lyons 2013; McNiven and Russell 2005; Silliman 2008; C. Smith and Wobst 2005; L.T. Smith 2012; Steeves 2015; Watkins 2001). Doing so may contribute, in some small way, to descendant communities achieving their self-defined heritage goals, which relate to larger issues of ownership, self-governance, sovereignty, and cultural stewardship. Global and local movements surrounding Indigenous rights have political implications for what we do in British Columbia, and they "pose real challenges to traditional practice of archaeology" (Hammond 2009, 14). This is the subject of the next chapter.

4
Indigenous Rights

Indigenous rights are entangled within archaeological practice. This is because, in British Columbia, archaeology is performed on unceded Indigenous lands where descendant communities thrive and is encapsulated in colonial legislation regulating what happens on this land. Sonya Atalay (2006b) captures this entanglement when she says:

> the colonial past is not distinct from today's realities and practices, as the precedents that were set continue to define structures for heritage management practices and have powerful continuing implications for Indigenous peoples in North America and elsewhere precisely because they disrupted the self-determination and sovereignty of Indigenous populations with respect to their abilities to govern and practice their own traditional forms of cultural resource management. (282)

Most archaeologists should be well aware of this disruption, since archaeology examines the *longue durée* of many cultures worldwide. Or perhaps they picked it up through George Orwell (1949), who wrote that those who control the present control the past. Stephanie Irlbacher-Fox

(2009) discusses this attitude in Canadian governance, noting that, by "conflating specific unjust events, policies, and laws with 'history,' what is unjust becomes temporarily separate from the present, unchangeable" (33). For Canada, this means placing any settler colonial abuses or atrocities firmly in the past (Coulthard 2014, 22, 120–21). The idea is that what's past is past, and everyone just needs to get over it. This sentiment puts the onus on Indigenous peoples to adapt to the current conditions set by the colonizer (Irlbacher-Fox 2009, 34). When Indigenous heritage is discussed within the scope of Indigenous sovereignty, reconciliation, and human rights (see Nicholas 2018b), it becomes apparent that the treatment of Indigenous heritage is another form of continued colonization, part of the same wave eroding Indigenous trust.

Ultimate power in Canada rests with the federal and provincial governments, "leaving the present structure of colonial rule largely unscathed" (Coulthard 2014, 22). This chapter looks at three major publications that aim to challenge these structures and guide informed action toward reconciliation and overturning power imbalances between Canadian governments and Indigenous peoples: the report of the Royal Commission on Aboriginal Peoples (RCAP), the ninety-four calls to action of the Truth and Reconciliation Commission (TRC), and the United Nations Declaration on the Rights of Indigenous Peoples (UNDRIP). Will settler-colonial governments at all levels embrace the substance of these publications and pivot to include Indigenous voices in decision making and restructure existing power relations, given the uncertainty this would bring for settlers (Mackey 2014; Tuck and Yang 2012)? Either way, how can archaeologists in their daily practice honour the calls to action and UNDRIP articles – especially Articles 11 and 31, which address Indigenous sovereignty and explicitly state that Indigenous peoples have the right to maintain, control, protect, and develop their cultural heritage? Can archaeologists contribute in some small way through daily practice to normalizing conversations around Indigenous sovereignty?

THE ROYAL COMMISSION ON ABORIGINAL PEOPLES

The Royal Commission on Aboriginal Peoples (RCAP) was established in 1991 by the federal government as a reaction to two events: the failure of the Meech Lake Accord and the "standoff" at Oka. Both events reflected years of Indigenous frustration with a government that refused to uphold Aboriginal rights that had been recognized and affirmed in Section 35(1) of the Constitution Act, 1982 (Coulthard 2014, 116; A. Simpson 2014, 152–53). The purpose of the RCAP was to investigate the evolution of the relationship between Indigenous peoples, the Canadian government, and Canadian society as a whole. It produced a five-volume, nearly 4,000-page report, which was informed by five years of research and public hearings in ninety-six communities. With the report came 444 recommendations and the proposition that the relationship between Indigenous and non-Indigenous peoples be profoundly restructured. Indigenous scholars believe that a renewed relationship "based upon a realization of a postcolonial vision and not a perpetuation of colonialism through the creation of negotiated inferiority and an unequal partnership" is the way forward (Ladner 2001, 261). However, the report did not always seem to be consistent with this approach. For example, it stated that "there is every reason to believe that with access to resources, to development capital and to appropriate skills, Aboriginal people can participate successfully in the globally oriented southern market economy and in the increasingly self-reliant mixed economy of northern communities" (RCAP 1996, 5: 3). Critics argue that this assessment of Indigenous potential and engagement in the world still situates Indigenous being – and land – under colonial authority, with assimilation as a goal (Coulthard 2014, 119; Ladner 2001).

The RCAP recognized that involving Indigenous communities in meaningful engagement with heritage was a pragmatic way to help counter past grievances and destruction of Indigenous heritage. Among the commission's recommendations are sections that relate to cultural heritage, offering "archaeologists, bureaucrats, and businesses a chance to engage in a kind of archaeology freed from accusations of curiosity-seeking and self-interest" (Hammond 2009, 142).

Noteworthy recommendations made by the RCAP regarding heritage include the following:

> 3.6.1 – Federal, provincial and territorial governments collaborate with Aboriginal organizations and communities to prepare a

comprehensive inventory of historical and sacred sites, involving elders as expert advisers, before negotiations on designation of lands in accordance with our recommendations in Volume 2, Chapter 4.

3.6.2 – Federal, provincial and territorial governments review legislation affecting sacred and historical sites to ensure that Aboriginal organizations and communities have access to urgent remedies to prevent or arrest damage to significant heritage sites such as the Mnjikaning Fish Fence, whether they be threatened by human actions or natural processes.

3.6.3 – Federal, provincial and territorial governments in collaboration with Aboriginal organizations review legislation affecting historical and sacred sites and the conservation and display of cultural artifacts to ensure that:

(a) Aboriginal interests are recognized in designing, protecting, developing and managing sites significant to Aboriginal culture and heritage and in conserving, repatriating and displaying Aboriginal cultural artifacts;

(b) Aboriginal people are fully involved in planning and managing heritage activities relevant to their cultures; and

(c) Aboriginal people share the economic benefits that may accrue from appropriate development of relevant heritage sites and display of cultural artifacts.

3.6.4 – Museums and cultural institutions adopt ethical guidelines governing all aspects of collection, disposition, display and interpretation of artifacts related to Aboriginal culture and heritage, including the following:

(a) involving Aboriginal people in drafting, endorsing and implementing the guidelines;

(b) creating inventories of relevant holdings and making such inventories freely accessible to Aboriginal people;

(c) cataloguing and designating appropriate use and display of relevant holdings;

(d) repatriating, on request, objects that are sacred or integral to the history and continuity of particular nations and communities;

(e) returning human remains to the family, community or nation of origin, on request, or consulting with Aboriginal advisers on appropriate disposition, where remains cannot be associated with a particular nation; and

(f) ensuring that Aboriginal people and communities have effective access to cultural education and training opportunities available through museums and cultural institutions. (RCAP 1996, 3: 560–61)

These four recommendations, with their detailed actions, showed a path toward a new relationship between settler governments and Indigenous governments with respect to heritage. With the ideas of collaboration in 3.6.1 and reviewing legislation in 3.6.2, the recommendations proffer the co-management of Indigenous heritage. Although not a complete overturn of colonial power, co-managing heritage would have been a new step in the relationship between provincial governments and Indigenous communities. Discussions about topics such as protection of archaeological sites, developing processes to protect cultural places, and sorting out how to resolve past, and cumulative, impacts to archaeological sites would certainly be welcomed by Indigenous communities and archaeologists alike – especially if they included an understanding of accountability by provincial and Indigenous governments. Such discussions could have put heritage management onto another path, one that was more equitable, particularly if both Indigenous and settler governments had embraced the recommendations to co-manage heritage. The potential to shift power back into communities, and the potential for descendant peoples to access the land as they saw fit, could have begun much earlier if all governments in Canada had recognized that "in the core areas of jurisdiction Indigenous peoples have the capacity to implement their inherent right of self-government by self-starting initiatives without the need for agreements with the federal and provincial governments, although it would be highly advisable that they negotiate agreements with other governments in the interests of reciprocal recognition and avoiding litigation" (RCAP 1996, 5: 147).

Any notion of decolonization within the "settler colonial context must involve the repatriation of land" (Tuck and Yang 2012, 7). Land is integral to Indigenous heritage because it forms Indigenous identity through teachings and law: knowledge dwells there. Languages were born from these spaces, the landscapes and seascapes. These spaces hold stories and mark events; they are where children are enculturated into customs. Indigenous epistemology shapes an identity of the known world from the land to rivers, lakes, and sea. Land is essential to the cultural, spiritual, and economic health of Indigenous communities, and relationships reside there. Heritage figures prominently in Indigenous identity, with archaeology being one of many components that connects individuals to their history. Those who maintain "legal" control over Indigenous heritage betray a deep lack of understanding of Indigenous world views, and thus do not value them: this is why the RCAP recommendations related to heritage have not been implemented in the daily practice of heritage management. Coulthard (2014, 119–20) remarks that, at the very least, the RCAP report was an entry point for challenging conversations that need to happen if the relationship between Indigenous and non-Indigenous peoples in Canada is to be decolonized. Yet this conversation, as he correctly notes, has yet to happen.

THE TRUTH AND RECONCILIATION COMMISSION CALLS TO ACTION
If, in the estimation of some, the RCAP report was "dead on arrival" (Ladner 2001, 241), one wonders how the Truth and Reconciliation Commission's calls to action, published almost twenty years after the Royal Commission's report, will play out. The TRC was established in 2008 to document the violent history of residential schools and their lasting impacts on Indigenous peoples. These impacts, which are felt to this day, were a product of a genocidal nation-building program to remove Indigenous peoples from the land (S. White 2021). In 2015–16, the TRC published its findings in multiple volumes, including the *Truth and Reconciliation Commission of Canada: Calls to Action* (2015). The calls to action are intended to redress the legacy of residential schools and advance the process of reconciliation. Heritage is mentioned in Call to Action 79, but the focus is to integrate Indigenous history, values, and memory practices into Canada's national heritage and history. It's a start. But actions need to follow words. Canadian law still doesn't have

a single definition for *cultural heritage*, despite earlier attempts to codify the term (Burley 1994). Rather, it is defined in specific provincial statutes, which, in British Columbia, at least, narrowly focus on pre-1846 tangible heritage. More significant for the present discussion is Call to Action 43, which falls under the headings "Reconciliation" and "Canadian Governments and the United Nations Declaration on the Rights of Indigenous People[s]": "We call upon federal, provincial, territorial, and municipal governments to fully adopt and implement the *United Nations Declaration on the Rights of Indigenous Peoples* as the framework for reconciliation" (TRC 2015, 4).

UNDRIP comprises forty-six articles, which set a standard for the treatment of Indigenous peoples around the world (UNDRIP 2007). Among them are many articles relevant to cultural heritage, especially within development capitalism, that call upon governments to address power imbalances and their positions on Indigenous ownership. Honouring these UNDRIP articles would require a sincere effort on the part of governments in Canada to acknowledge past and continuing injustices related to Indigenous heritage and the descendant communities who have suffered as a result of Canadian colonizers' actions to remove them from the landscape and limit their voices in heritage management.

Call to Action 44 calls upon the government of Canada to develop a plan and strategies to implement UNDRIP. The call to action does not stipulate how that is to be done, but it seems that both Indigenous communities and the government of Canada will have to clearly state expectations, accountability, and goals. Call to Action 57 calls "upon federal, provincial, territorial, and municipal governments to provide education to public servants on the history of Aboriginal peoples" (TRC 2015, 7). Archaeologists can contribute to this goal by educating proponents and advocating each day for Indigenous communities when in conversation with proponents and government representatives. But more importantly, Call to Action 57, should force archaeologists to reflexively think on how they will educate others on archaeology by examining how non-Indigenous peoples have become the primary authors and stewards of Indigenous pasts that has led to Indigenous erasure

(Supernant 2020, 11). Within most hallways of academia, professors are beginning to include Indigenous authors on their syllabi, but these readings also need to find their way onto the desks of CRM archaeologists. Digesting alternative perspectives and experiences can lead to self-reflexivity, where archaeologists internally examine how they have learned archaeology, how they have taught it in the field, and how they have written about it. Such an exercise in self-examination can help practitioners develop and maintain a grounded approach, one where archaeologists put Indigenous people and their heritage first, an approach that can then be reflected in the results of their work.

The TRC's calls to action demand tangible outcomes and approaches that archaeologists can employ. If reconciliation is about righting power imbalances between Indigenous peoples and non-Indigenous peoples, then it requires a shift in power and knowledge. United Nations declarations aren't legally binding on signatories unless a jurisdiction chooses to make them so by incorporating them into law. (And one might ask how meaningful an act of decolonization it is when a nation-state must follow rules set out by an international body to acknowledge that Indigenous peoples are equal to all other peoples.) On November 28, 2019, the government of British Columbia passed Bill 41, the Declaration on the Rights of Indigenous Peoples Act (DRIPA). The new legislation requires the province to embark on a process of legislative reform to ensure that provincial laws are consistent with UNDRIP. As yet, there seems to be no indication that the provincial regulator of Indigenous heritage, the Archaeology Branch, will embrace DRIPA and change how it approaches that heritage. It could well be up to archaeologists and their colleagues within Indigenous communities to think how UNDRIP applies to the world of heritage and then develop and implement practices and advocacy for the Archaeology Branch to support.

UNDRIP

UNDRIP was adopted by the United Nations on September 13, 2007. According to the UN, it "is the most comprehensive international instrument on the rights of indigenous peoples. It establishes a universal framework of minimum standards for the survival, dignity and well-being of the indigenous peoples of the world and it elaborates on existing human rights standards and fundamental freedoms as they apply to the specific situation of indigenous peoples."[1] UNDRIP protects collective rights that may not be addressed in other human rights charters that emphasize individual rights, and it also safeguards the individual rights of Indigenous people. As stated in Article 43, the articles constitute the minimum standards for the survival, dignity, and well-being of the Indigenous peoples of the world.

In British Columbia, the recent conflict with Wet'suwet'en over the Coastal GasLink pipeline completely diluted an opportunity for the province to engender meaningful change in the spirit of UNDRIP. Despite the inaction of the state, archaeologists can take some initiative, which could begin with an awareness of the content of the forty-six articles of UNDRIP and their implications for archaeological practice. Table 4.1 lists nineteen articles relevant to cultural heritage, which archaeologists might use when formulating a plan of action to modify their daily practice and methods so they align with UNDRIP commitments.

TABLE 4.1 UNDRIP ARTICLES RELEVANT TO INTANGIBLE AND TANGIBLE HERITAGE

ARTICLE 3 – Indigenous peoples have the right to self-determination. By virtue of that right they freely determine their political status and freely pursue their economic, social and cultural development.
ARTICLE 4 – Indigenous peoples, in exercising their right to self-determination, have the right to autonomy or self-government in matters relating to their internal and local affairs, as well as ways and means for financing their autonomous functions.
ARTICLE 8 – 1. Indigenous peoples and individuals have the right not to be subjected to forced assimilation or destruction of their culture.
ARTICLE 11 – 1. Indigenous peoples have the right to practise and revitalize their cultural traditions and customs. This includes the right to maintain, protect and develop the past, present and future manifestations of their cultures, such as archaeological and historical sites, artefacts, designs, ceremonies, technologies and visual and performing arts and literature.

ARTICLE 11 – 2. States shall provide redress through effective mechanisms, which may include restitution, developed in conjunction with indigenous peoples, with respect to their cultural, intellectual, religious and spiritual property taken without their free, prior and informed consent or in violation of their laws, traditions and customs.

ARTICLE 12 – 1. Indigenous peoples have the right to manifest, practise, develop and teach their spiritual and religious traditions, customs and ceremonies; the right to maintain, protect, and have access in privacy to their religious and cultural sites; the right to the use and control of their ceremonial objects; and the right to the repatriation of their human remains.

2. States shall seek to enable the access and/or repatriation of ceremonial objects and human remains in their possession through fair, transparent and effective mechanisms developed in conjunction with indigenous peoples concerned.

ARTICLE 13 – 1. Indigenous peoples have the right to revitalize, use, develop and transmit to future generations their histories, languages, oral traditions, philosophies, writing systems and literatures, and to designate and retain their own names for communities, places and persons.

2. States shall take effective measures to ensure that this right is protected and also to ensure that indigenous peoples can understand and be understood in political, legal and administrative proceedings, where necessary through the provision of interpretation or by other appropriate means.

ARTICLE 15 – 1. Indigenous peoples have the right to the dignity and diversity of their cultures, traditions, histories and aspirations which shall be appropriately reflected in education and public information.

2. States shall take effective measures, in consultation and cooperation with the indigenous peoples concerned, to combat prejudice and eliminate discrimination and to promote tolerance, understanding and good relations among indigenous peoples and all other segments of society.

ARTICLE 18 – Indigenous peoples have the right to participate in decision-making in matters which would affect their rights, through representatives chosen by themselves in accordance with their own procedures, as well as to maintain and develop their own indigenous decision-making institutions.

ARTICLE 19 – States shall consult and cooperate in good faith with the indigenous peoples concerned through their own representative institutions in order to obtain their free, prior and informed consent before adopting and implementing legislative or administrative measures that may affect them.

ARTICLE 22 – 1. Particular attention shall be paid to the rights and special needs of indigenous elders, women, youth, children and persons with disabilities in the implementation of this Declaration.

2. States shall take measures, in conjunction with indigenous peoples, to ensure that indigenous women and children enjoy the full protection and guarantees against all forms of violence and discrimination.

ARTICLE 25 – Indigenous peoples have the right to maintain and strengthen their distinctive spiritual relationship with their traditionally owned or otherwise occupied and used lands, territories, waters and coastal seas and other resources and to uphold their responsibilities to future generations in this regard.

ARTICLE 26 – 1. Indigenous peoples have the right to the lands, territories and resources which they have traditionally owned, occupied or otherwise used or acquired.

2. Indigenous peoples have the right to own, use, develop and control the lands, territories and resources that they possess by reason of traditional ownership or other traditional occupation or use, as well as those which they have otherwise acquired.

3. States shall give legal recognition and protection to these lands, territories and resources. Such recognition shall be conducted with due respect to the customs, traditions and land tenure systems of the indigenous peoples concerned.

ARTICLE 27 – States shall establish and implement, in conjunction with indigenous peoples concerned, a fair, independent, impartial, open and transparent process, giving due recognition to indigenous peoples' laws, traditions, customs and land tenure systems, to recognize and adjudicate the rights of indigenous peoples pertaining to their lands, territories and resources, including those which were traditionally owned or otherwise occupied or used. Indigenous peoples shall have the right to participate in this process.

ARTICLE 28 – 1. Indigenous peoples have the right to redress, by means that can include restitution or, when this is not possible, just, fair and equitable compensation, for the lands, territories and resources which they have traditionally owned or otherwise occupied or used, and which have been confiscated, taken, occupied, used or damaged without their free, prior and informed consent.

2. Unless otherwise freely agreed upon by the peoples concerned, compensation shall take the form of lands, territories and resources equal in quality, size and legal status or of monetary compensation or other appropriate redress.

ARTICLE 29 – 1. Indigenous peoples have the right to the conservation and protection of the environment and the productive capacity of their lands or territories and resources. States shall establish and implement assistance programmes for indigenous peoples for such conservation and protection, without discrimination.

2. States shall take effective measures to ensure that no storage or disposal of hazardous materials shall take place in the lands or territories of indigenous peoples without their free, prior and informed consent.

3. States shall also take effective measures to ensure, as needed, that programmes for monitoring, maintaining and restoring the health of indigenous peoples, as developed and implemented by the peoples affected by such materials, are duly implemented.

ARTICLE 31 – 1. Indigenous peoples have the right to maintain, control, protect and develop their cultural heritage, traditional knowledge and traditional cultural expressions, as well as the manifestations of their sciences, technologies and cultures, including human and genetic resources, seeds, medicines, knowledge of the properties of fauna and flora, oral traditions, literatures, designs, sports and traditional games and visual and performing arts. They also have the right to maintain, control, protect and develop their intellectual property over such cultural heritage, traditional knowledge, and traditional expressions.

2. In conjunction with indigenous peoples, States shall take effective measures to recognize and protect the exercise of these rights.

ARTICLE 32 – 1. Indigenous peoples have the right to determine and develop priorities and strategies for the development or use of their lands or territories and other resources.

2. States shall consult and cooperate in good faith with the indigenous peoples concerned through their own representative institutions in order to obtain their free and informed consent prior to the approval of any project affecting their lands or territories and other resources, particularly in connection with the development, utilization or exploitation of mineral, water or other resources.

3. States shall provide effective mechanisms for just and fair redress for any such activities, and appropriate measures shall be taken to mitigate adverse environmental, economic, social, cultural or spiritual impact.

ARTICLE 34 – Indigenous peoples have the right to promote, develop and maintain their institutional structures and their distinctive customs, spirituality, traditions, procedures, practices and, in the cases where they exist, juridical systems or customs, in accordance with international human rights standards.

ARTICLE 39 – Indigenous peoples have the right to have access to financial and technical assistance from States and through international cooperation, for the enjoyment of the rights contained in this Declaration.

Clearly, these articles are steeped in respect, dignity, and compassion. In this regard, UNDRIP represents a lens through which we can reimagine archaeology in a way that contributes to a more equitable future. Doing so runs up against pressure from development capitalism on both archaeology and Indigenous peoples, but not doing so is a failure to recognize and act on what we know to be true. Of the articles listed above, a few are particularly relevant to this process of reimagining and remaking CRM, as discussed in the balance of this section.

Article 15

(1). Indigenous peoples have the right to the dignity and diversity of their cultures, traditions, histories and aspirations which shall be appropriately reflected in education and public information.

(2). States shall take effective measures, in consultation and cooperation with the indigenous peoples concerned, to combat prejudice and eliminate discrimination and to promote tolerance, understanding and good relations among indigenous peoples and all other segments of society.

If British Columbia is serious about implementing UNDRIP through provincial law, as signalled by DRIPA, then a transformative shift must occur in both personal and institutional ideologies in government, business, and archaeology. Non-Indigenous people must acknowledge differences in world views and work to better understand the local Indigenous communities they live among. On a more general level, it is incumbent on all settlers to know the history of the colonized state, which is a prerequisite to understanding present conditions and finding ways toward reconciliation through UNDRIP and the TRC calls to action. While Article 15 calls on the state to take effective measures to promote understanding, archaeologists can contribute by developing close relationships with Indigenous peoples in every project and ensuring that Indigenous voices are heard. We live on unceded Indigenous land: archaeologists can begin each project, each conversation, from this position.

> Article 19. States shall consult and cooperate in good faith with the indigenous peoples concerned through their own representative institutions in order to obtain their free, prior and informed consent before adopting and implementing legislative or administrative measures that may affect them.

A major takeaway from UNDRIP is the requirement for Indigenous communities to exercise free, prior, and informed consent (FPIC) with respect to any projects that would potentially affect them, including their lands, territories, or resources. Indigenous communities have had only limited opportunities to provide input into heritage management legislation and practice. That must change: before any work can happen on indigenous lands, proponents and governments must engage in meaningful consultation with local First Nations to determine if they consent to a proposed project. Consultations and planning regarding heritage cannot be items that proponents tick off the to-do list at the last minute; proposals must be planned years in advance of a project and must conform to timelines that Indigenous communities are comfortable with and that give them the time and space to review each project thoroughly, not the project's "critical path" timeline. The timelines of the fast-paced world of development capitalism must be slowed so that Indigenous communities are not under time pressures to make decisions that could harm their heritage: they have the "right not to be subjected to forced assimilation or destruction of their culture" (Article 8).

Ian McNiven and Lynette Russell's "host/guest" model (2005, 236–42) is a useful framework for archaeologists seeking to develop sustainable partnerships. In contrast to approaches in which Indigenous heritage is the object of research, this framework specifically centres power in the community, allowing the people affected to decide whether (and how) to actively participate with the archaeologist (and/or company) to co-produce knowledge. This model is consistent with the sentiments expressed in Article 19 as well as Articles 8, 11, and 12. Archaeologists can cite these articles with proponents to impress upon them how best to proceed if they want to work within Indigenous lands, especially as DRIPA has direct implications for cultural heritage. The exact requirements of the HCA with respect to DRIPA are part of the Provincial DRIPA Action Plan 4.35 (British Columbia 2022, 27). Under the action plan, the province must "work with First Nations to reform the Heritage Conservation Act to align with the UN Declaration, including shared decision-making and the protection of First Nations cultural, spiritual, and heritage sites and objects" (British Columbia 2022, 27). First Nations must be consulted and free, prior, and informed consent must be acquired before any potential impacts to an archaeological site. The action plan contains strong, progressive language about Indigenous rights relative to their heritage (and FPIC) in Articles 11, 12, 18, 19, 25, 26, 29, and 31.

In cases where full consensus does not yet exist in a community regarding a proposed development project, then any pre-development archaeological program to assess the potential impacts must have the support of the community and, ideally, would be co-managed and co-produced, if not completely directed, by the descendant community. Otherwise, the program and project should not proceed. Development projects need to be assessed in terms of environmental impact, cultural impact, economic viability, long-term vision, and how Indigenous communities (and local non-Indigenous communities) affected by the development will benefit, including the sustainability of those benefits. This is supposedly done through the environmental assessment process, but results vary (Noble 2016).

Development is destructive to heritage. Analysing potential impacts on a descendant community's cultural heritage requires considerable thought, research, and community knowledge, all of which can slow the speed at which development moves across Indigenous lands. Archaeologists can help slow down the process: they can educate clients and advocate for Indigenous communities. This education may include explaining the steps of archaeological assessments to proponents. Assessments begin at the request-for-proposal stage, followed by planning meetings with proponents, discussions with Indigenous communities, and applications through the nation's (or nations') permitting system, if they have one in place. The archaeologist can ask the client whether they have brought the project forward to the nation or nations affected by the proposed development. They can ask the client about the level of engagement and then approach the nations as well. FPIC is key, especially for archaeologists. Within an archaeological assessment (whether an archaeological overview assessment or an archaeological impact assessment), the opportunity exists to co-develop, co-execute, and co-write archaeological reports with local Indigenous communities. The level of involvement can be established at the planning and budgeting stage with proponents with a cost estimate that is inclusive and illustrates to proponents that, if archaeology is going to be done, it must be done the right way, with a focus on Indigenous needs, wants, and values.

> Article 11(1). Indigenous people have the ... right to maintain, protect and develop the past, present and future manifestations of their cultures, such as archaeological and historical sites.

Indigenous communities already know their past. But some communities engage archaeologists because they see the value of their unique skills, methods, and knowledge. Archaeologists can help challenge archaeological colonialism by working with, beside, and for First Nations, under the heritage policies drafted and implemented by each nation.

Archaeologists can be facilitators or tools for nations to use. In lower mainland Vancouver, many First Nations have developed their own permitting system, along with fees, for any archaeological work that will be conducted within their territories (the permit fees support infrastructure positions, with money put aside for future research).[2] These permits are applied for by individual archaeologists and evaluated and commented on by the communities' themselves and then assigned to the archaeologist if their application is successful. Permits, once approved, outline expectations and responsibilities of the archaeologists who are undertaking work within the nation's territory. The focus is the nation, not the client.

Another aspect of Article 11(1) that those involved in heritage management should consider is the recognition of their own limitations, expertise, and voice – that is, Indigenous peoples have the right to maintain and protect archaeological sites. Archaeologists can remind all involved in CRM that archaeological knowledge is only one way of knowing, and that there are experts within Indigenous communities who are knowledgeable about protocols, laws, practices, and customs (Nicholas 2018a). By making proponents aware of the need to acknowledge these sources, archaeologists can support Indigenous sovereignty.

> Article 11(2). States shall provide redress through effective mechanisms, which may include restitution, developed in conjunction with indigenous peoples, with respect to their cultural, intellectual, religious and spiritual property taken without their free, prior and informed consent or in violation of their laws, traditions and customs.
>
> ...
>
> Article 28
>
> (1). Indigenous peoples have the right to redress, by means that can include restitution or, when this is not possible, just, fair and equitable compensation, for the lands, territories and resources which they have traditionally owned or otherwise occupied or used, and which have been confiscated, taken, occupied, used or damaged without their free, prior and informed consent.

(2). Unless otherwise freely agreed upon by the peoples concerned, compensation shall take the form of lands, territories and resources equal in quality, size and legal status or of monetary compensation or other appropriate redress.

In British Columbia, under the HCA, archaeological sites are protected from damage or desecration, whether known or unrecorded, on Crown and private land. Despite these protections, Indigenous communities and archaeologists have recorded significant and ongoing damage and impacts to archaeological sites (Inlailawatash 2020a). There is a major gap between what the HCA is legislated to protect and how that protection is applied or enforced. The most obvious limitation of current HCA enforcement is identification of non-compliance – typically from development-driven industries such as logging, residential development, and tourism – which creates cumulative impacts on archaeological sites. The province has not considered the cumulative effects on Indigenous heritage from years of non-compliance as destruction: indeed, the province exhibits a general neglect toward and lack of accountability for past impacts. It needs to consider the cumulative effects of impacts and develop regulatory tools to address this gap. Articles 11(2) and 28 have the potential to show the pathway forward to resolve continued impacts. Fundamentally, archaeological and cultural sites represent Indigenous cultural history, and, despite provincial laws, Indigenous peoples, ultimately, hold stewardship responsibilities for their territories.

Research indicates that the province either does not understand or is indifferent to how impacts to cultural heritage and identity hurt First Nations (Inlailawatash 2019b, 2020a).[3] In face-to-face interactions with archaeologists, enforcers of the HCA (provincial compliance and enforcement officers) have betrayed a wanton indifference to impacts to heritage sites, revealing that the province, in its role as regulator and enforcer of heritage legislation, is simply continuing a process of colonialism (Inlailawatash 2020a). If the objective of the HCA is "to encourage and facilitate the protection and conservation of heritage property in British Columbia," then the province needs to increase staff and resources and, particularly, promote the involvement of the Indigenous peoples. The province does not have a right to control, own, and manage heritage resources, particularly those that it is not protecting from constant and cumulative impacts. And reparations are warranted under Article 11(2) to each community for past transgressions. Restorative justice may be an appropriate avenue to determine the appropriate monetary value and/or act of reconciliation required to rebuild the damage to Indigenous identities.

> Article 31(1). Indigenous peoples have the right to maintain, control, protect and develop their cultural heritage, traditional knowledge and traditional cultural expressions, as well as the manifestations of their sciences, technologies and cultures, including human and genetic resources, seeds, medicines, knowledge of the properties of fauna and flora, oral traditions, literatures, designs, sports and traditional games and visual and performing arts. They also have the right to maintain, control, protect and develop their intellectual property over such cultural heritage, traditional knowledge, and traditional expressions.

Embedded in this article is the understanding that Indigenous heritage belongs to descendant communities and is not the purview of the colonizing government. Yet, in British Columbia, legislation positions the province as the owner of Indigenous heritage. The Archaeology Branch's management and control of data through the Remote Access to Archaeological Data means that local nations do not always have full and complete access to the locations, descriptions, and documented images and materials of archaeological sites (Gupta et al. 2020, 2023). The province maintains these records and regulates who can access them, who can input data to update site inventory forms, and how the data are used. Not only is the database not co-managed with Indigenous communities, but it does not include some aspects of archaeological sites, such as their intangible features.

Some First Nations have generated their own data, but nation-owned and -controlled databases are limited by insufficient infrastructure, resources, and training (Gupta et al. 2023). Indigenous communities are bombarded with referrals from proponents and governments (Hanson 2018), so digital management of their archaeological sites requires a skilled and experienced team. Some nations have developed organizations, such as the Stó:lō Research and Resource Management Centre, with the personnel, experience, and resources to maintain their own database, but the provincial government needs to provide more support, funding, and training for Indigenous protection of heritage similar to funding for non-Indigenous heritage.

Article 39 of UNDRIP, which states that "Indigenous people have the right to access financial and technical assistance" from the state, offers a way to support Article 31. The province could, for example, dedicate funds to on-the-ground programs such as the wonderful Guardian Watchmen, which serve as the eyes and ears for First Nations with respect to their heritage in the field. To support Guardians, the province could fund and help develop an in-house team to process, manage, and update heritage sites that the Guardians have assessed in the field, ensuring that such data collection can contribute to developing policies surrounding heritage and development that reflect Indigenous communities' needs and wants.

> Article 12
>
> (1). Indigenous peoples have the right to manifest, practise, develop and teach their spiritual and religious traditions, customs and ceremonies; the right to maintain, protect, and have access in privacy to their religious and cultural sites; the right to the use and control of their ceremonial objects; and the right to the repatriation of their human remains.
>
> (2). States shall seek to enable the access and/or repatriation of ceremonial objects and human remains in their possession through fair, transparent and effective mechanisms developed in conjunction with indigenous peoples concerned.

Material culture in the form of artifacts, objects, and belongings that are unearthed by archaeologists and that then sit in the basements of institutions collecting dust, or, worse, forgotten in tattered boxes, exist as an archive of loss for Indigenous communities.[4] When communities request that their material culture, and especially ancestral remains, be handed back to them, this should be honoured. If museums have permission from Indigenous communities to house curated items, then perhaps those institutions should organize a fund, financed by proponents, for future research by Indigenous community members and archaeologists on the excavated items. This way, as Barbara Voss (2012) explains, community members and "archaeologists can come into direct physical contact with material evidence, not temporally constrained by the fleeting encounter of excavation but in a sustained and systematic manner that has the capacity to kick back against applied ideas, models and theories" (149). Belongings then, will not be "unvisible," as Maura Finkelstein (2019, 33) conceives of the term, because their whereabouts will be known to Indigenous communities. Funding set aside from every project that unearthed items – ample funding negotiated between Indigenous communities, the institution housing the belongings, the province (granting HCA permits), and the proponent whose project disturbed them – may help ensure that future studies of belongings by communities, along with an archaeologist if they so choose, can take place outside the rushed timelines of CRM.

Article 13

(1). Indigenous peoples have the right to revitalize, use, develop and transmit to future generations their histories, languages, oral traditions, philosophies, writing systems and literatures, and to designate and retain their own names for communities, places and persons.

(2). States shall take effective measures to ensure that this right is protected and also to ensure that indigenous peoples can understand and be understood in political, legal and administrative proceedings, where necessary through the provision of interpretation or by other appropriate means.

In relation to language, a small way archaeologists can contribute to decolonizing reports is by using the local language for various things. This is easier to do in places where only one Indigenous language is spoken. In British Columbia, there are at least thirty-four Indigenous languages, which are mutually unintelligible, and becoming a fluent speaker in just one of them would be an accomplishment for any settler. In the lower mainland of Vancouver, hənqəminəm̓ is spoken by xʷməθkʷəy̓əm (Musqueam) and səlilwətaɬ (Tsleil-Waututh) peoples (although different languages would likely have been learned by individuals, given marriages, trade, and interactions deep in time). Some First Nations–owned archaeological firms are trying to infuse hənqəminəm̓ into archaeological reports when discussing artifacts, objects, and belongings. This needs to be done, generally, in careful consultation with language-speakers/users. The Archaeology Branch is open to this practice, in theory, although there has been recent push back when referring to artifacts as "belongings" despite literature to the contrary (J. Wilson 2016). So, a complete shift in reporting, using a varied lexicon for certain objects, places, and things, might prove challenging. But it is still worth the effort to try to be inclusive of local languages of descendant communities.

DECOLONIZATION AS A SETTLER PROJECT
Canadian nation building was based on the notion that Indigenous peoples were inferior to the colonizers. Such attitudes are reflected in Western principles like *terra nullius* and the "Doctrine of Discovery." These antiquated and fundamentally wrong notions have seeped into the mindsets of present-day non-Indigenous populations and governments, which espouse such rhetoric in politics and narratives around decolonization (Mackey 2014). Despite the promise of the Royal Commission on Aboriginal Peoples and the Truth and Reconciliation Commission, governments in Canada have been slow to endorse UNDRIP and even slower to implements its recommendations. Fear and uncertainty about what a decolonized world would look like surely contribute to the hesitation of non-Indigenous peoples, and especially governments, to act. Do settlers think that, if the power structures were reversed, Indigenous peoples will turn and do to them what colonial structures have been doing to their families, friends, and community members for generations? I have never been privy to such vengeful talk. Or is it more visceral, an emotional reaction to the vulnerability of not knowing one's future, following centuries of entitlement. It is true that certainty in regard to settler's own standing vis-à-vis Indigenous peoples – that is, in terms of access to land, property, and secure economic futures

– is being challenged in meaningful ways in Canadian society (Blackburn 2005; Mackey 2014, 237). This uncertainty makes settler populations, and colonial governments, uneasy.

Uncertain futures were reinforced by the 2014 Supreme Court of Canada decision *Tsilhqot'in Nation v. British Columbia*, which definitively established Aboriginal Title, regardless of the existence of a treaty. The implications of this case are not yet fully understood. If it is interpreted as recognizing rights that will render the HCA void on Tsilhqot'in land – and, presumably, the land of any other nations that can prove Aboriginal Title – it would affect archaeological practice throughout British Columbia.[5] Any legislation or government decisions that enable destruction of or alteration to a heritage site (for example, granting permits through the Archaeology Branch to do such things) are essentially infringements on Aboriginal Title and trigger the duty to consult the affected community. This creates the space for Indigenous roles, rights, and responsibilities with respect to stewardship within their ancestral places and among their belongings.

So, where does this leave non-Indigenous archaeologists?

Certainly, decolonization, reconciliation, and anticolonial approaches are work settlers must do – they cannot be left up to Indigenous communities alone. I do not know if archaeology, especially CRM, can be decolonized (see Lyons, Leon, et al. 2022 for some ideas), but I tend to be hopeful. Yet, even if such decolonization does occur, it will proceed at a glacial pace. In the meantime, to be proactive and break down barriers, archaeologists can study UNDRIP and cite Call to Action 43 when discussing projects with municipalities and other proponents. Archaeologists can be anticolonial each day. Normalizing these ideas in everyday discourse, and constantly thinking on them, will contribute to deconstructing the current model so that a new foundation can eventually be laid by Indigenous archaeologists with Indigenous epistemologies and with their own ideals, thoughts, concerns, needs, and knowledge regarding their cultural heritage.

Non-Indigenous archaeologists can provide support along the way. Many archaeologists are invested in putting Indigenous heritage first and would welcome the opportunity to transform the discourse and practice alongside local Indigenous community members while actively aspiring to uphold UNDRIP. To get there, to that imagined future of uncertainty, it is necessary to inject humanity and Indigenous expressions of being into a system that is currently without emotion or feelings. How do we transform CRM so it is compatible with a future where kindness and sustainability exist, where time and pace are slowed, and where heritage isn't altered for development? To do so, we need first to think through the consequences of implementing UNDRIP, so that archaeologists can begin to recognize the challenges Indigenous communities have faced for centuries in government-to-government relationships. Humbling ourselves to acknowledge the privilege that we have inherited from a racist system, one that has allowed us to have careers built on extracting Indigenous heritage, causes some to pause and feel anxious about their future. Asking for help in this process of reorientation, of praxis, is prudent. Within Nuu-chah-nulth communities along western Vancouver Island, asking for help is a strong teaching and an act of kindness (E.R. Atleo 2004, 12, 47). We could use more kindness in archaeology, and we need not be reluctant to ask our friends and colleagues for help so we can become more vulnerable practitioners (see Behar 1996), allowing us to imagine a different future.

Do archaeologists think that, if they participate in a decolonial process, they will erase themselves from archaeological futures in the same way that Indigenous pasts have been erased through colonization? Given that there is no collective strategy to challenge the system in which CRM resides, the question may be premature. But I'm not writing this book for complicity, it is a call for action. When Sonya Atalay (2012) talks about a community-first approach to doing archaeology, she says that "it means thinking hard about involving communities. And it means engaging with archaeological places and landscapes in ways that have long-term sustainability" (2). It will require imagining new modes of life, changes in archaeological practice and relationships, and futures rooted in Indigenous epistemologies (see Tabar and Desai 2017).

This chapter has provided a few instruments that lead to proactive choices and introspection within CRM. Introspection is an important process in archaeology: it can spotlight the issues inherent in the current system for non-Indigenous archaeologists. The recommendations of both the RCAP and the TRC can provide the basis for some hard thinking by archaeologists about their role and responsibilities within a field that privileges their experiences and knowledge over Indigenous experiences and knowledge. As archaeologists in settler Canada, we are currently implicated in a colonial system (Tuck and Yang 2012, 7), perpetuated by constant development-driven capitalism atop Indigenous heritage that is controlled by the province. Non-Indigenous archaeologists have benefited from this relationship in terms of power, employment opportunities, and influence. The UNDRIP articles I have discussed provide a framework for restructuring relationships and day-to-day practice in order to help redress these imbalances.

The values of corporate archaeology are in conflict with Indigenous lifeways as well as UNDRIP and the calls to action of the TRC. Bringing CRM into line with the values, needs, and wants of Indigenous peoples will be enormously challenging. The only way forward that I see is for change to come from compassionate, human values being inserted into archaeological practice. Descendant communities must be empowered to be the stewards of their heritage that they already know they are, even if the colonial powers do not recognize this stewardship. Archaeological projects that have placed community first, where the community has driven the work, with archaeologists as facilitators, have produced meaningful results for communities (Angelbeck and Grier 2014; Angelbeck and Jones 2019; Inlailawatash 2018, 2019, 2020b, 2021; Lyons 2014; Lyons, Dawson, et al. 2010). In other instances, archaeology has been shown as a vehicle for healing and love, even within CRM (Lyons, Hoffmann, et al. 2018; Schaepe et al. 2017; Supernant et al. 2020; Two Bears 2008). So, it can be done differently. But these examples tend to be the exception and not the rule.

Adrienne Maree Brown has a wonderful quote in her book *Emergent Strategies* (2017), which I think applies to all who participate in archaeology, and which we should all remember:

> When we are engaged in acts of love, we humans are at our best and most resilient. The love in romance that makes us want to be better people, the love of children that makes us change our whole lives to

> meet their needs, the love of family that makes us drop everything to take care of them, the love of community that makes us work tirelessly with broken hearts. (9)

We have to love what we do in order to change it: we have to have our passion drive us (McGuire 2014, 129). Keeping passion alive can be hard to do most days in CRM, which seems to pulverize our hearts and minds more than encouraging us to celebrate them. That's why we have to remember why we do this work and for whom because it's too painful to be in our industry if you don't have passion.

The First Peoples' Cultural Council recently produced a report, *Recommendations for Decolonizing British Columbia's Heritage-Related Processes and Legislation* (2020), on heritage policy in British Columbia, with the goal of supporting the development of more inclusive, collaborative opportunities for Indigenous cultural heritage management and stewardship in the province. Clearly, CRM needs internal structural change so that the industry is in line with what Indigenous communities want from archaeology (if they want it at all). While such structural change is critical, I maintain that commitment at a personal level to see, understand, and value another culture's world view is at least as important. It's on this level that we can engender change. And engendering change depends, really, on our outlook, values, and motivations. Is kindness and compassion important in how we do archaeology? Can we work toward an equitable archaeology that is steeped in meaningfulness, relevance, and compassion? Those questions are discussed in the next chapter.

5
A Matter of Values

In his book *Toward an Anthropological Theory of Value: The False Coin of Our Own Dreams* (2001), David Graeber explores anthropological theories of value. He engages the writings of Marcel Mauss, Karl Marx, Bronisław Malinowski, and many others, drawing on rich ethnographic examples to illuminate his thoughts on value (e.g., in exchange, in gift economies, in social creativity). Graeber explores many lines of inquiry, but his discussion of the early work of Clyde Kluckhohn's related to defining "value" (as in ethics/morals) is particularly relevant here. Kluckhohn (1951) set out to perform a comparative study of values in five different communities (Mexican-American, Mormon, Navaho, Texan, and Zuñi) in one county in New Mexico. He was interested in understanding how these communities, all with different systems of value, engaged with their world. Kluckhohn's early attempts at defining "value" led him and his graduate students to a theory of "value orientations." They tried to boil down a culture's values in terms of its beliefs about the purpose of existence, gods, the nature of knowledge, what humans can expect from each other, and notions of "success" and frustration, noting that differences in cultures were a product of how each culture choose to prioritize and respond to these beliefs. Graeber (2001) writes of Kluckhohn's definition of values:

> The central assumption though was that values are "conceptions of the desirable" – conceptions which play some sort of role in influencing the choices people make between different possible courses of action. The key term is "desirable." The desirable refers not simply to what people actually want – in practice, people want all sorts of things. Values are ideas about what they ought to want. They are the criteria by which people judge which desires they consider legitimate and worthwhile and which they do not. (3)

Although Kluckhohn's project was considered a "failure" by those who participated in it – because they felt it did not make a systematic comparative study of values possible – Graeber notes that there is something appealing about Kluckhohn's project, "that what makes cultures different is not simply what they believe the world to [be] like, but what they feel one can justifiably demand from it" (5).

When I talk of values, I mean how an individual's choices – and subsequent actions – reflect their conception of the world. Values form the basis of world views or cultural systems that shape a person's behaviour (Otto and Willerslev 2013, 3). In daily life, we are often placed in social situations where our world view is met by another's, often through their actions, words, and their choices (Belshaw 1959; P. West 2016, 111–12). Values are learned, tested, and confirmed or rejected based on people's experiences with other beings (be they human, animal, plant, supernatural, or some combination thereof) in the world they inhabit (Kohn 2013; Tsing 2015). These interactions are the ways in which we come to know the world we inhabit. They also inform our ability to reshape a world through actions driven by our sense of values.

I am in a constant state of existential crisis working in CRM. I ask myself daily, what can I demand from the space I occupy in the world of CRM? How can my set of values impact the work I do as an archaeologist within this sphere? Like others (see, e.g., McGuire 2014, 129), my motivation for an archaeology that centres Indigenous values and wants, compassion, dignity, and equity springs from my own passion as an anthropological archaeologist and my personal experiences of facilitating meaningful archaeology with, for, and by a community.

In discussing his understanding of Karl Marx's theory of value and of how we collectively make our world, and remake it daily, Graeber (2013) asks, "why is it that we somehow end up creating a world that few of us particularly like, most find unjust, and over which no one feels they have any ultimate control?" (222). When I thought about the world that I inhabit within commercial archaeology, this question echoed in my skull, leading me to ask, can we change the archaeological world that we inhabit?

From our colonial and capitalist predecessors, we have inherited a world that revolves not around the needs of the people who live in it but around the eternal expansion of production and profit. Individual economic gains matter, not the collective well-being of society. Commercial archaeology is situated within a colonial endeavour reinforced by capitalistic enterprises that are hostile toward Indigenous communities and their heritage (Grey and Kuokkanen 2020). Within this world, human beings have no value other than the instrumental: they are the means to an end that has long since ceased to contribute to their welfare. Commercial archaeology and Indigenous lifeways are two worlds that have different and often conflicting values.[1] In this chapter, I argue for the restoration of *human* values within archaeology, which have, at this point, largely been supplanted by economic values.

SAFEGUARDING INDIVIDUAL RIGHTS: LIBERALISM

For centuries, liberalism has held sway in Western cultures. Liberalism is a political ideology advocating civil liberties under the rule of law but with an emphasis on economic freedom. Its origins lie with many thinkers, including Thomas Hobbes, Thomas Malthus, John Stuart Mill, and particularly John Locke (1764), who espoused the rights to life, liberty, and property. The definition of and origins of liberalism, and how such thinking has evolved over time and space, have been widely studied by scholars (see, e.g., Bell 2014; Freeden 2005) who note that liberalism, as we understand it today – that is, as centring individual freedoms over other freedoms – emerged in the early twentieth century (Bell 2014, 699), perhaps in a predatory way.

Liberalism tells us that individuals have a right to pursue their own interests, within the bounds of the law, even if doing so comes at the expense of the welfare of others or of the natural world.[2] In particular, individuals have a right to pursue their *economic* interests – because, in Western culture, material wealth is a key marker of status. In North America, we tend to uphold values that support the acquisition of wealth. Terms like *individualism, exceptionalism,* and *self-made* contribute to a narrative of an independent self-determined actor whose existence is void of any relational context grounded in a community or larger society. Their marker of success is money, or capital, and their accrued wealth is falsely equated with intelligence. Learning is not valued in and of itself. As historian Harold Wilson (1996) laments, "so materialistic have we become, that unless the acquisition of knowledge, or more correctly information, leads directly or indirectly to the material betterment of the individual it is regarded as useless" (v). In this view, the collective (i.e., society) is a bunch of individuals who are basically in competition with one another and are responsible for their own wealth and capital. Any failure in acquiring wealth is the fault of the individual, not the structural systems or institutions of the society in which they reside (Fisher 2009). This rhetoric is espoused through a neoliberal ethos that asserts personal responsibility for economic wealth and attributes any lack of material success to inherent character flaws in the individual (e.g., laziness, unintelligence, lack of ambition) rather than examining the larger systems at play within a society – including factors related to gender, race, class, and so on – that may contribute to disparities in wealth.

CENTRING THE MARKET: NEOLIBERAL CAPITALISM

Emerging in the 1970s and 1980s, neoliberalism is an economic ideology and political project driven by the corporate capitalist class to, essentially, crush the power of labour (Fisher 2009; Harvey 2005). Neoliberalism seeks to advance individual human well-being through entrepreneurial freedoms within a system focused on free markets, free trade, and private property rights, with minimal state intervention (Harvey 2005). The rhetoric around neoliberalism is that the state's power should be limited, with responsibility only for "military, defence, police, and legal structures and functions required to secure private property rights and to guarantee, by force, if need be, the proper functioning of markets" (2). Neoliberal practices centre markets and transactions, with the hope of bringing social good through global human action within an open marketplace. Utilizing technology and information, the global reach of capitalism creates a dependency on exchanging labour (i.e., wages) for commodities, where commodities are produced on a global scale and are supposedly universally available through the internet. Yet, in reality, the global production and consumption of such commodities creates varying degrees of suffering worldwide (Robbins 2017). Those who subscribe to neoliberalism assume that individual freedoms are guaranteed by the freedom of a competitive market, the ethics of which are embodied in corporations, private-property owners, and extraction businesses. In the past forty years, the state has altered its function from supporting people (through education, social welfare, and healthcare, for example) to supporting capital and behaving as an agent of capital to subsidize corporations, banks, and industries (Desmond 2023; Harvey 2005, 2018). This shift has had deleterious effects on the human condition, and Indigenous communities are acutely aware of its impacts.

Cliff Atleo (2021) provides context for situating Indigenous peoples within settler colonialism and neoliberal capitalism. He points out how neoliberal capitalism affects Indigenous environmental politics, self-determination, resistance, and adaptation, and he discusses the nuanced and challenging decisions many Indigenous leaders and communities are forced to make with respect to natural resource extraction projects on their lands. He highlights cases from the Mackenzie River (in the Northwest Territories), Arizona, and British Columbia in which Indigenous leaders redefine self-determination as referring specifically to economic autonomy – which isn't autonomy at all but induction into Western capitalist exploitation (both of resources and of people). Atleo explains that "choosing" is not a "simple binary of those for and those against development, or those who have 'sold out' and those who have 'remained true' to their Indigenous values" (355). Rather, he understands their dilemma. And he certainly thinks "that all political and economic decisions should be debated and critiqued by Indigenous people" (367). His essay provides a balanced discussion around Indigenous resource management, one that illustrates real-life decisions that Indigenous leaders must make about the survival of their communities. Often, First Nations must weigh competing variables, such as the "loss of Indigenous ways of living and subsequent community poverty, relentless industrial development pressures, and hollow relationships with settler governments" (369). Indigenous peoples are caught in a situation begotten by colonialism and capitalism, where capitalism desacralizes culture (Fisher 2009, 6). Atleo (2021, 369) believes Indigenous leaders are doing the best they can for their communities, but the realities of proposed developments on Indigenous lands have forced communities to deal with limited options in a system that has not benefited them or recognized their sovereignty.

The socio-political-economic realities Indigenous communities endure can be observed within CRM. Commercial archaeology has an impact on Indigenous communities but is largely outside of Indigenous control. Archaeology functions as a business, commodifying heritage; the province, not the people affected, regulates the process; and a number of large transnational corporations employ archaeologists who perform assessments of Indigenous heritage on unceded Indigenous lands for large-scale extraction and development projects.

The dominance of neoliberalism within bureaucratic archaeology in British Columbia – that is, archaeology regulated by the state – can be understood by analysing policies that supposedly highlight the province's claim that archaeological sites are valuable provincial resources while underlining the value of mineral deposits, arable land, forests, fish, and wildlife (Archaeology Branch 2018). The province compares the value of resources for extraction that can be sold on the global market against the value of either preserving an archaeological site or destroying it for economic gain by clients. Indigenous heritage is consistently evaluated against the potential economic gains of a proposed project, which our capitalist benefactors frame as beneficial to all Canadians. Large-scale extraction projects do not truly benefit the masses; rather, the main beneficiaries are the minority who possess the wealth, "own" the property, and possess the means to access and convert natural resources into commodities. Extraction comes at the expense of Indigenous peoples, whose rights have been limited through Canadian legislation and governance since Confederation. Within this context, it is the province, as the self-appointed "owner" of Indigenous heritage – and not the descendant communities – that determines the value of archaeological sites. Yet, given its embrace of neoliberal and colonial structures, the province is actually "opposed to the effective preservation and promotion of Indigenous peoples' cultural heritage" (Grey and Kuokkanen 2020, 920). When the province offers co-management/shared decision-making with Indigenous nations on heritage projects – a few of which I have been privy to first-hand – what actually takes place is the subversion of Indigenous peoples' inherent rights, with the province reinforcing colonial systems and values (Grey and Kuokkanen 2020; Inlailawatash 2020a). The increase in the neoliberalization of commercial archaeology and general land-use in the past forty years reflects an opportunistic grab to extract as much as possible before Indigenous communities can curtail such greed-driven behaviour and suffering (Baker and Westman 2018; Irlbacher-Fox 2009; Robbins 2017).

SAFEGUARDING THE WELFARE OF THE COLLECTIVE: RELATIONALITY

In a relational world view, the individual is subordinate to the collective: I exist only because others exist, and the things I say and do have implications for the whole. Of course, people pursue their own interests (all human beings do that), but not if doing so harms others or otherwise disrupts the harmony and balance of the collective. With relationality comes a moral obligation to think of others and try to live a life that does not cause them suffering. Material wealth (of which there is only so much) is something to be shared: it is wrong of an individual to attempt to hoard it. Cultures with relational tenets tend to uphold values, such as reciprocity and respect, that support balance. They also tend to recognize that we are all dependent on the natural world for our survival and that no one person can "own" the land and its natural wealth. Such a world view is markedly different from that of neoliberal capitalism. And, even prior to the ascendancy of neoliberalism, settler colonialism was, and continues to be, a disruption to Indigenous lifeways, in its constant attempts to break down the relationships between people, ecosystems, and landscapes. To me, a big part of the shift in values required to transform CRM is learning to think in terms of the collective welfare, rather than immediately putting our own interests first (see Tax

1975). We won't suddenly embrace a fully relational world view, but we can learn to ask, what impact will this action have on other people and on the ecological balance of the world for future generations?

Wade Davis (2009) wrote that "a child raised to believe that a mountain is the abode of a protective spirit will be a profoundly different human being from a youth brought up to believe that a mountain is an inert mass of rock ready to be mined" (123). His statement illustrates how two people can look at a physical landmark and interpret its existence in two markedly different ways.[3] His experience living and working within Indigenous communities with radically different cultural values than his own taught him more about the world he came from than the one he was visiting. World views do not need to be in competition with each other – rather, learning to understand various world views may reignite the notion that the world is socially constructed, with a multitude of ideas existing within a realm of possible futures. Such introspection would produce empathy and compassion within individuals. There are many aspects of our local world that we may not particularly like or may find unjust. We needn't give up and say "it is what it is." It is what it is because of human construction, events, and history, but alternative world views and ways of thinking exist in different communities, which may provide solutions to contemporary problems (in part, caused by capitalism), if we expand our knowledge base to include them.

Ontologies and epistemologies that centre relationality exist in the world today, especially, in Canada, across diverse Indigenous communities. I witness such perspectives every time I work with descendant communities within their territories, where our pursuit of understanding past lifeways is a group effort focused on the collective or the community. The work we do as archaeologists binds us to communities in ways we may not immediate recognize, much in the way settlers do not understand when Indigenous peoples include the sacred with the secular when sharing stories on the land. Through my in-field learning and my exposure to Indigenous voices, both within communities themselves and those of Indigenous scholars, I am confronted with new ideas, perspectives, and interpretations. I am shown tangible markers of Indigenous innovations in the field, like cultivated meadows (from my friend Gina Thomas of Tlowitsis Nation) or forest gardens (Armstrong et al. 2021), and the importance of cultivated plants (Hoffman et al. 2016) and those transplanted across the province by Indigenous peoples (Turner et al. 2021). Opening ourselves up to other modes of thought, being, and practice offers alternative realities and different ways of thinking and relating to issues, which may provide potential solutions to problems inherent in the field of archaeology.

INDIGENOUS METHODOLOGIES

Over the past two decades, many Indigenous scholars have made a space for all archaeologists to explore more deeply how to decolonize archaeology (or practise anticolonial methods) and centre a community's needs, wants, and values into daily practice. Scholars such as Sonya Atalay (2006a 2006b, 2012), Lynette Russell (McNiven and Russell 2005), Linda Tuhiwai Smith (2012), Paulette Steeves (2015), Shawn Wilson (2008), and many others,[4] have been exploring the question of how to conduct research in accordance with the values embedded in Indigenous ways of being in the world. A number of themes have emerged in this work, including community-based participation in both design and research; centring Indigenous epistemologies; dialogue around "experts" and privilege; community consent for research; meaningful and relevant knowledge production; building trust and relationships through words and deeds; acknowledging existing relationships to people, land, animals, and plants; and a preference for communal discussion. Archaeologists who draw on the work of Indigenous scholars will gain inspiration and insight, and they can explore how to ground these approaches into everyday archaeological practice. Alternative realities already exist in the world: archaeologists working within the structures of CRM simply need to recognize the value in these world views, which will enable them to create the opportunity to be agents of change and to make the space for their Indigenous colleagues to lead, and thus transform, archaeological practice.

The critical take away, from both Indigenous scholars and local Indigenous representatives with whom many archaeologists work, is that *descendant communities should decide for themselves the kind of archaeology they find meaningful, relevant, and useful*. Archaeological knowledge is only one way of knowing the world. It is not greater than Indigenous knowledge, but it can contribute to a community's needs, wants, and desires. Meaningful archaeology for Indigenous communities requires archaeologists to pause, slow down, listen, and pay attention to the local rhythms and beats within a community in its own cultural landscape. If we are invited to practise archaeology together it needs to begin with humility, kindness, and building meaningful relationships.

An important text for me is Shawn Wilson's *Research Is Ceremony* (2008). Wilson is honest, intelligent, and vulnerable. He speaks directly to readers, which include his sons. Informed from his experiences in both Canada (he is Opaskwayak Cree from northern Manitoba) and Australia, he describes an Indigenous research paradigm that centres relationality and relational accountability, specifically for the connections that form when we search for enlightenment or knowledge (95). Relationality captures the essence of what I am advocating when I talk about transforming cultural resource management: the strength of my relationships (or bonds) with a community are an equally valued component of my work, not just the technical. Wilson discusses "relationality" with reference to people, land, the cosmos, ideas, and values expressed through creativity, equitability, and shared knowledge building (80–96). This is a vastly different approach than that of CRM, which begins with requests for proposals, bids, budgets, and contracts, all focusing on Indigenous land. Nowhere are relationships acknowledged or established based on shared values, collective goals, or mutual relationships. CRM is purely an economic exchange, supported by governmental regulations related to Indigenous heritage. In contrast, relationality situates a person in relation to people, landmarks, places, and/or events, with a goal of locating shared relationships in order to strengthen new relationships (84). In sharing the purpose behind relationality, Wilson highlights the spirituality of the relationship to land, which is often highlighted through ceremony (89–91). Ceremonies enable us to occupy the same space, and this closeness can strengthen connections on the ground, which can also contribute to relationality – which is why, as the title of Wilson's book notes, research is ceremony.

An important tenet of relationality is relational accountability, or axiology, which refers to the ethics or morals that guide one's search for knowledge and why we must be accountable to the relationships we develop in this search (Wilson 2008, 35, 77–79). As Wilson states, what is "important and meaningful is fulfilling a role and obligations in the research relationship – that is, being accountable to your relations. The researcher is therefore a part of his or her research and inseparable from the subject of that research" (77). Of critical importance is that the "knowledge that the researcher interprets must be respectful of and help to build relationships that have been established through the process of finding out more information" (79). The responsibility to secure respectful, reciprocal relationships becomes the axiology that binds these connections. Although Wilson focuses his discussion on Indigenous researchers working within Indigenous communities, his teachings are applicable to all archaeological relationships. This accountability should drive all archaeological practice, adding dignity and compassion to the process. Such an idea strikes a chord in my heart, as I have felt this and learned this in my early days in the South Pacific. My experience is embodied in Wilson's quote from a friend, "if research doesn't change you as a person, then you aren't doing it right" (83).

CRM cannot solely be a place of bottom lines, recommendations, and cold, descriptive details. CRM done on Indigenous lands exists in a human world – an Indigenous world – that includes laws, protocols, ancestors, knowledge, history, art, innovation, spiritual beings, animals, plants, and resilience. To seek out ways of being accountable that go beyond typical CRM practices, we should strive for equitable relationships by identifying shared relationships – in this instance, Wilson (2008, 84) is talking about identifying mutual friends, acquaintances, or even landmarks or places through which to establish a connection – when in the field working with community members. I crave a meaningful connection with the people I am engaged with, hoping that the work we co-produce can (and will) improve the reality for their community. This could mean assessing archaeological sites that have been impacted by humans (e.g., by logging) and working together to provide solutions to protect and conserve sensitive sites. It could also mean demonstrating how archaeologists construct a narrative around material remains and contextual information while in the field. If archaeologists can highlight the opportunities that archaeological theory and methods offer knowledge seekers within a community, we can then be of service and help develop and facilitate a program to answer questions a community may have about its past. This process helps create accountable relationships, as archaeologists demonstrate our commitment to Indigenous communities, and they, in turn, show us how heritage and archaeological inquiry can provide deep meaning to them and their local community. This exchange may help improve their reality and relationship to heritage and eradicate the us-versus-them approach so common in the field of archaeology. For my part, through dialogue and facilitation, I hope to inspire Indigenous youth and elders who are looking for ways to integrate archaeology and traditional knowledge within their lifeways.

In an essay on the plurality of pluralisms, Alison Wylie (2015) challenges everyone who conducts archaeology to question their interactions and intentions. Archaeologists need to cultivate an awareness of how they learn and critically evaluate research goals in order to ensure that constant learning takes place in the field within communities. Wylie challenges archaeologists to elevate the discourse and recognize other experts, those whose lives are shaped by other conditions (e.g., social, economic, cultural) (12). The idea of the "expert" needs to be challenged in archaeological practice. I do not consider myself the expert: *I am a facilitator*. I possess one way of knowing (i.e., through archaeological method, theory, and practice). Introspection about expertise, and thinking on how to resituate oneself in the process, creates equitable space for people with multiple world views to participate and have ownership of and accountability within the process. Indigenous community members bring forward their knowledge and skills on projects: they too are experts. Those in positions of privilege and power working in descendant communities should feel a moral obligation to lift up marginalized voices that typically go unrecognized in CRM (since the colonial settler government determines and "authorizes" who can manage and oversee heritage, those who are unheard are overwhelmingly Indigenous peoples). The provincially recognized "experts" have to be the ones to make the space for knowledge holders of various backgrounds and experiences to come forward so we can, together, truly contribute to learning and co-producing knowledge within a CRM that meets a community's needs.

Wylie's challenge is related to Wilson's concept of relational accountability, for the former engenders the kind of change in archaeological practice required to enact an Indigenous axiology – by letting go of ego and expertise and by engaging in an Indigenous process where the archaeologist must relinquish control. Things like timelines, micromanagement, and costs privilege the project over the community, its ancestors, and its heritage. For archaeologists to be accountability to their relationships means a profound change in practice, because the relationship to an Indigenous community is the primary concern. I firmly believe that the ancestors, Indigenous heritage, and descendant communities come first before non-Indigenous clients. I tell proponents this in meetings: if you centre Indigenous communities and their heritage, then you will create a stronger working relationship with the nation. This framework is my praxis, but it is an uphill battle, given the predominate way of thinking about projects, industry, and results that is structured by capitalist frameworks supported by colonial governance. All too often, a project's "critical path," rather than local communities' timeframes, concerns, or conditions for a project, is the priority. A larger industry transformation requires education about other values and Indigenous world views, and a commitment to Indigenous communities having full and complete participation and, at a minimum, shared decision making in proposed projects.[5]

Relationships need execution; otherwise they are meaningless (S. Wilson 2008). They need to be demonstrated and enacted, and they need to be based in trust: all of these elements allow the relationship to grow and promote action to create accountability. I'm largely talking about social, emotional, spiritual values – intangibles that comprise of "good" character within a particular society observed through actions and being. Sometimes tangible items, such as gifts, can be a part of acknowledging relationships, but "no accounts need to be kept because the relationship is not treated as if it will end" (Graeber 2001, 218). Creating value through our being and, more specifically, through actions that are received as meaningful and relevant to Indigenous peoples, particularly results that are useful to an Indigenous community, or individuals, clearly outweighing any disturbance to them (Tax 1975, 515) exemplifies the definition of a "good" person within the local cultural setting.

When I am in the field, it is important to me that what I say matters. That I listen. That I take in an alternative view of the world, and that I honestly share my thoughts, too, when asked. That I follow words that I have spoken with action (Tax 1975). Such action does not need to be a production performed in front of a group of people. It can be rooted in small moments with an audience of one. It can be ordinary: a picture you took and sent to a friend; a PDF of an article on a subject a friend expressed interest in; a lunch bought or a truck ride offered; delivering grandma's jars for canning fish. It can be simple acts of kindness but may also include advocating for friends and colleagues through thoughtful action, such as including recommendations in policy papers to engender change in legislation or helping to protect archaeological sites and places (see Tax 1975, 515). Positive acts are ultimately how we establish trust, which allows the relationship to grow and enables us to begin to discuss more difficult subjects together.

ACCOUNTABLE PRAXIS: WORKING WITH THE DA'NAXDA'XW/ AWAETLALA GUARDIANS

The traditional territory of the Da'naxda'xw/Awaetlala Nation is within Knight Inlet, with major villages in Glendale Cove and at the head of the inlet. While conducting field projects directed by the Da'naxda'xw Guardians, I often stay at the Knight Inlet Lodge in Glendale Cove as a field base. The lodge caters to eco-tourists, many of whom are international, and grizzly tours. It also serves as a research base for studying the impacts of tourism on bear populations. Each night at 8:30, the lodge puts on a talk, typically given by one of the guides and/or bear researchers. In June 2018, I was working with the Da'naxda'xw Guardians Harold Glendale Jr. (Guardian manager) and Nolan Puglas Glendale. Harold asked me to give a talk to the lodge guests on the archaeology we were doing that summer. With permission from Harold and Nolan, I developed the talk to showcase some of the work we had accomplished and to highlight the role the Guardians play. I felt it was important to show the guests at the lodge why the Guardians worked and stayed on the premises within their territory. The term "First Nations" masks the diversity that exists within the province, and I wanted to highlight the diversity of cultures and languages within British Columbia.

At the end of my talk, there was a question-and-answer period, which went reasonably well. As guests funnelled out of the room, one gentle-

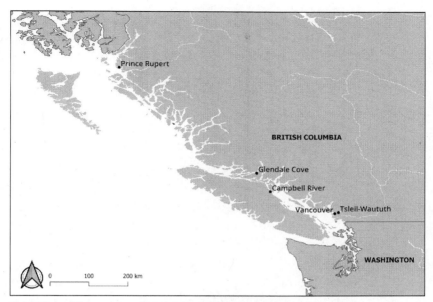

FIGURE 5.1 Places in British Columbia mentioned in the text. | Created by Walter Homewood via Natural Earth.

man stayed to discuss some issues with me. He was in his early sixties, I reckoned, and from Australia. We had a revealing, and at times intense, conversation that encompassed notions of Indigeneity, ownership, sovereignty, Indigenous law, and world views. He began with an example from Australia, in which he asserted that the idea of Aboriginal Australians crying over the repatriation of Mungo Man, ancestral remains that were some 40,000 years old, was unfathomable.[6] I asked if he thought those emotions were disingenuous. He replied that he found it hard to understand why someone would be emotionally moved during a ceremony to return to the ground an ancestor who lived so very long ago. I tried to highlight that those emotions weren't for him to understand, for he is not tied to that place, that "country" (in the parlance of local Aboriginal communities in Australia).

He wanted to know when "enough is enough." What this exactly meant, I am not sure, but I think he wanted to know when "white people" would be forgiven and "we can all move on" from the genocide committed under settler colonialism. This notion of forgiveness then segued into how he defined traditional practice. He used hunting dugong along coastal Australia as an example for how Aboriginal Australians use "non-traditional technology" such as aluminium boats, outboard motors, and rifles.[7] This, in turn, he claimed was a direct cause in declines in dugong populations. The subtext here is that this type of hunting was cruel and that it was not "traditional" and was not a practice that was necessary for food.

This man may have been misinformed: I do not know where it is legal to hunt dugong with rifles – both the Torres Strait Fisheries Act 1984 and the Queensland Animal Care and Protection Act state that traditional killing (i.e., spear/harpoon) must be done in a humane way – but, regardless, his underlying assumptions highlight a few fundamental issues. First, who defines what is traditional? Does a middle-age, white male get to define what Indigenous communities can or cannot do? Granted, this has long happened through legislation (in both Australia and Canada, among other settler states), but, for the rest of us, when we have such discussions, why do we presume to make moral assessments about what should and should not be done, based on our own view on another culture?

Second, though still related to defining traditional practice, it is important to recognize that tradition is not completely fixed. Cultures change through time. Yes, some practices demonstrate continuity through time, but ideas and things – both tangible and intangible things – change, including technology (i.e., motorized boats replacing dugout canoes). What matters here is social practice, the things that keep communities culturally alive, the things taught and learned between generations through continued practice – like hunting dugong (McNiven 2023). In this case, through hunting, knowledge is transmitted, stories are told, connections are reimagined, a culture thrives and continues – that is what is traditional (McNiven 2023). Communities are within their homeland hunting, surviving, and thriving.

Finally, as is common among privileged members of settler society who are unwilling to actually acknowledge their privileges, this gentleman used misinformation and political talking points to devalue Indigenous behaviour. His arguments betrayed a complete lack of understanding of Indigenous practice (and ideology), and he conflated all Aboriginal Australians (as if they are all one ethnic/linguistic community). He also clearly failed to understand the complexities of the reasons for dugong population decline, or that this decline did not extend to areas under Indigenous stewardship. He seemed not to be aware of the fact that Torres Strait Islanders (and other Aboriginal Australian communities) have continually hunted dugong, sustainably, for at least the past 4,000 years (McNiven 2010; McNiven and Bedingfield 2008; Urwin et al. 2016). The research shows that the Torres Strait is estimated to contain the largest single continuous seagrass meadow in Australia (Hagihara et al. 2016, 4). This region also has the largest dugong population in the world. The continued practice of hunting in the Torres Strait has not impacted local dugong populations: monitoring of these animals over the past thirty years has indicated that populations have been stable and sustainable (Delisle et al. 2018; Marsh, Harris, and Lawler, 1997; Marsh, O'Shea, and Reynolds 2011; Marsh and Sobtzick 2015). There has been a decline along the urban coast of Queensland (especially in the Great Barrier Reef), but this is due largely to gill netting, habitat (i.e., seagrass) loss, human settlement, pollution, and extreme weather events exacerbated by climate change (Marsh and Sobtzick 2015). Marsh and Hamann (2016) point out that traditional owners manage coastal waters, and they have the most to lose from any decline in the dugong population. Accordingly, Aboriginal Rangers and Management Plans have been developed to maintain these species and their habitats.

While this conversation was taking place, most of the guests had exited, as had most of the guides – but not everyone. Harold and Nolan were sitting on the couch in the back of the room, listening. They heard the questions asked, the tone in which they were asked, and the heated discussion that took place. They heard him belittle Indigenous emotions with respect to the dead, and belittle Indigenous ways of hunting and living on the land and sea. They listened to my counterpoints, my call for compassion, and my attempt to get him to understand another world view, another experience, another way of knowing and interacting with the world. They heard it all. They sat quietly and listened to one of the guests at the lodge, a guest who was within the traditional homeland of their people, put down Indigenous values and Indigenous ways of being.

Unprovoked. He saw no need to watch his words or consider how others know the world. His incredulity was such that no explanation of alternative realities would find a safe place to be understood.

The next day, Harold, Nolan, and I went out for the day to conduct an archaeological survey. On the boat, the *Knight Guardian*, they spoke about the prior evening. They were interested in the kind of questions the Australian man asked me and the tone in which he asked them. They know that most people wouldn't speak to them that way – or, rather, that most non-Indigenous people would have a hard time discussing such topics with them. This led to a discussion on the types of conversations and experiences they have had with other non-Indigenous people. For me, it was an opportunity to discuss sensitive topics and to hear what their lives have been like when not in their village (Tsatsisnukwomi) but in the small towns that dot the eastern coast of northern Vancouver Island. Aboard the *Knight Guardian*, we shared in our collective experience of the night before. As we navigated toward *dzwadi* at the head of Knight Inlet, we laid down the trowel to discuss experiences they both have had and to get at a deeper understanding of the gulf between disparate world views. The guest would not have believed the work Harold and Nolan were doing that day, for he knew of only one way of being for Indigenous peoples.

Centring Indigenous communities within CRM will lead to more formalized ways of conceiving of and practising an archaeology done with, for, and by descendant communities. This is not a new idea (see Atalay 2012; Nicholas 1997, 85), but transforming CRM into a community-first practice would lead to radical changes in the industry. Guardian Watchmen programs, like the one Harold and Nolan are part of, serve as the eyes and ears of a nation within their territory and are actively caring for its resources and ways of life. They document, record, and assess archaeological sites. The Guardian program seeks to proactively conserve and protect heritage by actively conducting archaeological surveys and collecting and curating data for its nation, not for the province. This is the kind of work archaeologists can help facilitate.

Suffice to say, Indigenous communities aren't necessarily sitting back idly waiting for archaeologists to make the right move regarding their

FIGURE 5.2 Harold Glendale Jr. and the author in Glendale Cove, Knight Inlet, British Columbia, August 2020. | Photo courtesy of author.

heritage. Many communities possess knowledgeable and engaged members who have eyes on proposed projects and who are active before, during, and after archaeological fieldwork. If archaeologists are in the field with them, they'll hold us accountable – and they should. Sometimes, a community member may want our advice or specialized knowledge. Sonya Atalay (2012, 72–80) discusses this engagement in more detail, and how such interrelationships are possible when projects begin from a place of equality, democratizing knowledge, and building capacity. Other times, a community member may disagree with our interpretation of a site or proposed recommendations. Enabling multiple but equal voices is the goal of an equitable practice of archaeology, but, in the end, the descendant community must drive the archaeology, the interpretations, and the heritage recommendations. But such processes are not the ones favoured by CRM clients, who always regard the consulting archaeologist – not the community or any of its members – as the "expert." And, if they didn't do so, why would they pay archaeologists?

MAKING SPACE

Archaeology's empire is dirt. We dig into the earth, and we screen the soil with our hands. The soil is alive with earthworms and other organisms. It breathes and needs water. Chemical processes are happening below our boots. The earth also possesses history, meaning, and cultural importance within its layers. We can discover stories built upon stories, if we know how to decipher them together. Shawn Wilson's *Research Is Ceremony* (2008) presents one path that creates space for Indigenous perspectives within archaeology, from research design to data collection, analysis, interpretation, and dissemination. Since his approach is built on relationships, this also enables it to be brought into all kinds of archaeological practice. Yet, relationality alone does not provide a roadmap to more equitable archaeological practice: this is uncharted territory. Still, it is through our relationships – our commitments – that we learn and grow and realize that the work archaeologists do has consequences. Being accountable to our relationships offers a more full-bodied archaeological experience. By asking you, dear reader, to imagine a world of archaeology that prioritizes improving the existence of Indigenous peoples, I am also asking you not to look out for your own self first. I believe we can collectively bring forward to clients, company managers, and regulators (i.e., the Archaeology Branch) alternative ways of doing archaeology. If we draw on our collective backgrounds, values, creativity, passion, and world views, we can put into practice anticolonial ideas supporting a more inclusive and compassionate archaeology built from relationships with our peers in Indigenous communities.

The space that we currently share in British Columbia as Indigenous and non-Indigenous peoples is contentious. It represents violence and erasure, but it is also a space to learn from, one that can help us understand how to heal from trauma inflicted by settler world views. For non-Indigenous peoples, the relationship to land may not be spiritual, but that doesn't matter, for such relationships exist whether or not they are visible to the non-Indigenous eye. Within commercial archaeology, tight timelines, intrusive demands, and tangible results are sought by proponents on unceded Indigenous lands. To disrupt this normative behaviour, archaeologists need to educate proponents and regulators, advocate for shared decision making with Indigenous communities (at a minimum), slow down the pace of development, and replace proponents' economic goals with collective goals when the project may impact Indigenous heritage. We need a new model. We need to think in new ways and work with new passions. Those in CRM may say, "Sean, this is all well and good, but it's not easy." Of course, it's not easy: nothing worth doing is. I agree with Atalay (2012) when she talks about a community-first approach to doing archaeology, that "it means thinking hard about involving communities. And it means engaging with archaeological places and landscapes in ways that have long-term sustainability" (2).

Making space for our Indigenous colleagues is not theory – relationality is a reality, one that is implicit in my archaeology. While archaeology is a science that deals with the tangible, its practice integrates numerous intangible qualities tied to ideologies, emotions, and connections. Without relationships framing archaeological practice, what are we doing as archaeologists? Do we do it so the Archaeology Branch can say the proponent's project is compliant with provincial standards? Do we do it so a proponent can replace their bridge as quickly and cheaply as possible, or extract natural resources out of the ground at a rampant pace and pump them out as commodities?

IRRECONCILABLE DIFFERENCES?

I acknowledge the difficulty of decentring power within both CRM and the academy. Academically, archaeology and anthropology have a checkered past, a history that all anthropologists must learn, reconcile with, and think through clearly. Archaeology has been dominated by white males and has accrued a great deal of nasty baggage over the course of its history and development (Trigger 2000). Many archaeologists, particularly over the past thirty years, have recognized that their craft possesses this colonial baggage with its built-in power imbalance and other complexities.[8] By acknowledging the historical development of the discipline, archaeologists can think more deeply about how to conduct their work today, so as not to continually be an extension of colonialism (Atalay, Clauss, et al. 2014; Deloria 1969; Denizen et al. 2008; Franklin et al. 2020; McNiven and Russell 2005; L.T. Smith 2012; A.C. Wilson 2004).

As a discipline, we are nowhere near being finished with the work of decolonizing archaeology. If decolonization is not a metaphor as stated by Tuck and Yang (2012), how do archaeologists ensure their discipline does not perpetuate innocence? Clearly, decolonization within settler Canada "must involve the repatriation of land simultaneous to the recognition of how land and relations to land have always already been differently understood and enacted; that is, *all* of the land, and not just symbolically" (Tuck and Yang 2012, 7). Archaeologists do not possess the power to directly give land back. So, the question becomes, how do we conduct ourselves on the land with and within communities in order to be something more than simply sympathetic settlers fighting for others in a "fantasy of mutuality based on sympathy and suffering" (Tuck and Yang 2012, 20)? This is a challenging, even unsettling, question for archaeologists, as "decolonization is accountable to Indigenous sovereignty and futurity," not to settlers' futures (Tuck and Yang 2012, 35). Uncertainty for the discipline is part of the process of decolonization. Maybe archeologists should not use the word *decolonize*. Following Max Liboiron (2021), perhaps the term *anticolonial* better reflects methods to challenge current practice, because they "do not reproduce settler and colonial entitlement to Land and Indigenous cultures, concepts, and knowledge" (27). It is up to archaeologists to relinquish control, power, and exclusive "expertise" and to step aside and support (when asked), lift up (when needed), and champion our First Nations colleagues who should be setting the goals within archaeological practice and driving the change to protect their heritage. In this sense, archaeologists can contribute to an anticolonial praxis that "describes the diversity of work, positionalities, and obligations that let us 'stand with' one another as we pursue good land relations, broadly defined" (Liboiron 2021, 27).

Structurally, a major obstacle for transformation in CRM is the fact that archaeology is conducted as a business, and therefore is entangled with development-driven capitalism, which privileges non-Indigenous perspectives and values (especially Canadian economic interests writ large). Indigenous peoples have had brutal experiences with archaeology as result of development-driven capitalism (Atleo 2021; Robinson 1996; Steeves 2015, 2017; Watkins 2003; Yellowhorn 2012). The exploitative nature of archaeology as a business within development-driven capitalism will likely never change. Archaeology tied to capitalism will always be about the bottom line: it is the only thing that matters to the majority of project managers within companies behind development projects and archaeological firms. There is no morality or ethics within capitalism (Fisher 2009, 16–20; Robbins 2017, 55–56): profits are its ethos and influence decisions. Being beholden to profit makes the archaeologist a tool of the marketplace, and there are no morality points for thinking critically about how to create equity within the current structure of CRM. For archaeologists, then, a key questions is, how can we rage against the machine when we're a cog in it? Although we cannot change the exploitive nature of capitalism itself, we can – and must – align to overcome structural forces of oppression in our daily practice as archaeologists, where we relinquish control and power so others are empowered.

While corporate archaeology and Indigenous lifeways are two worlds that have different and often conflicting values, they are not binary positions (Atleo 2021). The current challenge is one of history, structure, and agency. We all organize the present as we understand the past (Binney 1986, 529). But, like history, the structures presently in place are not static – they are dynamic and respond internally to changes in politics and other events (Sahlins 1985). As actors in our world, we are "under no obligation to conform to the logic by which some people conceive it" (Sahlins 1985, 138). Changes to legislation, policy, and procedures can be advocated by archaeologists to lift others up and promote alternative solutions. Political activism through organizations (e.g., the British Columbia Association of Professional Archaeologists and the Archaeological Society of British Columbia) and independent grass-roots archaeological councils (e.g., the Council of Elrond) can challenge provincial legislation, rules, and bulletins.[9] These organizations, made up of practitioners in the field, can advocate for practical changes in heritage management policies and, through their advocacy as well as their work on the ground, highlight for bureaucrats who currently control and regulate Indigenous heritage the importance of relationality and compassion.

The subtext of this chapter has been the distinction between Western and Indigenous ways of knowing and how they reflect and are exercised through values. Discussion around this issue is continually unfolding in heritage management around questions of privilege and power (see

Nicholas 2018a). Cultural values influence different approaches to heritage management. In some cases, archaeologists and Indigenous members share similar ideas, but they have each been educated differently; they are like streams braiding together then separating but both pouring into the same ocean. In such cases, relationships between individuals on the ground create the momentum to change daily practice. In other instances, the values of archaeologists and specific Indigenous communities impacted by development do not align. In still other cases, nations may support development, as they determine that they have other needs greater than archaeological ones. The opportunity remains, nevertheless, for archaeologists to be agents of change, to advocate for transformations in policy, practice, and the profession with direction from Indigenous colleagues and nations.

As a settler archaeologist, I can't speak for any Indigenous community, because, first, it's not my place, and, second, there are diverse individual experiences and perspectives within Indigenous communities. But, from the relationships I hold with individuals from many First Nations, I think I can safely say that, generally speaking, Indigenous values markedly differ from the corporate values evinced by the settler state. Such differences are, of course, obvious from the historical record, which reveals how the colonialist state removed Indigenous peoples from the landscape in order to acquire land and extract resources (a process that continues today, as illustrated by the Wet'suwet'en and the land defenders).[10] Colonial legislation continues to dominate Indigenous lives, but, despite the settler government's abuse of Indigenous peoples and the barriers the state has placed before them, efforts toward self-determination are ongoing. Indigenous communities have pushed back and are reclaiming their rights, identities, and languages, as well as the sovereignty that they never ceded, even if the colonial state considered it to be extinguished. Communities are reasserting themselves on the land – culturally, socially, economically – and momentum is building. Culture is not stagnant: it changes, adapts, and evolves, and core Indigenous values within communities can thrive as a form of resistance (L.B. Simpson 2017).

The techniques within archaeology don't have to be colonial. Tools are available to construct and design research with, for, and by descendant communities (Nicholas and Andrews 1997b, 3). Doing so shifts power from the privileged few and to the many who have a vested interest in and right to their heritage. While many archaeologists have put forward methods to shape practice and discourse by centring Indigenous voices to shift power and help engender equity (Atalay 2006b; Atalay 2012; Nicholas 2006; L.T. Smith 2012), such approaches have yet to be fully undertaken in the academy or certainly within CRM. Still, the incorporation of alternative values into the dominant system is possible. Working toward relationality will build understanding and trust, and create a safe space for difference, even when the process may be unsettling for settler archaeologists. Relationality begins with establishing an audience, even an audience of one, and is followed by action and acknowledgment. Once acknowledgment occurs, the foundation for a meaningful relationship with another is set. Relationality is a slow process and must be curated. But moments build on each other, and, with time, more audiences come into the fold; relationships are maintained through accountability (S. Wilson 2008), so that each one matters.

In a way, this book is a manifestation of my own self-critique and action. I have gained knowledge of the CRM world, I am critiquing that world, and I am taking action in it (McGuire 2008, 38). Influenced by my time in Polynesia, I have spent time building relationships with my Indigenous colleagues from the time I first met them along the Fraser River at the village site of səẃq̓ʷeqsən – the hən̓q̓əmin̓əm̓ place name for both the Glenrose Cannery and St. Mungo archaeological sites. In late August 2011, the archaeological team I was on had begun a major excavation, working with seven different First Nations communities, and we were all getting to know each other. The ancestral Central Coast Salish village provided the backdrop for excavation in our one-by-two-metre excavation unit. We were nearly forty-five centimetres below the surface, finally passing through the remainder of recent human residential occupation and disturbances, what Terry Point of xʷməθkʷəy̓əm called "white-man midden." Terry continued to excavate as I scribbled notes. Clyde Adams (scəẃaθən məsteyəxʷ/Haida), Dennis Paul (xʷməθkʷəy̓əm), Tia Williams (scəẃaθən məsteyəxʷ), and Jordan Wilson (xʷməθkʷəy̓əm) labelled bags, prepared level forms, and filled buckets for the wet screen.

Terry abruptly stopped digging, looked up at me, and asked, "Hey, Sean. Do you know why Indians hate the snow?"

"No, I don't know. Why?"

"Because it's white, and it's on our land."

Many Indigenous peoples know this joke, but a lot of archaeologists do not.

Archaeology is not performed in a vacuum, and archaeologists have a responsibility that extends beyond the excavation. We are privileged to work on ancestral lands, but this privilege was afforded to us through colonial violence, and so we should always be seeking approval and consent from the nations themselves. Holding the space I am privileged to hold, my writing is an engagement with archaeological praxis, which is not just about changing the way we do things, but is transformative, theoretically informed action (McGuire et al. 2005, 356). I want transformation within CRM, and I want those who are like-minded to see that they have colleagues who are willing to try to engender such change. Indigenous communities want to work with individuals who care for and respect their heritage and who will do the right thing to respect and honour their ancestors. A commitment to work this way can be demonstrated in many forms in the field, from having open, honest conversations, sharing food, and creating a space for multiple voices along with levity and good feelings. But it also needs to be demonstrated in technical and scientific proficiency, and in recording and mapping belongings correctly and working together to co-produce knowledge through interpretations and stories of past events and histories, as directed by Indigenous communities for their own needs.

If archaeologists put Indigenous communities first, everything else will fall in line. When the client is served first, archaeology and Indigenous communities suffer. Maybe this is what capitalism's true currency is in the colonial state: suffering. If so, archaeological practice will always be subject to irreconcilable differences. Archaeologists need to be the agents of change, to incorporate, think through, and execute a reimagined archaeology. To do so will take courage and the support from Indigenous colleagues and friends who have been consistently working toward self-determination since placed under the Indian Act.

6
Reimagining Archaeology

Indigenous communities in Canada are resurgent communities. They have called the good faith of governments into question and are determined to restore their autonomy. A small but important part of this process for self-determination is gaining control over their heritage.[1] For Indigenous nations, the long-term plan is to take over management and protection of their cultural heritage. Indigenous communities possess the inherent knowledge to care for their ancestors and their past and present belongings. Their history, identity, and teachings are imbued in the landscape, in the places that surround them. Archaeological sites are the touchstone for their songs, masks, languages, and values. In talking about heritage, I am not referring to an antiquated long-ago past (a misconception held by many settlers). For descendant communities, songs, entities, teachings, and knowledge still reside on the land and within the sea, rivers, mountains, and lakes. The humanity that created an archaeological record, one with deep history, across the land cannot be removed from contemporary archaeological practice.

In British Columbia, current legislation presents opportunities for nation-driven initiatives. For example, Section 4 of the Heritage

Conservation Act (HCA) and Section 7 of the Declaration on the Rights of Indigenous Peoples Act (DRIPA) but initiatives have yet to be developed under such legislation. Potential relationships between the province and First Nations are being explored together by archaeologists and First Nations archaeologists around co-decision-making, heritage stewardship, and ownership. In the meantime, nation-driven initiatives to control and manage their heritage are moving forward (whether legislated or not) in order to proactively care for their heritage. Some First Nations have archaeological departments, and some (e.g., Inlailawatash [Tsleil-Waututh Nation], xʷməθkʷəy̓əm [Musqueam] Archaeology Department, KDLP [Katzie], Sugar Cane Archaeology [Williams Lake First Nations]) have nation-owned heritage firms. Others work with specific archaeological consultants who respect their rights to control their own heritage. These structures, positions, and practices enhance capacity, amplify voices, and contribute to new archaeological outcomes that (I hope) will transform the field. In certain parts of the province, Indigenous-led archaeological research is advancing knowledge that informs internal nation-led management of archaeological, heritage, and cultural sites, and illustrates Indigenous stewardship of natural resources (Atlas et al. 2021; Atlas, Housty, et al. 2017; Connaughton, Hill, et al. 2022; Duffield et al. 2022; Inlailawatash 2017, 2020b; Klassen 2013; Morin et al. 2021; Thomas 2019). Many nations' internal teams are working to resolve issues, including impacts and insults to their heritage, by using archaeology to inform, protect, and rehabilitate local ecosystems. Many are also working on heritage policies, rights and title, and sovereignty.

Given the enactment of DRIPA in 2019, with its commitment to bring provincial legislation in line with the United Nations Declaration on the Rights of Indigenous Peoples (UNDRIP), I hope that the province will take practical steps to support the re-assertion of Indigenous peoples' autonomy over their heritage, both on the basis of UNDRIP and the applicable calls to action of the Truth and Reconciliation Commission (TRC). Despite these developments, though, larger structural forces in the form of development-driven capitalism and colonial legislation and attitudes still influence and direct much of current CRM. The discipline of archaeology and CRM are undergoing a change, with Indigenous communities asserting control within the CRM process, but archaeologists must support Indigenous-led initiatives if we are to fully transform practice.

A reimagining of archaeology is occurring now: it is taking place within nations' offices and among their members and their archaeologists. Some of it is even taking place in the hallways of the pedantic and the pretentious (I kid). But knowledge is not housed solely in the academy: it's on the ground, in the community, among Nation members, in stories, plants, and animals. The tools to reimagine our world are in front of us in the form of Indigenous knowledge, Indigenous scholarship, and Indigenous science. Over the past twenty-five years, Indigenous scholars and writers have produced important, thought-provoking works that settler archaeologists should engage with and, through them, explore ideas, help inform experiences, understand trauma, and recognize innovations, and adaptations. The human condition is right on the page, whether in scholarly articles, non-fiction, or fiction, written by Indigenous authors. There is no excuse for not reading and listening to these voices, for not learning, linking ideas, and finding inspiration. Before they engage in archaeological practice, every archaeologist should draw on these ideas while they ask themselves these three questions (Nicholas 2014, 137): Why do we do archaeology? For whom do we do it? How best can it be done?

Admittedly, we cannot immediately strike down the suffocating structural inequities that entangle CRM, but a lot of good can come from inserting compassionate, human values into archaeological practice, beginning today. Drawing on Indigenous scholars' work to explore more fully how to ground these approaches into everyday archaeological practice is one step. Fieldwork too offers an opportunity to create strong bonds within a field crew. Working in a community offers the opportunity to forge meaningful relationships and to listen to and learn from nation members during fieldwork. This recursive and self-reflexive exercise in reading Indigenous scholars and working within Indigenous communities on the ground provides a path forward, to reconsider current practice and to be an agent of change in the archaeological world, and to critique and help dismantle the hegemonic forces that control Indigenous heritage.

INDIGENOUS CRITIQUES OF ARCHAEOLOGY

Indigenous scholars have provided a great deal of criticism of and insight into the discipline of archaeology. With a few exceptions, such as Vine Deloria Jr., such voices were not present within the archaeological canon as recently as forty years ago. But within the past twenty-five years, assessments by Sonya Atalay, Paulette Steeves, and Eldon Yellowhorn, among many others, have provided readers with an opportunity to explore and confront the injustices of archaeological practice through an Indigenous lens. These critiques, which situate archaeology within the ongoing colonial experience, including the access that archaeologists (and the state) have had to Indigenous heritage for decades, help prepare non-Indigenous archaeologists for the challenge of making archaeology meaningful to descendant communities today. To support them in this challenge, archaeologists have a robust body of literature to engage with and contemplate, works that can help refine their thinking when it comes to the practice of a compassionate, kind, and caring form of archaeology.

VINE DELORIA JR.

Vine Deloria Jr.'s book *Custer Died for Your Sins: An Indian Manifesto* (1969) contains a scathing chapter on anthropologists and other "friends." By describing what an anthropologist is – how they look, dress, and behave – Deloria paints a picture of their privilege, hubris, and ignorance, and of their attitudes toward the people they study. He notes how anthropologists objectify Indigenous peoples – for they are objects, not human, and thus ripe "for experimentation, for manipulation, and for eventual extinction" (86). Deloria's brutally insightful piece illustrates the intrusiveness of anthropologists into local Indigenous territories and how their presence, with their prodding and pernicious questions, have not contributed to resolving the socio-economic ills Indigenous communities feel but have contributed to the anthropologists' social standing and status within the academy. Anthropologists publish books and articles that define "authenticity" and who the "real Indians" are and are not. They do this in abstract ways, removed from the daily effects of colonial systems on the people they study. Anthropologists never give to the local community, they never listen, they never share, they never contribute to the well-being of those who allow them inside. Perhaps most fundamentally, the work of the anthropologist is not relevant to the community they study (97). Such a statement is still true today, fifty-odd years later. It is a reminder to anthropologists and archaeologists alike that much remains to be undone by the discipline and its practitioners.

Deloria provides a larger context for thinking through archaeological practice alongside Indigenous peoples today. In a later article, he takes on theory and method in archaeology. There, he illustrates why Indigenous peoples have been suspicious of archaeologists, humorously noting that "people who spend their lives writing tomes on the garbage of other people are not regarded as quite mentally sound in many Indian communities" (Deloria 1992, 596). Such tomes are filled with language that is "derogatory and demeaning" to Indigenous peoples, for they were never the intended audience (598). Current generations are still wrestling with such language and are taking ownership of the narratives and contributing new ideas, concepts, and data to dispel previous assessments and speak to an audience with Indigenous peoples in mind (Atalay 2006a, 2006b; Hunter 2008; Million 2005; Steeves 2021; Thomas 2019; E. White 2006). Deloria acknowledges that among Indigenous communities there is a want to know truths about North American history, the deep history so many archaeologists have undertaken in the past. His assertion is that, until Indigenous peoples are understood and treated with dignity as any human with complex thoughts, emotions, and feelings, they will be rendered as "other" by a larger public.

Dignity is central here. Deloria critiques the notion that Indigenous peoples were stone-age savages frozen from the dawn of time until their "discovery" five hundred years ago. He argues that such a trope must be extricated from public discourse and public education (Deloria 1992, 597). The ignorance that surrounds Indigenous being, knowing, and existing is one many settlers have never critically self-examined.[2] Governments have failed to implement educational opportunities and curriculum that would enable settlers to garner an appreciation for and understanding of Indigenous world views.

Deloria (1992) is hopeful that, in future projects, like-minded archaeologists and Indigenous scholars, nation members, and knowledge holders will work cooperatively "to rework and restate the findings of major importance in terms and language that eliminates cultural bias and attempts to give an accurate summary of what is known" (598). Archaeologists can bring their particular skills to assist Indigenous peoples in protecting sites, such as sacred sites, where ephemeral materials may or may not be present. Archaeological evidence has been used in the courts (Martindale and Armstrong 2019), but archaeology shouldn't always be the primary evidence to support Indigenous claims. Archaeology can illuminate how a sacred site is situated within a larger cultural landscape where archaeological sites exist, but oral traditions (as evidenced in *Delgamuukw v. British Columbia* 1997), place names, and stories must also be used to help nations protect and conserve their heritage from developmental impacts. Yet, in the end, archaeology and the courts may be the only avenue to protect Indigenous rights under UNDRIP/DRIPA within the current colonial system.

ELDON YELLOWHORN

Eldon Yellowhorn has rightly stated that archaeology was designed for non-Indigenous peoples and has failed to count Indigenous people as "part of its constituency" (2006, 197). This is illustrated in the dichotomy of history/prehistory and the use of culture histories in North America such as the Archaic Period and Paleo-Indian Period to define a period of time that stretches across a massive landscape based largely on projectile points (199). Granted, archaeologists study the material culture of what is left behind by people, but such terms imply a crudeness within human development and mask a rich world full of diversity and innovation. Furthermore, the history of archaeology's ignoring oral traditions, as narratives that may explain past phenomena but cannot be confirmed through "scientific explanation," has stunted the development of the discipline. This has all led Indigenous communities to regard archaeology and its practitioners with suspicion.

Yellowhorn (2002, 2006) does not view archaeology as the antithesis of Indigenous history; rather, he proffers an internalist approach – that is, one where phenomena in the archaeological record can be understood as a manifestation of past local histories through which local community members can glean a sense of their past because they are best positioned to interpret the archaeological record. Archaeological methods and data accumulation are the mechanisms used within archaeology to acquire knowledge. Depending on the practitioner, the role of oral traditions in these processes is disputed. Settler scholars have referred to oral traditions as "myths" that do not constitute plausible sources to help explain or understand the past and have relegated them to the fringes of archaeology. By contrast, oral traditions, for Yellowhorn (2006), are the motivation to undertake archaeology as an Indigenous person. Local cultural knowledge, including that arising from oral traditions, should be used to gain an understanding of local history. The insertion of an Indigenous voice into archaeological practice, then, is not only appropriate but key.[3] Framed as an "internalist archaeology," this kind of archaeology is a bridge between the secular and the sacred: "it emanates from an internal dialogue on the nature of secular antiquity. This dialogue on heritage is a symptom of modern life" (195). Internalist archaeology is an analytical tool to "rehabilitate" oral narratives by deploying methods to identify their signatures in the archaeological record (197). This process starts with a frame of reference from local knowledge within a community. The archaeology is designed within local foundations, traditions, customs; from this lens, aspects of local knowledge can be reimagined by peering into the past to identify patterns of continuity. There are some similarities between internalist archaeology and middle-range theory or the direct historical approach, where oral narratives and customs can be illuminated by archaeology, generating new insights to better understanding past lifeways (e.g., Connaughton, Tache et al. 2010; Hall 1997; Yellowhorn 2002, 137–89).

Prior to the development of the discipline of archaeology, Indigenous peoples for millennia would have constructed their own concepts and ideas about the past within their communities. Yellowhorn (2006, 206) believes that internalist archaeology can validate traditions by constructing theories based on folklore, myth, and oral traditions to determine the antiquity of a culture system in order to find archaeological reflections of it. These intangible data sources are reservoirs of knowledge and explanation that exist within the social milieu of a cultural community. As an example of this approach, Robert L. Hall's *An Archaeology of the Soul* (1997) uses both archaeology and local knowledge within single communities to explore ceremonialism across the Midwest and plains of the United States. He traces the interconnectedness of various practices across space and time, situating the roots of ceremony deep in time. He draws on local knowledge, histories, and teachings to interpret the archaeological record.

Yellowhorn's work establishes the parameters for an internalist archaeology. He provides a practical guide for imagining the past from a local, Indigenous perspective and uses relational connections to ancestors and their lifeways grounded in Indigenous knowledge networks to interpret the archaeological record. Internalist archaeology brings Indigenous thought into the contemporary world: it conveys Indigenous perspectives about the ancient past through holistic research centring local Indigenous communities. This dialogue between past and present provides alternative narratives to mainstream talking points, upsetting the gatekeepers of archaeology (traditionally non-Indigenous scholars who are seen as the "experts") and engendering a richer explanation of the past by exploring cultural knowledge, traditions, and oral histories. As a settler archaeologist, I am what Yellowhorn says I am: an externalist archaeologist in North America. Space must be made for new voices and future generations to tackle archaeology as a discipline in ways that fit their teachings and local epistemology. By creating space for alternate explanations led by Indigenous scholars, including those generated by an internalist archaeology, we can better understand the material observed in the archaeological record through collective, community-driven explanations drawn from oral traditions, language, stories, and mythology.

PAULETTE STEEVES

Like Deloria and Yellowhorn, Paulette Steeves (2015) recognizes that the practice of archaeology and CRM is an exclusionary one that privileges a "western-only lens" while not making the space for Indigenous ways of knowing, being, and doing (130). Steeves initially aimed her critique at American universities but then applied it to the CRM world as well, recognizing that most practising archaeologists are university-trained. The combination of how archaeologists are trained, how they behave in the field, and how they continue exclusionary practices as they gain experience rewards Western-centred perspectives on Indigenous heritage. Steeves acknowledges that some archaeologists are doing good work (and listening to First Nation members), but she argues that they are the exception. From her own field experiences as an archaeologist working for various CRM firms across the United States and Canada, what she witnessed was "disturbing" and "heartbreaking" (127). Her central criticisms focus on the following: (1) a lack of Indigenous representation on archaeological field projects; (2) a failure to give equal weight to Indigenous voices and perspectives on projects, even if Indigenous representation was on site (i.e., their presence did not stop heritage destruction); (3) overt racism by archaeological practitioners; and (4) a lack of understanding by practising archaeologists of state or federal regulation pertaining to heritage. She explains these shortcomings as arising from the current pedagogy in academic institutions across North America. When these teachings are put into practice on the ground by CRM firms, work in the field continues the suppression of Indigenous values and dehumanizes and harms Indigenous peoples (130). Based on her experience, Steeves argues that non-Indigenous archaeologists will not have the ability to approach archaeology related to sacred spaces across the Indigenous landscape from an internalist perspective, because Indigenous voices are not taught or valued in the academy or within CRM.

Steeves believes that many of the unethical practices she witnessed arose from a lack of training in heritage laws and ethics in university. Very few academic programs specifically train students for careers in CRM and/or in federal, state, or provincial laws and practices associated with such work (129). Training, teaching, and developing courses that centre Indigenous history, traditions, and law are critical to producing young archaeologists who will open themselves to Indigenous perspectives and world views (Hunter 2008, 165). The problem is that this teaching is likely to come from Indigenous archaeologists or representatives in the field, rather than from CRM firms or university professors. Indigenous world views, modes of thought, values, and interpretations are not part of the curriculum within universities.[4] Nor is there an element of academic rigor related to introspection and self-reflexivity in the day-to-day practice of CRM. Engaging with many field archaeologists who were undergraduates or recent graduates, Steeves (2015) observed how "happily oblivious to the laws and statutes regarding CRM and the protections of cultural sites" they were while on site (128). She attributes this mentality (and the underlying ignorance) to anthropology and archaeology university programs where traditional archaeological praxis is derived from colonial frameworks of discrimination against Indigenous peoples (129). In the United States, legislation like the Native American Graves Protection and Repatriation Act has not led to inclusionary practices. Rather, Steeves has experienced racial microaggressions, overt racism, and full-on dismissal of Indigenous ideas. Colonial perspectives are embedded in the academy and are then transferred into the field where, additionally, capitalistic factors influence archaeological practice.

In the United States, one place where different practices may be able to flourish and contribute to making space for Indigenous perspectives and world views is Tribal Historic Preservation (THP) programs. Local Indigenous communities have been the ones caring for their ancestral heritage since time immemorial, long before CRM firms came on the scene. Through THP programs and offices, Indigenous peoples have an opportunity to reinsert themselves into archaeology (on tribal lands – that is, federal lands) and be compensated for their time. They can have a career doing things they have been taught by prior generations, including following Indigenous protocols and customs and caring for the ancestors and places important to them. These programs provide participants with the opportunity to express Indigenous values through teachings, oral traditions, and ideology (Steeves 2015, 132). Tribal archaeologists contribute to rewriting archaeological scholarship by centring Indigenous knowledge networks and can have more ownership in the construction of the archaeological process (e.g., methods, analyses, interpretation, reporting). Such participation is critical if practice is to change (Alfred 2008; Hunter 2008; L.T. Smith 2012). Yet, even with this opportunity, "these practitioners are still marginalized within an industry that privileges settler perspectives" (Steeves 2015, 136).

This marginalization is part of larger structures that control, own, and manage Indigenous heritage – that is, regulators, law makers, principal investigators, the Register of Professional Archaeologists (RPA) – along with ineffective consultation process between Indigenous communities and proponents. According to Steeves (2015),

> What is missing in CRM is a connection between the offices where regulations become law, the offices where paper work and reports are completed, and the field where archaeology is carried out. The departments and people responsible for creating the regulations, requirements, and standards of professional qualification and affiliations for archaeologists in CRM have no way of knowing what actually goes on in the field. That is, they currently have no agenda or program that links them in any way to a system of quality control or a process where the actual work done or not is checked. (136)

Although THPs are a positive step toward Indigenous sovereignty over their heritage, the fact remains that many archaeological sites are outside tribal jurisdiction. Steeves sees that the "lack of formal training in Federal regulations, heritage management, ethics, and Indigenous histories and world views has a negative impact on the quality and completeness of fieldwork and thus also on knowledge production" (136). Similar structures of oppression plague CRM in British Columbia (and Canada more broadly), with provincial legislation, regulators, field directors, permit holders, and proponents possessing too much power and influence over the process of archaeology on Indigenous lands.

Steeves illustrated the "dis-linkages between academies of higher education, governmental institutions, CRM, and THP programs" (137). Given these disconnections, it is unsurprising that the practice of archaeology fails to reflect Indigenous values and Indigenous knowledge and understanding of local heritage, and fails to address issues around local protocols, consent, shared decision making, and co-production (at least) of the results from fieldwork. Uninformed interpretations of the past and preferencing only Western-based knowledge systems learned in university, where a bachelor's degree in anthropology serves as a licence to practise in CRM, contribute to the mismanagement of Indigenous heritage, resulting in impacts to sites. Archaeological assessments should make space for the equitable integration of Indigenous knowledge networks and not continue to privilege Western theory and knowledge production for proposed projects. By conducting proper surveys and assessments steeped in local Indigenous knowledge, archaeology can be used to explore many questions about the past and to find ways to protect sites from impacts. In addition, all practitioners should have a grounding in heritage law, ethics, and Indigenous law. Steeves provides an example of mismanaged heritage in the damage to the Effigy Mounds National Monument in northeast Iowa (134). By presenting examples of disconnections in archaeological pedagogy and practice, she hopes to engender meaningful discussion among all practitioners to curb impacts on and devastation to cultural heritage sites.

Indigenous critiques of archaeology and CRM as they are currently practised are not anti-science, anti-knowledge, or even anti-development. What they highlight, and what should be cause for embarrassment among archaeological practitioners, is the clear imbalance of power within archaeology and, even more so, within archaeology as a business.[5] CRM in British Columbia privileges settler archaeologists who maintain legal control and ownership of the process of archaeology, making recommendations with consequences for heritage existing within a colonized space. Colonialist structures regulate archaeologists and, ultimately, own and decide the fate of Indigenous archaeological materials and sites. Indigenous communities, who are proactively asserting their rights for control, are left out of the final decision-making process and kept on the sidelines, with no legislatively endorsed opportunity to co-design the fieldwork or methods, conduct analyses, provide interpretations, disseminate data, or authorize recommendations (Connaughton, Leon, and Herbert 2014; Ferris 2003; Hammond 2009).

Clearly, archaeology needs to be relevant for local community audiences. One mechanism to ensure this is through representation in the field. A concentrated effort to increase Indigenous representation in positions like field directors and permit holders would help shift power to Indigenous archaeologists conducting work within their territory (and shared territories). Indigenous field directors and permit holders would have a direct role in designing methods, analysis, interpretation, decision making, and recommendations. This is only one small, if tangible, step in responding to the many critiques of archaeology from Indigenous scholars, and even this step will not be easy, given CRM gatekeeping in British Columbia. To influence the philosophy surrounding heritage management in provincial decision making, archaeologists need to follow Steeves's guidance and look within legislation for ways to advocate for and lift up Indigenous colleagues so that heritage management truly reflects Indigenous values and ideals.

KEEPING PROMISES

An archaeologist's practice should embody a collective set of values and lift up those around them. The articles of the United Nations Declaration on the Rights of Indigenous Peoples and the calls to action of the Truth and Reconciliation Commission can help direct those values. Archaeology can facilitate multiple perspectives, articulating the many ways to know the past. How best do we perform archaeology so we can transcend the practice through shared collective values that have deep meaning to the communities we work within and that help dismantle inequity? One strategy is for archaeologists to normalize talk around Indigenous governance and drive home at every opportunity when in dialogue with proponents, managers, or the Archaeology Branch, for example, that any development projects conducted in Canada are on unceded Indigenous lands. Archaeologists can also highlight for clients the local Indigenous laws, protocols, and governance that guide behaviour and decorum. Archaeologists should themselves be familiar with relevant calls to action (e.g., call to action 43) and articles of UNDRIP (e.g., Articles 3, 4, 11, 12, 18, 19, 26, 29, 31) and can review them with upper management and also with subcontractors and crews on the ground when undertaking fieldwork projects. In this way, archaeologists can actively be a positive force in constructing an awareness that centres Indigenous being and rights on the land. In addition, they can listen to their Indigenous colleagues when in the field, and lift them up in front of those with authority on the ground during fieldwork by directing decision making to them when a representative of the proponent asks about recommendations or next steps. These are small, practical things archaeologists can do in the field. But what about the larger structural forces at play, including those reflected in legislation?

On November 28, 2019, the government of British Columbia passed Bill 41, the Declaration on the Rights of Indigenous Peoples Act (DRIPA). This legislation requires the province to embark on a process of legislative reform to ensure that provincial laws are consistent with UNDRIP. This is a big undertaking, requiring the transformation of colonialist world views, values, and ideals. Subsection (1) of Article 11 of UNDRIP calls for a complete reframing of heritage management in terms of power, ownership, and equity:

> 11(1). Indigenous peoples have the right to practise and revitalize their cultural traditions and customs. This includes the right to maintain, protect and develop the past, present and future manifestations of their cultures, such as archaeological and historical sites, artefacts, designs, ceremonies, technologies and visual and performing arts and literature.

In addition, Articles 3, 4, 18, 19, 26, and 31 completely resituate the power to manage heritage (and lands) to Indigenous communities. Thus, under DRIPA, proponents, governments, and lawyers will have to fall in line with Indigenous policies, laws, governance, and timelines on projects within their territories, a situation that will be further complicated when First Nations share overlapping territories. Given resistance within the settler state – evinced, for example, by the ongoing violence perpetrated against Wet'suwet'en land defenders – it is hard to imagine that the government will embrace the ideals behind UNDRIP and change legislation and practices in wise and meaningful ways (Bracken 2020).[6] DRIPA appears to be a progressive policy, but it requires follow through. Otherwise, what will really change in terms of processes and procedures?

Of DRIPA's ten sections, Section 7, on decision-making agreements between government and Indigenous governing bodies for joint decisions, has particular promise:

7 (1) For the purposes of reconciliation, the Lieutenant Governor in Council may authorize a member of the Executive Council, on behalf of the government, to negotiate and enter into an agreement with an Indigenous governing body relating to one or both of the following:
  (a) the exercise of a statutory power of decision jointly by
    (i) the Indigenous governing body, and
    (ii) the government or another decision-maker;
  (b) the consent of the Indigenous governing body before the exercise of a statutory power of decision.

(2) A member authorized under subsection (1) to negotiate an agreement may enter into the agreement without further authorization from the Lieutenant Governor in Council unless the Lieutenant Governor in Council restricts the initial authorization to only the negotiation of the agreement.

(3) Within 15 days after the Lieutenant Governor in Council authorizes the member to negotiate an agreement under subsection (1), the member must make public a summary of the local governments and other persons the member intends to consult before or during the negotiation.

This section provides for an agreement between the province and an Indigenous government for joint decision making when exercising a statutory power of decision. In theory, joint decision-making power between the province and a First Nations government offers equal weight to both governments. Shared decision making is only part of what nations want in terms of sovereignty, ownership, and equity. Indigenous peoples have always considered themselves as the rightful owners and sovereign managers of their heritage. The right expressed in Article 11 of UNDRIP is recognized by DRIPA but not by the Archaeology Branch who regulate archaeology under the Heritage Conservation Act (HCA), and not DRIPA. Although the Branch claim to respect the province's ongoing commitment to reconciliation with First Nations (Archaeology Branch 2020), the HCA (and other acts) have not yet been revised to be consistent with DRIPA. At the moment, the systematic and effective protection of cultural sites within Indigenous territories requires coordinated planning and action on behalf of the province and First Nations independently to care for archaeological sites. By contrast, under Section 7 of DRIPA, the province and First Nations can explore a collaborative management relationship, with the province offering First Nations a meaningful role in discussions prior to as well as following permit applications, thus helping ensure First Nations engagement and centrality in decision making at all phases of cultural heritage management.

Does Section 7 of DRIPA require the province to enter into agreements with First Nations so they can accomplish their own self-determined goals relative to their heritage? That has yet to be seen. And it is uncertain whether the province actually wants to enter into shared decision making with First Nations, DRIPA notwithstanding. Another area of uncertainty regarding this new legislation is how will it affect the HCA. At present, the Archaeology Branch has little to say on the subject, beyond a footnote in its policy guide (Archaeology Branch 2020) that observes, "presently the province and First Nations Leadership Council are setting priorities and identifying opportunities for future alignment of laws in accordance with *DRIPA*" (9).

Section 4 of the current HCA can be interpreted as partially reflecting the heritage management rights in Article 11 of UNDRIP. Section 4(1) says that "the province may enter into a formal agreement with a first nation with respect to the conservation and protection of heritage sites and heritage objects that represent the cultural heritage of the aboriginal people who are represented by that first nation." To date, however, the province has never acted on this section, despite having added it to the HCA in 1985 at the behest of Indigenous communities. A pilot project with Stó:lō Nation has been ongoing since 2012, with no conclusion yet determined. In any case, the pilot project is not technically a Section 4 agreement. Given the delays, lack of transparency, and other challenges currently being faced by Stó:lō Nation in its agreement with the province, it seems reasonable to assume that the provincial government will not easily give up power over Indigenous heritage. To do so would lessen its control over development in the province. Yet, Section 3 of DRIPA, entitled "Measures to align laws with Declaration," states that, "In consultation and cooperation with the Indigenous peoples in British

Columbia, the government must take all measures necessary to ensure the laws of British Columbia are consistent with the Declaration." How is this to be done?

To ensure that the laws of British Columbia are consistent with DRIPA will require a profound self-reflexive exercise to radically shift Western world views so that institutions vested with authority redesign the heritage management process and procedures collaboratively, directed by voices from Indigenous scholars, knowledge holders, and cultural experts. Given the diversity of Indigenous cultures across British Columbia, years of meetings and discussions will be required to ensure that varied perspectives are reflected in rewritten heritage legislation. Such a process is an exercise in the relinquishment of power by the province and reimagining relationships vested in the ideals of reconciliation. The HCA will have to be amended or perhaps completely rewritten by Indigenous members to reflect Indigenous values, wants, and needs. Revisions may allow for intangible heritage such as spiritual and cultural sites (and belongings) within Indigenous lands to be afforded the same protection as tangible heritage. In this way, cultural landscapes and environs may be afforded more powerful protection from developmental destruction. In addition, amending/rewriting the HCA so that agreements can be established for joint decision making between the province and First Nations would address free, prior, and informed consent (FPIC) with respect to proposed developments on Indigenous lands and/or the conditions for which a heritage permit (for example, a site alteration permit) can be issued. Such changes would be in line with Articles 19 and 32 of UNDRIP. Ultimately, these changes could provide nations more equitable control and ownership over their heritage within their lands.

It is yet to be understood how Section 3 of DRIPA can or will be implemented. Legal scholars and Indigenous lawyers will have to sort out this process. But through my experiences as an archaeologist, I can confidently state that power will not be given up easily by the province. Compromise will likely be the first path taken when revising current legislation. The compromise will more than likely be tilted toward maintaining power within the province, and First Nations may have to accept shared decision making, for the time being. Yet, perhaps by codifying the principle of involving First Nations in decision making, such principles may become more normalized within heritage management.

There are examples of shared decision making that Indigenous communities and the province can look to as a model. In December 2009, the province and the Haida Nation created a unique management council for exercising shared decision making on Haida Gwaii. This was done under the Kunst'aa guu – Kunst'aayah Reconciliation Protocol (*Kunst'aa guu – Kunst'aayah* means "the beginning"), which acknowledges the Haida Nation's authority over Haida Gwaii, enabling that nation to ensure sustainable use of its territory by its people and for its people, and to protect Haida Gwaii's natural resources, ecosystems, and heritage for future generations. Bill 18, passed on June 3, 2010, gave effect to this protocol, and committed the province to engage in joint decision making with the Haida Nation through the Haida Gwaii Management Council. The management council is made up of two representatives of the Haida, two from the province, and a neutral chair agreed upon by both parties. The appointed representatives serve two-year terms. Decisions are made by consensus; however, if consensus cannot be reached, the chair casts the deciding vote. The goal of the protocol is to find consensus when making decisions about resource management on Haida Gwaii. This includes implementing the Haida Gwaii Strategic Land-Use Agreement (2007), establishing land-use objectives for forest practices, determining the annual allowable cut for Haida Gwaii, conserving heritage sites (tangible and intangible), and approving management plans for protected areas.

Can such reconciliatory protocols and joint decision-making councils be developed between the province and every First Nation within British Columbia? That remains to be seen. No other nations claim territory that overlaps with that of the Haida Nation, so the province has to deal directly with only one nation in negotiations over Haida territory. Indigenous territories with overlapping claims present a far more complex challenge, one the province would prefer to avoid.

Until all the legislative angles can be smoothed out, proponents will continue to put forward projects on Indigenous lands, and they will state that they are following the law, that they are compliant, and that archaeological resources (i.e., Indigenous heritage) are important to them, while, in reality, most regard archaeology and archaeologists as a hindrance to their economic project. What can archaeologists do to shift the status quo while we all wait for the province to act? For one thing, we can embrace being a hindrance: archaeologists can slow development down by laying out appropriate timelines for projects, both for the Archaeological Branch to do their job and for First Nations to have ample time to review archaeological permit applications and reports for proposed projects. Timelines are a central issue in CRM, forced onto archaeologists and First Nations by proponents who have planned their project poorly. Archaeologists can collectively say no to a proponents' timelines and advocate for consultation, realistic expectations, and meaningful results. By slowing down projects, we can do better work and can educate proponents through the entire heritage management process. Explaining concepts surrounding colonization, legislation, heritage, archaeological methods, and power imbalances falls largely on archaeologists and nation members, and archaeologists can increase their share of this load so nation members aren't overburden by it (which they have been). Collectively, we can show proponents a better process by explaining how we are doing the work.

One final suggestion: lawmakers, Indigenous relations "experts" within the varied ministries, and all politicians need to read Indigenous scholars and authors to gain a sense of the narratives and dialogues within Indigenous communities. In addition to the academic writings discussed earlier in this chapter, Indigenous authors such as Billy-Ray Belcourt, Alicia Elliot, Linda Hogan, Sterling HolyWhiteMountain, Stephen Graham Jones, Helen Knotts, Tracey Lindberg, Terese Marie Mailhot, Tommy Orange, and Joshua Whitehead, among others, illustrate the challenges, beauty, and complexities within Indigenous communities and their world views. Indigenous scholars have been thinking on and writing about the shortcomings of archaeology as a discipline for decades. Indigenous writers, whether fiction or non-fiction, create meaning through storytelling, humanizing individuals within complex situations. It is time to read these authors, listen to them, and be moved by them to act.

INCORPORATING INDIGENOUS VALUES INTO ARCHAEOLOGICAL FIELDWORK

Indigenous scholars have made the space for archaeologists to explore more deeply how to decolonize archaeology. They have illustrated methods through which to incorporate a community's needs, wants, and values into the discipline, leading to a new form of practice. Scholars such as Sonya Atalay (2006a, 2012), Lynette Russell (McNiven and Russell 2005), Linda Tuhiwai Smith (2005, 2012), Paulette Steeves (2015, 2017, 2021), and Shawn Wilson (2008), among many others,[7] have provided thoughtful discourse to engage our minds and bodies as we conduct archaeology. For example, Linda Tuhiwai Smith (2005) discusses the drivers for and definitions of Indigenous research that actively pursues "social and institutional change, that makes space for Indigenous knowledge, and that has a critical view of power relations and inequality" (89). Understanding the desire for transformative praxis is to witness the ethical, accountable, and holistic approaches inherent in Indigenous ways of knowing, being, and existing. In order to reimagine archaeology and develop "models of improved practice," we have to critically examine current archaeological practice, as Indigenous scholars have done (Atalay 2008, 129). Through this lens, we can then think more deeply about improving the process of archaeology.

In *Community-Based Archaeology*, Sonya Atalay (2012) explores community-based participatory research (CBPR), which she illustrates through various examples worldwide. She outlines five principles required for CBPR: (1) pursuing a community-based partnership process that (2) is participatory in all aspects, (3) builds community capacity, (4) engages in a spirit of reciprocity, and (5) recognizes the contributions of multiple knowledge systems (24). Ultimately, CBPR, in terms of methods, is about creating both theoretical and ethical guidelines for conducting archaeology, with the goal of creating an archaeology that is "engaged, relevant, ethical, and, as a result, sustainable" (3). Performing aspects of CBPR archaeology within CRM is a challenge, given that archaeology as a business is entangled with legislation, state-supported development capitalism, and colonialism (Connaughton, Leon, and Herbert 2014; Connaughton and Herbert 2017; McNiven and Connaughton 2019). CRM archaeologists face pressures tied to business solvency, multiple stakeholders (especially if they privilege clients over Indigenous heritage and descendant communities), and a regulator that works to both undermine Indigenous wants and enable archaeological site impacts. This complicated web precludes the performance of CBPR archaeology in its most idealistic form.

What to do, then? At a minimum, some CBPR principles can certainly be applied to the CRM world. To do so requires archaeologists to give up power and decentre themselves as experts – and maybe even to decentre archaeology as a discipline, in a Western sense, in order to lift up Indigenous scholarship and knowledge, in terms of values and ideals, all in an effort to work toward building something new that is relevant to the nations affected by proposed development projects (Alfred 2004).

As an example, Atalay (2008, 135) discuss *gikinawaabi*, which is an Ojibwe concept that describes knowledge transfer or knowledge reproduction from the older generation to the younger one through experience and teaching. It is learned through oral traditions and face-to-face interactions and is practised daily. Although degrees of knowledge may differ between individuals, there remains a sense of shared knowledge related by shared histories. Knowledge is possessed internally, within the people, and is not for external public consumption. In contrast to CRM archaeology, marked by non-disclosure agreements, secrecy, a lack of transparency, and the commodification of culture, *gikinawaabi* focuses on open, shared knowledge production. It has the power to draw on Indigenous history to shape a "model of knowledge stewardship" developed through collaboration with local communities, centring descendant communities but enabling archaeologists to co-contribute as storytellers (Atalay 2008, 135–36). In this application, archaeology is more than technical science: it is humanized to influence a larger audience's understanding of Indigenous heritage and why protection and stewardship can lead to more sustainable archaeological practice in the face of development.

My colleague and friend Charlene Everson published a report (2021a) that was conceived with the intention to address destruction of ancestral burial sites and other archaeological sites within Kwakwaka'wakw territories. Destruction included handling ancestral skulls from burials, pillaging bentwood burial boxes for regalia and other personal belongings, and setting fires to ancestral village sites. The HCA is supposed to protect these places, but it fails to do so. Consulting elders and knowledge keepers, Everson came to the idea of using *tłik'sala*, meaning "to show how to do things in the right way" or "to show the right way to live," to ground the report. She writes:

> tłik'sala is a method of teaching important life lessons through repetition. The "classroom" could be anywhere, but often it was in the home in the evenings. As a child, one learned to sit quietly and listen while you were taught in this manner. Though many subjects were taught, for the Ni'noxsola we spoke with, the activity centered around knowing who they are (what namima they were a part of), where they come from (origin stories), and how they are related to others. Knowing and understanding connections to the people and the world around one is central to Kwakwaka'wakw law and governance. (3)

Everson's report explores the idea of leveraging UNDRIP and DRIPA in order to incorporate Indigenous law into efforts to protect sacred places (such as burials) and thus put Indigenous law into practice. Instead of simply looking to protect archaeological sites, her project explores the implementation of Indigenous law and traditional resource management through a new strategy, the creation of Indigenous Protected and Conserved Areas (IPCAs) in British Columbia. IPCAs are Indigenous-led acts of self-determination through Crown governments. Through Everson's consultation and interviews, she realized that a guidebook was needed to place Indigenous law – including concepts and values – in a modern context for readers to better understand Indigenous world views (Everson 2021b).

Both *gikinawaabi* and *tłik'sala* are Indigenous concepts rooted in and relevant to their respective cultural contexts. As Atalay (2008), notes, they are "an example of the way in which traditional Indigenous knowledge holds contemporary relevance for the larger global community" (136). These concepts, and others like them, promote transparent, compassionate, and trusting relationships built through respect and reciprocity. Both CRM practice and archaeology curriculum would benefit greatly if they incorporated such concepts and values as well as the ideas of scholars, writers, and thinkers such as Deloria (1992), Hunter (2008),

McNiven and Russell (2005), L.T. Smith (2012), Steeves (2015, 2017), S. Wilson (2008), and Yellowhorn (2006). Grounding in such ideas enables archaeologists to process what they are seeing and living each day as they work with Indigenous communities and to recognize how we can begin to create change.

Living and working within descendant communities both in the South Pacific and across British Columbia have allowed me to get to know individuals and families who have taught me, continue to teach me, and help me learn and grow. I believe, then, that fieldwork can be a starting point from which to reimagine archaeological practice. From the ground up, we can collectively infuse fieldwork practices with ethos, values, and ideals reflective of our relationships with community members so their needs and wants are applied in our collective work. Such efforts are recognizable to the communities archaeologists work within. Practising an archaeology led by Indigenous values may generate momentum to actually transform the discipline. But in this process, the archaeologist must take care not to appropriate the voices of Indigenous peoples: we can lift others up, but the work must be represented by Indigenous practitioners, with ultimate authority and decision making from descendant communities.

Archaeologists can draw lessons from both scholarly, theoretical works and community-based interactions within Indigenous nations to develop strategies for incorporating Indigenous values into CRM. Six practices are of particular importance: establishing relationality; ensuring that work is relevant to the community; prioritizing Indigenous heritage; supporting representation of Indigenous practitioners; relinquishing control; and ensuring that timelines respect the needs of communities.

1. PUTTING RELATIONALITY AND RELATIONAL ACCOUNTABILITY INTO PRACTICE

An underlying theme of much of this book is the importance of relationships built in the field: they are a source of trust, knowledge, and accountability. Archaeologists can build meaningful relationships through their conduct in the field, day to day, over time. This ongoing process is grounded in respect, resiliency, humility, and humour. As discussed by Shawn Wilson (2008), it begins with the commitments archaeologists make to members of an Indigenous community and develops through accountability to the feelings, ideas, and input of those members. Creating the space for an open and safe exchange of information facilitates the development of a sustainable partnership. Fieldwork provides the opportunity for people to start the process of braiding together different world views through understanding and appreciation. Such engagement and experience can – and should – cause us, as archaeologists, to question everything we know about heritage, archaeology, and knowledge production.

I deeply value the experience of co-working with community members and building relationships and, in many cases, friendships with them. This work is forged through hard lessons learned, through the incorporation of alternative viewpoints that enable a meaningful practice. Here, I'm speaking about the intangible stuff, the spaces in-between that slowly fill with sweat, blood, tears, and beer: the rapport more than the report. These are not the things that make for successful peer-reviewed articles. These sorts of discussions get cut from technical reports (although perhaps they shouldn't). Building such relationships doesn't get someone tenure or a promotion at work, nor does it resonate with granting agencies. These relationships are built on personal victories and failures gained through practising archaeology with others. In this process, we project our sense of self, a way of being and doing while in the field, that is seen, felt, and heard by others. By demonstrating respect for Indigenous values – respect for the descendant community, ancestors, and heritage – and incorporating them into archaeological methods in the field, we demonstrate relational accountability.

If productive fieldwork is the result of acquiring knowledge through rapport (which archaeologists do even if they're not necessarily conscious of it), we must start from a place of honesty and respect. To build trust, we need to be honest and open, always. We need to convey through both words and actions that we're not here to treat heritage – both tangible and intangible – lightly, that we know *it matters*. We need to listen so we understand, as best we can, the Indigenous community's voice and vision. Heritage matters because those who have invited us into their territory say it matters. So, we can act accordingly. We can eat fry bread (bannock). Stop and pick some plants (medicine). Not interrupt elders. Make jokes. Have fun. Share food. We can listen, learn, and teach – share ideas, explain concepts, discuss perspectives, feel emotion – and do these things with respect and from a commitment to understand each other. These actions contribute to the joy of working together and lead to results that everyone on the crew is happy with. For me, a primary measure of success on any given project is the fact that the community is happy with the process in which the work took place. A positive project is one where everyone participating had ample space to contribute to the pre-planning, methods, analysis and interpretation, and the writing up of the results. Full participation of Indigenous communities in telling the story of what came before is only right: after all, these are their ancestors.

2. ENSURING ARCHAEOLOGY IS RELEVANT TO INDIGENOUS COMMUNITIES

Descendant communities should decide on the kind of archaeology they find meaningful, relevant, and useful. They must be the audience for archaeologists, even though, under current CRM, proponents, the Archaeology Branch, and the public are also audience members. Making archaeology meaningful begins by asking nations what they want from projects. With each project in their territory, we must ask, what are their goals or objectives? Within the CRM world, not all projects are the same in terms of impact, scale, and results. In a project that focuses on revitalizing streams for fish habitat, the archaeology is important and requires care, but the goal is protecting the local environment for the descendant community. Other projects will be larger in scale, with potential impacts across a landscape that affect current lifeways of descendant communities. Yet other projects involve infrastructure in an urban setting. In such cases, heritage may yet be impacted because no archaeological assessment was ever conducted in the proposed project area, or it has been buried or displaced. Possessing an understanding of a First Nation's wants, needs, and values, accrued over time by working for years in the area (and having built relations whereby archaeologists learn directly from nation members) is one path toward advocating for Indigenous archaeologists and assuring them that they are recognized and heard.

Ultimately, the focus of any project is finding the approach that makes archaeology relevant for the descendant communities whose heritage is under assessment.

I have learned to appreciate Indigenous peoples' relationships to the landscape (places) which they were born into. Each community has a unique cultural reality shared by its members. For some, it is a spiritual relationship that serves as an internal sense of connection to ancestors, beings, and entities draped across a landscape. For others, its lifeways, lessons, and languages serving as a nexus between the mundane and the fantastic. Generally speaking, Indigenous praxis embodies local science, protocols, laws, and a cosmology of their inhabited universe. The land is imbued with meaning, stories, sacredness, teachings, all of which are learned through relationships with people, flora and fauna, inanimate objects, and supernatural beings. Stories of place – the homelands of descendant communities – abound with rich cultural identities that are socially constructed by the people who reside in them and know them (Harris 2005; Low and Lawrence-Zúñiga 2003; Two Bears 2008). Indigenous communities have a reciprocal relationship with places where their ancestors reside (McNiven 2016, 31). The ancestors shaped the world for their descendants today by leaving behind material evidence of their existence through physical adaptions (e.g., ancestral villages, forest gardens, cultivated meadows, clam [sea] gardens) and technologies but also teachings orally passed down that reflect lessons learned on the landscape. Place is enveloped within a larger, connected world that offers well-being – emotional, physical, and mental health – and impacts to these places affect the lifeways of communities who have cared for them through time.

Acknowledging the importance of a place makes archaeological work relevant to Indigenous peoples. Illustrating the importance of a place through reporting to proponents, clients, municipalities, and even homeowners can help awaken within them a new appreciation of Indigenous lands. Perhaps it may even engender compassion and contribute to an understanding of the importance of heritage and of Indigenous-centred archaeology. Until landback acquires structural momentum, writing about an Indigenous landscape upon which descendant communities thrive could create allies in unlikely spaces, that is, non-Indigenous people, who may now afford protection by possessing an appreciation and deeper understanding of the land they occupy. Writing to inspire and educate others, and make archaeology relevant to both descendant communities (and a larger public), begins by creating the space on the ground, so the work is amplified (e.g., in the news, online videos, interviews) for others ignorant of such world views.

3. PRIORITIZING INDIGENOUS HERITAGE

Prioritizing heritage means thinking about three things: (1) the ancestors, (2) descendant communities whose heritage is being assessed, and (3) Indigenous colleagues in the field who possess direct ties to their heritage. If our focus is on the fieldwork – that is, the on-the-ground work to identify, record, protect, and conserve the archaeological record that is the heritage – then we will succeed in all aspects of a project. There won't be room for the proponent to apply pressure with respect to timelines (they will try, but we need to have the strength and knowledge to explain why this is not a good idea), nor will they be able to find quick solutions to subvert archaeological efforts to do what is right. Heritage inspection and the results of fieldwork require Indigenous nations review and comments: archaeologists should always remind proponents of this critical component. If we can slow the demands of timelines and put Indigenous heritage and descendant communities first, we can avert mistakes and poor decisions.

CRM archaeologists or clients may well push back at the idea of prioritizing Indigenous heritage over the client's project. But such a reaction doesn't change the fact that community-centred archaeology is the correct and ethical path. In most cases, clients are not centring Indigenous heritage and are not engaging Indigenous nations in clear, honest, and transparent ways. They want their project to succeed more than they value Indigenous heritage. And, as an added potential conflict, they are often the ones paying the archaeologists. I do not want to underestimate the challenge of identifying and balancing multiple audiences – I had enough difficulty figuring out who my audience should be for this book. Yet this simple truth remains: we are working on unceded Indigenous lands with heritage that is not ours, conducting archaeology for projects that could potentially damage that heritage. It seems obvious that, ethically, Indigenous heritage and the ancestors must be put first. From that premise, everything else will follow. Putting into practice Indigenous concepts, methods, and philosophies within a CBPR approach will open a space for multiple voices and perspectives within the fieldwork and the larger project.

4. SUPPORTING REPRESENTATION

Archaeological knowledge is only one way of knowing the world, and it is not more important or valid than Indigenous knowledge or teachings. Archaeology can facilitate multiple perspectives, articulating many ways to know the past, one of which is through fieldwork. Fieldwork offers an opportunity for knowledge exchange: by being present in the same space, archaeologists can listen to and learn from ideas within a population largely marginalized in Canadian governance. Engaging with and making the space for multiple voices – in terms of input, interpretations, and recommendations – results in on-the-ground work that is meaningful for everyone. Indigenous knowledge as a body of collective teachings has served to sustain many communities across the globe in a variety of environments (Harris 2005, 37). Moreover, Indigenous knowledge reflects innovation, ingenuity, and technological adaptations through time. Why, then, wouldn't Indigenous epistemologies enhance archaeology in both practice and interpretation? Increasing the representation of Indigenous people in archaeological practice can only support meaningful archaeology and effective heritage management.

Currently, CRM lacks Indigenous representation in positions of authority and power, such as field directors, permit holders, report authors, and Archaeology Branch officers. The presence of First Nations field representatives (and let's call them archaeologists as opposed to field techs or monitors) is fundamentally important. They are the origin of a good deal of my learning, but such learning requires listening and paying attention to the local rhythms and beats within the cultural landscape in which we practise archaeology together. What, then, can the archaeological community do to increase Indigenous representation in positions of power? Archaeologists can – indeed, have a responsibility to – support and build capacity among Indigenous practitioners and stand up for them in a system that undervalues and ignores them. We can advocate for Indigenous field directors and permit holders, as well as for positions within the Archaeology Branch (e.g., permit officers, site inventory officer). Archaeologists are capable of helping to facilitate the development of nation members who have a passion for archaeology and who can contribute to a heritage stewardship that reflects their community's needs, wants, and values.

5. RELINQUISHING CONTROL AND POWER

When it comes to archaeology on Indigenous lands, the experts are the elders and knowledge keepers in a community, not the archaeologists. I'm not an expert; I'm a facilitator (but with a touch of grey). I take my skills and apply them to situations for descendant communities. As a facilitator, I can champion and help bring to life what descendant communities want from archaeology, not my own goals or research questions. This does not mean that my archaeological skills are not valued by Indigenous communities – I have experienced the opposite. But, in addition to those skills, being a facilitator requires listening, thinking through the problems as presented by the local community, and co-developing solutions. I liken a facilitator to the guest in McNiven and Russell's (2005) host-guest model. Being a facilitator requires archaeologists to give up power and decenter themselves, and to seriously centre Indigenous epistemologies and descendant community members. Doing so enables archaeologists to loosen their grasp on the elitism of "expertise" and ground archaeology in more community-focused, heterarchical practice. For example, archaeologists typically manage tangible heritage; they often don't find creative ways to protect intangible heritage. Archaeologists need to ask Indigenous communities themselves how they define cultural heritage, how it fits into their world view. This way, a more inclusive and holistic understanding of heritage can achieved, with methods co-designed to protect it during archaeological assessments. As more communities choose to engage in this process, it may lead to reforming the legislation to protect heritage based on a more Indigenous definition.

A thought: imagine if archaeological impact assessments were under the jurisdiction of First Nations and archaeologists, and not the

Archaeology Branch. This would free up time and resources for the Archaeology Branch so it could focus more effectively on protecting known archaeological sites from potential impact (as currently allowed under site alteration permits). It would also enable First Nations and archaeologists to assess areas with no known archaeological sites, with the archaeology directed by local Indigenous communities with support from non-Indigenous archaeologists (if they so choose).

6. ENSURING THAT TIMELINES ARE SET BY INDIGENOUS COMMUNITIES
British Columbia is unceded Indigenous land. This fact alone must be front and centre in the minds of each archaeologist in order to transform thinking around archaeology as currently practised. As Max Liboiron (2021) writes, "to change colonial land relations and enact other types of Land relations requires specificity" (13). Proponents who continually dispossess Indigenous peoples from the land through development-driven capitalism by acquiring and developing the land betray an insatiable appetite for more land to produce commodities for exchange (by extracting natural resources and through residential and industrial development). Their relationship to the land is one of accumulation and, in effect, colonial dispossession (Coulthard 2014; Liboiron 2021; P. West 2016). Such "development" on dispossessed lands reflects non-Indigenous world views and expectations. Under CRM, engagement, consultation, and goals all heavily favour the proponent, instead of involving dialogue and discourse with Indigenous communities, even on Indigenous land. The provincial government, through the Archaeology Branch, does not want to impede development, they would rather assist the development industry in making decisions to ensure land use and development (Archaeology Branch 2018).

Indigenous communities want to restore opportunities for themselves within their own territories and seek control and ownership over their heritage (see Hammond 2009; Klassen 2013; McNiven 2016). This struggle is not new. Klassen et al. (2009) nicely illustrate the convergence of Indigenous political activism, legal decisions, booming industrial development, and shifting disciplinary ethics that have transformed archaeological practice in British Columbia. By highlighting the boom in forestry-related assessments and the increased participation of Indigenous communities in archaeological heritage management during the late 1980s and into the 1990s, these scholars speak to the challenges consulting archaeologists have faced relative to ethical, political, and theoretical issues when confronted by active and engaged communities who assert their own rights and title to the lands proposed for development. These challenges are even more pressing today, given the abundance of proposed liquid natural gas projects and pipelines snaking across British Columbia.

Nations are doing the work themselves to build capacity, or they work closely with trusted firms. But such work is made all the more difficult by the weight CRM gives to proponents' perspectives on time and urgency. Proponents are, basically, setting the timelines for projects. This should not be. For any proposed development situated on Indigenous land – which, in British Columbia, is *all* development – First Nations should be setting the timelines, so that the proper time and space is available for heritage assessment. In my years in CRM, proponents have historically demonstrated poor planning for projects and assigned a low priority to heritage. Some clients engage with the rhetoric of reconciliation, but proponents need to demonstrate that they understand what reconciliation truly means. One way of doing so is by letting First Nations and their archaeologists determine the time needed for archaeological assessments. When the timelines for a project – whether it be a watermain, a pipeline, an industrial facility, a new plaza, or a highway – are so tight as to preclude a meaningful assessment of Indigenous heritage, it's clear that heritage is not important to a proponent. When project team meetings that are setting the agenda are held with no presence from any First Nations, it's apparent that heritage does not matter. In such cases, it's our obligation as archaeologists to advocate on behalf of the Indigenous communities.

INDIGENOUS-OWNED HERITAGE FIRMS

In recent years, many First Nations have been growing capacity internally by creating positions and structures to support nation-based archaeological departments to manage heritage in their territories. In the lower mainland of Vancouver, for example, Katzie Nation, sәýeṁ qwantlen (Kwantlen), xʷmәθkʷәẏәm (Musqueam), Skwxwú7mesh Úxwumixw (Squamish Nation), Stó:lō Nation, sәlilwәtaɬ (Tsleil-Waututh), and scəẃaθən məsteyəxʷ (Tsawwassen First Nation), among others, have been pursuing this strategy. Some of these departments have developed First Nations permit systems, heritage policies, and ancestral remains policies, and have built repositories and hired staff to perform archaeological assessments as well as review and comment on archaeological reports conducted within their territory by other heritage firms. Such capacity enables a nation to mould a vision for protection and conservation of its own heritage as it sees fit. For example, the Stó:lō Nation's Stó:lō Research and Resource Management Centre (SRRMC) has been active for over twenty years, offering a range of professional and technical capabilities in areas such as archaeology, fisheries, education, geographic information systems (GIS), land management, treaty, and rights and title, among others. SRRMC's Heritage Stewardship and Archaeology Program adopts a holistic and multidisciplinary approach to cultural heritage research and management that recognizes both tangible and intangible heritage (Schaepe 2007, 248). SRRMC regulates archaeological projects within Stó:lō territory through permits but also actively participates in all aspects of archaeology, from research to resource management, collections curation, and repatriation. Its role helps influence archaeological practice in Stó:lō territory, but that is only one nation. It seems self-evident that archaeological practice would be greatly influenced if all nations had the capacity to do what the Stó:lō Nation is doing. This is exactly what has been happening in recent years in the lower mainland and elsewhere in the province.

Inlailawatash is a səlilwətaɬ Nation–owned company established in 2004. *Inlailawatash* is hənq̓əminəm̓ for "the go inside place," referring to a village located beyond the mouth of the Indian River at the head of the Indian Arm in Burrard Inlet. Inlailawatash provides integrated cultural and renewable resource services to Indigenous and Crown governments and private-sector clients, organizations, and institutions. Inlailawatash has departments focused on forestry, natural resources, fisheries, archaeology, and GIS. The Archaeology Department became active in 2014 after taking on a large-scale project in the Indian River watershed. All profits go back into the nation to be used as determined by the community. Thus, profits derived from assessing Indigenous heritage benefit the community that is actually affected by the development. This is radically different than with non-Indigenous heritage-assessment firms, whose profits go to corporate shareholders.

In many respects, the Inlailawatash model is one that is common in Western companies, and Inlailawatash behaves like most companies that are encapsulated within the capitalistic system. However, the current Inlailawatash archaeological team members choose to practise archaeology in meaningful ways. (Full disclosure: I work for Inlailawatash.) They are a unique team of educators, activists, and scholars who are efficient, adaptive, and flexible, which allows them to meet the interests of both the nation and their clients. Inlailawatash has been able to serve the needs of descendant communities and their heritage by respecting the place in which they work, building meaningful relationships with their colleagues and nation members, keeping an eye on their long-term goals and vision, and not being afraid to stand up for what they believe in when in communication with proponents or governments. They do not do this job for money: they do this job for the ancestors. They do this job for their nation-member colleagues whose interests are not served by development-driven capitalism proponents who are not looking to protect Indigenous heritage, Indigenous identity, or Indigenous futures. Inlailawatash holds the line for First Nations and advocate on their behalf through Indigenous teachings and values. When Inlailawatash archaeologists are in the field, people see them as representing səlilwətaɫ. To some degree this is true, but not all of them are members of səlilwətaɫ. First Nation–owned companies are sometimes accused of bias – as if non-Indigenous companies are apolitical and free from bias! In reality, a central difference between First Nation–owned firms and typical consulting firms is that the former place Indigenous heritage first ahead of non-Indigenous proponents' needs. And, on Indigenous lands, who better to do archaeology than a firm grounded in Indigenous values?

An Indigenous-owned heritage firm enables nations to insert themselves directly into the heritage management system as it currently operates. Such firms can engage potential clients for proposed work within their territory, offering an alternative to the typical transnational corporations or other non-Indigenous-owned firms that take on such work. A community can choose the right archaeologists to facilitate its needs, wants, and values related to overseeing, assessing, and protecting its heritage. As part of Inlailawatash archaeology's code of ethics, engagement with local First Nations, on whose unceded territories they are working, is initiated through First Nations archaeology permits. These permits allow archaeologists to work within a nation's territory but also encourage representatives from the local nation to work alongside the archaeologists. This practice contributes to First Nations economies through wages and permit fees, but also ensures that Inlailawatash is following local protocols and laws.

Inlailawatash works at arm's length from the nation, so the archaeological team is able to exert passion in practice by protecting Indigenous heritage across British Columbia and elsewhere by serving many different and unique clients (both non-Indigenous entities and Indigenous nations). Educating the public and clients and centring Indigenous heritage while balancing the needs of local First Nations and clients ensure that the work can be done in accordance with nations' standards and expectations. Inlailawatash is thoroughly committed to sustainable environmental practices and resource stewardship that are in accord with səlilwətaɫ Nation values and practices. Sustainability depends on developing meaningful relationships over time, and the Inlailawatash archaeological team does its best to be mindful of and implement the articles of the United Nations Declaration on the Rights of Indigenous Peoples in its work. In addition, the team advocates for the calls to action of the Truth and Reconciliation Commission, especially Call to Action 43, which asks the federal, provincial, territorial, and municipal governments to fully adopt and implement UNDRIP as the framework for reconciliation. Positive relationships with local communities build trust and contribute to successful projects. Recognizing that we work on unceded Indigenous lands underlines the need to act in a sustainable way on all projects.

The regulations that structure archaeology in the province also apply to nation-owned archaeological firms. The challenge is creating the space to raise up nations members who want to participate in archaeology, to advocate for equality, and to build capacity so interested members can take on the roles of professional archaeologists. In addition, səlilwətaɫ, through Inlailawatash, can hire the type of archaeologists that it wants to work in its territory: it can choose who can and cannot conduct archaeology in sensitive səlilwətaɬ areas. Being an Indigenous-owned company means seeking out opportunities to hire not only Indigenous peoples but also people from other backgrounds and underrepresented communities (e.g., women, ethnic minorities, 2SLGBTQIA+ people). Representation is important in the field of archaeology, and, ultimately, a goal for Inlailawatash is to have a fully Indigenous archaeological team. However, if Inlailawatash chooses to continue working with settler archaeologists, it has the prerogative to do so.

In the end, Inlailawatash is a business, one that is owned by a First Nation and that possesses a set of values within a collective world view. But it is a company, and companies are institutions with inherent flaws and are only as good as their employees. I value my colleagues within Inlailawatash archaeology because they centre Indigenous heritage, expend the emotional labour to do what is right, and are transparent and honest.

ARCHAEOLOGY AWAKENS

Bringing together ideas from this chapter and the previous ones, I want to offer some practical answers to the question of how we can begin to reimagine archaeology. As illustrated in Figure 6.1, most fundamentally, everyone involved in CRM must centre Indigenous heritage and descendant communities within a proposed project. This requirement applies to proponents who wish to propose any work on unceded Indigenous land; the Archaeology Branch, which regulates archaeology through legislation; and the archaeologists who are currently empowered by the province to make recommendations regarding Indigenous heritage. Proponents must commit to meaningful engagement (and reconciliation) and to seek free, prior, and informed consent for all projects on Indigenous land. They must exercise deep listening and commit themselves to following Indigenous world views, values, and law in any project that is on Indigenous land. If a nation requires an archaeological impact assessment prior to determining if it will approve a project, a proponent can demonstrate good faith by putting heritage ahead of the project's goals and timelines. If, after the heritage field assessment and any other

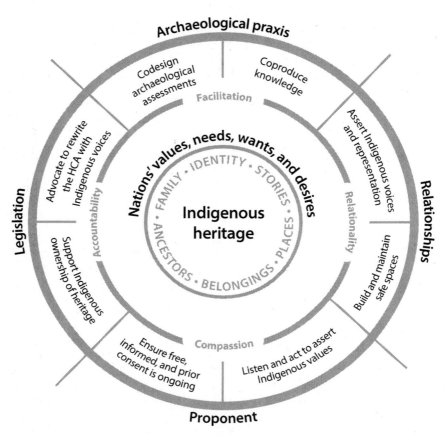

FIGURE 6.1 A framework for centring Indigenous heritage within CRM. | Original conceived by author and drawn by Walter Homewood; redrawn by Julie Cochrane.

environmental and socio-economic assessments are conducted, a nation decides it does not want to approve the project, those wishes should be honoured – to do so is a part of reconciliation.

Figure 6.1 illustrates a framework for centring Indigenous heritage within CRM but doesn't focus on a single path. Rather, it suggests an archaeology in which human values supplant economic ones, something that could occur if the CRM world were to prioritize Indigenous heritage over its own projects, wants, and goals. A transformation in practice will not take place if Indigenous heritage and descendant communities are not centred in this process. Focusing on a collective effort that engenders compassion for and supports the well-being of those under pressure from colonialism or development-driven capitalism to extract resources, at the expense of Indigenous heritage, helps counter the stark egotism of the capitalist system. Many outcomes could transpire if Indigenous heritage were put first, but this first step has to happen.

Currently, the Archaeology Branch is the self-appointed owner of Indigenous heritage. This inequity in power and ownership must change. Both the government and bureaucrats must be accountable to each First Nation in the province. They must begin to implement DRIPA and, in the process, support Indigenous ownership of heritage by creating positions and opportunities for Indigenous roles and oversight within the regulatory framework (if not completely reforming it). The Declaration on the Rights of Indigenous Peoples Act Action Plan, 2022–2027 released in March 2022 cannot simply be a horizon plan.[8] The Heritage Conservation Act requires a massive overhaul, one in which Indigenous voices co-write or completely rewrite the legislation, so it reflects Indigenous values, world views, and ideals. Among the changes would be redefining Indigenous heritage (both tangible and intangible) more expansively. Concurrent with those changes, the province could do more to actively protect heritage, like funding and otherwise supporting nation-driven initiatives such as Guardian programs and other forms of Indigenous stewardship.

For archaeologists, efforts to continually build meaningful connections steeped in relationality must be at the forefront. Relationality creates safe spaces for asserting Indigenous voices and representation, both in the field and in products co-produced with nation members. Co-designing and co-producing archaeological assessments where descendant communities determine what they find meaningful and relevant is critical for facilitating an archaeology that is useful for First Nations.

Within the complicated realm of CRM, there are many factors that local First Nations cannot control at the moment: the number of proposed projects on their lands, the provincial regulator of archaeology, the values archaeologists possess. The focus will have to be on what they can control within their territory and community: the types of development projects they support, which archaeologists can work in their territories (if a nation has a permitting system), and which archaeologists they employ and send to the field. First Nations must give time and thought to heritage policies, including the relationships they want to build with federal, provincial, and municipal governments and the protocols for outsiders working within their territories. Internal Indigenous politics and provincial politics, as well as economics, public perceptions, timelines, and urgency, will be variables for each First Nation to consider. All Indigenous Nations are within a colonial system encapsulated by capitalism: the choices they make have to be prudent, particularly as, at least for now, the options are not great. Archaeologists should help facilitate nation-driven initiatives, wants, values, and desires with respect to Indigenous heritage. We can start by acknowledging the power inequity and a lack of Indigenous control and ownership over Indigenous heritage within the CRM world. Finally, archaeologists can lift up others by listening to and reading works by Indigenous peoples to develop a sense that the world they inhabit can be otherwise.

Conclusion

In Coast Salish ceremonies and events, being called to witness is critically important. It is an honour and responsibility within the community. Witnesses are gifted items (e.g., money, blankets). Words are spoken to them, about them, in front of an audience. Witnesses observe the ceremony and record the events in their mind. When time moves forward, and people disband from the day's ceremony, the witnesses carry forth the events: they are the knowledge keepers. They will be the guardians of oral history. They will tell of the event years into the future. And when they pass, their stories will become oral tradition, and the meanings and knowledge will live on, continuing the grand narrative for future generations.

Through a colonial legacy that is still active, I possess a privileged position within this industry. But I can bear witness to the inequities of power, ownership, and abuse, and this means I have to speak up about it daily in order to empower others. Bearing witness to the world of CRM forces one to inhabit a space fraught with complications and contradictions. It is space where Indigenous heritage has been commodified under capitalism, auctioned off by proponents to heritage firms, and regulated by the province, which has a vested interest in large-scale economic projects to succeed. Through this system, Indigenous communities are continually dispossessed of their land.

HARM

As presently practised, CRM archaeology does little to support social, economic, and environmental justice for descendant communities. CRM – and the entire industry (proponents, government, and for-profit archaeological companies) – does not honour the wishes of Indigenous communities whose cultural heritage is in jeopardy. Instead, it exists to serve the interests of capital and, in particular, to aid project proponents in subverting the spirit of legislation that ostensibly claims to protect and conserve cultural heritage. It privileges economic values over human values. These values and practices are profoundly harmful to Indigenous peoples. By centring a project's critical path over Indigenous heritage and their ancestors, thus reducing Indigenous heritage as meaningless to the overall project's goals, relegates heritage to unimportant and causes suffering to Indigenous peoples when it is not cared for. In these circumstances, non-Indigenous archaeologists have a choice: they can uphold the status quo, or they can try to be the agents of change. Some of us who are embroiled in CRM look to serve the descendant communities whose heritage is under threat by trying to practise a community-first approach to reconstitute the industry, and ultimately, the discipline of archaeology. This effort helps provide our colleagues in Indigenous communities with a safe space in which to assert their voices and their own sovereignty. For archaeologists, such a process means working from the ground up in a system that is top down, mired in hierarchy that devalues and decentres Indigenous world views.

I underline two more realities: CRM is demanding, and it is harmful to the practitioner – physically, mentally, and emotionally. It offers no space for respite or introspection but, rather, constant pressure from unrelenting proponents. An archaeologist is often on the ground working with individuals who have experienced trauma and is placing strenuous demands on their labour. This labour is performed within a system that possesses a military history, in terms of archaeology's birth as a discipline, evinced in the form of organization, logistics, and fieldwork (Trigger 2000). It's not warfare by any stretch of the imagination, but CRM can expose individuals to rigid hierarchy as well as to violent sensory overload on sites, with loud, harsh sounds and sometimes real physical dangers (e.g., monitoring in a port environment, at the heart of commerce and trade, within a physically limited space in which to move, and surrounded by large excavators, dump trucks, trains, cranes, and an aggressive supervisors). Other times, archaeologists find themselves deep in remote mountains, hiking rugged terrain with other people whose personalities and experiences they may not fully comprehend, stuck together on an eight-kilometre trek to assess archaeological potential and then make it to a landing zone for a helicopter pick up, all the while navigating the forests and watching for animal signs and natural hazards. And often, archaeologists know the inequities which surround their work and do their best to be mindful. Emotional labour is a large part of our practice.

ACCOUNTABILITY AND COLONIALISM

Like everyone, I am responsible for the predictable consequences of my own actions. Through relationality, I am also accountable to others. The additional challenge posed by archaeology is accountability to those who lived long ago and who, in many cultures in British Columbia, are still here guiding us. Although legislation and bureaucratic oversight claims that the Archaeological Branch is responsible for the protection of Indigenous heritage, it lacks accountability. Descendant communities are impacted by legislation, policies, and procedures surrounding their heritage. I see this firsthand in the field. On Berry Island in the Broughton Archipelago, for example, alongside Jake Smith (a former manager of Mamalilikulla Guardians) and Chip Mountain (senior Guardian member), I see bentwood boxes plundered by eco-tourists. Ancestors' skulls have been held, moved, and placed about the site – to be clear, a legislatively protected place – as visitors rummaged through the boxes. This is a sacred place, next to a bathing well adorned with ancient artwork painted with ochre. I have visited this site many times over the years, recorded and documented the destruction, and helped report it. The emotions displayed by the Mamalilikulla Guardians who visit this place only to see new damage – frustration, anger, pain, sadness – hurt their hearts and minds. In 2022–23, the Guardians took action into their own hands, under direction from their chief (John Powell), and conducted a ceremony with knowledge holders to reinter remains, carve a new burial box, construct a burial house, and fence the area off (Inlailawatash 2023).

These activities required a site alteration permit (under Section 12.4 of the Heritage Conservation Act) granted by the Archaeology Branch. What a painful irony that provincial policies and procedures prevent protection through community direct-action but turn a blind eye to destructive impacts to heritage, in this case, a graveyard, year after year, with no oversight or efforts to do anything about it for over thirty years.[1]

Government legislation and regulation have repeatedly failed to protect Indigenous heritage in British Columbia, and the province shows few meaningful signs of taking accountability for these failures. Archaeologists cannot perpetuate this legacy. Instead, we can commit to prioritizing Indigenous interest in any project, and develop an understanding of those interests through our relationships with nations whose heritage is threatened. Being accountable to those relationships in the field enables archaeologists to create and maintain a connection with colleagues within the nation and prioritize their needs, wants, and desires for the project. Caring for Indigenous heritage and ancestors is caring for the descendant community.

Look – if the biggest threat to my existence is that the archaeological world I inhabit isn't changing quickly enough to a more equitable practice, then I'm pretty fortunate. I didn't grow up tied to the Indian Act. I wasn't the target of legislation constructed to assimilate me (or my ancestors) into a foreign world view. My history of place – that is, my identity and being – wasn't confiscated; agents weren't assigned to live in my community and to grant (or refuse) me passage to come and go; my songs, dances, celebrations, ceremonies, names, and belongings were not stolen from me. I wasn't confined to a postage stamp–sized reserve. My siblings weren't taken from me. I didn't lose my language or, worse, never have the opportunity to hear it. My ancestral knowledge wasn't denigrated. My places of heritage and identity have never been destroyed by development. Genocide didn't happen to me or my ancestors. Colonialism doesn't continue to happen to me.

I didn't commit the atrocities, but I have benefited from them, and that matters (see Robbins 2017, 148–49). I benefit from violent injustices that continually happen on Indigenous lands. I have obtained degrees and met provincial standards to conduct archaeology in British

Columbia, both reflections of my position of privilege and power. I can't be ignorant of the historical processes that led us to here. The first step is acknowledgment, but the road is long and unsettling. Many of those along the route never make this simple acknowledgment while they benefit from injustice. Yet despite the injustices, exclusion, colonialism, and attempts to assimilate, Indigenous values persist. Indigenous voices are heard. Babies are born to Indigenous mothers. Indigenous knowledge continues to be shared with younger generations.

RESPONSIBILITY

Indigenous identity is celebrated among all Canada's First Peoples. Some members live in urban centres, others on reserves; but no matter where they call home, their spirit continues. Indigenous cultures did not vanish, as Franz Boas and his cronies once thought while they were conducting "salvage ethnography" across British Columbia. Languages continue to be spoken, even if they are at risk. Community members are going forth with their lives, continuing ceremonies and exercising both resistance to colonialism and control over their needs, wants, and aspirations. Their voices are finding a way into archaeology.

As archaeologists, we have the responsibility to listen by opening up to new teachers so the next generation of archaeologists can do better, and we can be better. James Baldwin (1993 [1962]) said, "I know that people can be better than they are. We are capable of bearing a great burden, once we discover that the burden is reality and arrive where reality is" (91). The reality is that CRM is part of a colonialist system that functions to repress Indigenous sovereignty in managing their heritage. We need to arrive at this reality. Then, collectively, we can go about transforming it through anticolonial action.

We can become responsible for changing practices within our field, where a lack of time rather than a lack of will sometimes precludes committing to overturning problematic aspects of the field and the industry. Inaction means that others continue to suffer. And action promises benefits for all. To paraphrase James Baldwin (1993 [1962], 97), the price of the liberation of non-Indigenous people is the liberation of Indigenous people. As settlers/colonizers who live in a colonial world, we cannot be free from tyranny, but I am an anticolonial boy. Markers on the path forward include landback, sovereignty, and the opportunity for descendant communities to engage their traditional territories within a system of local Indigenous law and practices. But it will take unending pressure to release the power the colonial nation-state controls. And if heritage is but one aspect to spotlight within colonialism, then we have major work ahead of us.

Archaeologists have the capacity and responsibility to develop new approaches to archaeological fieldwork that are both respectful of and responsive to Indigenous values, customs, and ways of understanding the world. Archaeologists can be facilitators and help drive nation-led initiatives to protect, conserve, and assess Indigenous heritage, and they can educate clients about the need to adopt new approaches as a matter of routine practice. Indigenous scholars and local First Nation members who work with archaeologists have been providing, and continue to provide, perspectives, insights, and examples of how to challenge current archaeological convention. Change can be accomplished through the co-development and co-design of fieldwork programs, lifting up voices both in meetings and fieldwork, co-interpretations of fieldwork results, co-development of recommendations, and dissemination. I use co- not because archaeologists need to be at the centre but rather, Nation-members have relationships with archaeologists and value their input when invited to comment.

ACTION (PRAXIS)

The system archaeologists operate within is colonial. Moving toward anticolonial approaches and methods, inspired by Indigenous scholars and nation members, will contribute to transforming CRM (Atalay et al. 2014; Denzin et al. 2008; Gonzalez et al. 2018; Liboiron 2021; C. Smith and Wobst 2005; L.T. Smith 2012). The first thing all archaeologists need to do to begin this process is to centre Indigenous heritage and descendant communities – not the client, not the proponent, not the project, however big or small it may be. Prior to the start of a project (whether research-based or commercial), the archaeologist should ensure that field programs, budgets, interpretations, reporting, and timelines presented to the proponent reflect an archaeology that prioritizes the needs and concerns of the Indigenous community and clearly outline what the nation wants from the project and the process. In this way, the archaeologist can manage expectations.

Archaeologists – especially those employed by CRM firms – have the opportunity to press for greater equity within the profession. This can be accomplished by hiring Indigenous archaeologists in positions of influence and power, and supporting their development, and by empowering others who also have not had an equal seat within archaeology (women, including women of colour, visible minorities, individuals from the queer community). Additionally, archaeologists can advocate for changes in policies governing hiring and promotion within the industry. It is not acceptable that only non-Indigenous archaeologists are seen as experts, and Indigenous archaeologists (and/or representatives, technicians, monitors) are treated like second-class citizens, particularly when it is their heritage that is at stake. Indigenous words, voices, experience, and desires cannot be ignored. Archaeological firms can hire from and build capacity within communities, thereby increasing opportunities for nation members as practitioners doing the archaeology and in governmental positions within the Archaeology Branch.

Archaeologists need to speak up about current legislation, Archaeology Branch bulletins, and practices that violate professional integrity and the principles of inclusion and mutual recognition that we claim to uphold every year at professional member meetings and at the Community of Practice put on by the Archaeology Branch in Victoria every two years. By calling for the meaningful implementation of the Declaration on the Rights of Indigenous Peoples Act (DRIPA), archaeologists can advocate for the transformation of power inequities and for placing decision-making authority over heritage into the hands of First Nations. Archaeologists can reinforce the significance of DRIPA and the March 2019 amendments to the Heritage Conservation Act (HCA) with both proponents and government regulators, speaking out when decisions about whether to allow a project to proceed appear to violate the spirit of DRIPA or when timelines preclude meaningful Indigenous engagement.

To date, the province has not taken any meaningful steps to implement any articles of UNDRIP or align provincial law with DRIPA.[2] This is especially problematic for heritage, since British Columbia's heritage is overwhelmingly Indigenous and it is owned and managed by a non-Indigenous government with overwhelmingly non-Indigenous decisions makers. The key piece of legislation needing overhaul, with major input by Indigenous communities, is the Heritage Conservation Act. At the time of writing, the province is apparently in consultation with First Nations about revising the HCA. Under Article 11 of UNDRIP, Indigenous peoples possess the sovereign right to manage their heritage as they see fit. Both Section 4 of the HCA and Section 7 of DRIPA authorize the province to enter into agreements with First Nations regarding their heritage and shared decision making. Although the province may well not want to give up its power, to fail to act is to perpetuate inequality and suffering.

Archaeologists can advocate by working with First Nations governments, and their archaeological or lands and resources departments, to encourage the province to end gatekeeping and the denial of Indigenous rights in heritage management. Within the profession, archaeologists can impress on their colleagues that serious efforts to implement the Truth and Reconciliation Commission's calls to action and the UN Declaration on the Rights of Indigenous Peoples must be accompanied by a change in values and behaviour.

Fieldwork and legislation are two areas in which archaeologists can have tangible input. For fieldwork and the day-to-day practice of archaeology, archaeologists seeking change must become agents of education and activists with insight into the tactics that are most likely to prove fruitful in a particular set of circumstances. They can begin in client meetings, by being vocal about Indigenous heritage and consultation; asking questions related to requests for proposals and timelines; asking clients if they have engaged with First Nations about the proposed project before seeking an archaeological consultant; and standing up for nations' participation and active role in decision making. Archaeologists may need to explain colonialism to clients and certainly should call out prejudice if it presents itself in meetings, in the field, or on site. To gain the confidence to implement these actions effectively will require reading Indigenous scholars and listening to and learning from Indigenous colleagues; being accountable to relationships formed in the field with

First Nations; integrating Indigenous methods and perspectives by co-designing fieldwork programs; relinquishing control and power by being a facilitator of, rather than the "expert" in, the archaeological process; centring Indigenous heritage; making archaeology relevant for the descendant communities; and supporting nations to direct heritage work on their own timelines that reflect their relationships on the land. While some archaeologists are already doing this work, we all need to be doing it each day, and collectively (not in competition with each other).

Input by archaeologists into legislation reform begins by asserting that Indigenous communities should define heritage, as both tangible and intangible. Such definitions must be incorporated into the HCA (or completely new legislation co-written by Indigenous communities with the current government). Definitions of heritage cannot be amended without First Nations consent. Nor can non-Indigenous peoples define intangible heritage. There is room in our workday to put into practice articles of UNDRIP but with the province still maintaining ownership and control over Indigenous heritage this poses a real-life threat to archaeologists who advocate for change under the current colonial system (as they will be seen as agitators). In advocating for First Nations' wants surrounding heritage management, archaeologists must align their values with those of descendant communities. Such advocacy may be reflected in changes in practice, reporting outputs, representation in the field, interpretation in reports, and final recommendations for heritage driven and directed by Indigenous peoples. Archaeologists can write policy papers, unconventional reports, letters to the province, and letters or articles for the media. Activist archaeologists – those with the courage to speak out, to join protests and blockades, to push their professional associations to take a stand – can expect to encounter resistance and even hostility. They may put their jobs at risk. Then again, they could have the opportunity to join forces with Indigenous archaeologists or to start their own consulting operations dedicated to supporting cultural heritage rather than planning its destruction. By all indications – delays in implementing DRIPA, business as usual within the Archaeology Branch, decisions favouring economic development at the expense of Indigenous heritage – the province is not the ally archaeologists and First Nations need to usher in transformative change to overcome colonial mindsets and legislation.[3] Sustained advocacy and activism will be needed to prod the province into taking meaningful action.

HOPE

Archaeologists – whether non-Indigenous or Indigenous – working within CRM may take many different paths. Some may prove fruitful, while others may lead to dead ends. Making change will require all of our efforts on many fronts. I want anyone interested in archaeology, anthropology, First Nations, or development to know this world of CRM that we inhabit, its personalities, cadence, values, behaviour. I hope such knowledge makes plain why CRM needs to be remade in ways informed by Indigenous engagement.

This book is a small form of activism and a humble reflection of the kindness bestowed upon me as an archaeologist. In my writing and in my work as an archaeologist, I want to be a positive force for change that honours my relationships by utilizing the principles, ideas, and experiences of community-first archaeology. I am aware of falling into the tropes laid out by Tuck and Yang (2012), but I want communities, and my colleagues, to understand my values expressed in this book so we can start a process of transformation. The future isn't ours; the future is Indigenous. Sharing stories of what I learned from living and working within Indigenous communities, expressing these values and experiences, helps teach others but also challenges me to bring this working knowledge into CRM and to maintain reflexivity. My experiences have manifested themselves into different expressions of my being that radiate from me, so I can be accountable to my colleagues, peers, and friends. There is a value in doing archaeology, but we should not simply do archaeology: we should be archaeology – an archaeology that is equitable, inclusive, dignified, compassionate, and kind. We should engender closeness and care. With time, being steeped within such values through daily practice may bring the archaeological praxis I crave into being.

It is a truism to say that everything is political. But some things are more political than others. In this time and place in history, archaeology is inevitably and deeply political, whether individual archaeologists like it or not. As archaeologists, we can live in the past, or we can move forward toward a more just and equitable archaeology.

Notes

Introduction

1 I recognize that no term is ever ideal for all peoples. Since I am situated in British Columbia, I work largely with First Nations communities. Where communities may include Métis or Inuit as well, I use the term *Indigenous* or *First Nations, Métis, and Inuit*. When I can be more specific, I use the term for members from an individual nation, while aware that their own heritage is often greater than that of a single nation. In many cases, I use *First Nations* and *Indigenous* interchangeably, but I use only the latter term when referring to First Nations and Métis (who are present in British Columbia) and/or Inuit.

2 In fact, Aboriginal Title is much more complex than this and, for the most part, is still being worked out in colonial legal regimes across Canada from which Indigenous lands were stolen.

3 The exceptions are a few colonial-era treaties on Vancouver Island and Treaty 8 in northeastern British Columbia. Treaties have been negotiated in the past twenty years by some First Nations, but most Indigenous communities in the province never signed treaties with the federal government.

4 In general, archaeology is split into two camps: academics and consultants (Trigger, 2000). In the opinion of many, consulting archaeology cuts corners and functions only to meet the client's needs and therefore is not sufficiently responsive to the heritage archaeologists are supposed to protect (Carmen 2015; Kirch 2015). Critics have charged that it is descriptive, sloppy (in terms of method and rigor), and lacking any research paradigm through which to analyse and interpret the data, and that it generates poor reporting, which is hardly ever read or cited by academics (Black and Jolly 2003). Although approaches may vary, depending on the

corporation, the archaeologists, and the project, this is, essentially, an accurate assessment. On the other hand, academic archaeology is sometimes considered privileged and elitist, and has been charged with disturbing archaeological sites that were never in jeopardy of being impacted. Consultants like to bring forward this last point, as they are managing only those sites that are under threat, making CRM necessary. I believe that there should be no difference between academic archaeology and consulting archaeology: we are all archaeologists and should be more collegial. Archaeology is archaeology. But, the reality is that the world of North American archaeology continues to be divided into these two factions, each with their own attitudes and priorities.

5 In a casual search to locate a few samples of reports, I identified three reports – Archaeology Branch reports 2016-0329, 2016-0249, and 2017-0057 – that were written by either foresters or biologists. In report 2017-0057, 50 percent (n=55) of the culturally modified trees (CMTs) identified were harvested, 35 percent (n=39) were stumped above the cultural scar, and only 15 percent (n=17) were left intact. No data about a windfirm buffer were provided in the two-page report, written by a non-archaeologist, which means the CMTs left standing could have all fallen, and no information is provided about whether First Nations consented to the harvesting of CMTs.

6 Such egregious acts of violence to Indigenous heritage that have been permitted under legislation in British Columbia include c̓əsnaʔəm in Vancouver (2012), Poets Cove on South Pender Island (2003), Grace Islet near Salt Spring Island (2013), Lightning Rock in Abbotsford (2015), and the recent episode in Wet'suwet'en Territory (2019–present) to name just a few.

7 One could also argue that there were mega-projects from the moment Europeans colonized North America – they didn't emerge in the 1980s or 1990s.

8 Academia is not completely outside capitalistic bounds, of course.

9 Here, I am being careful not to glorify academic archaeology over CRM, but to note possible differences.

10 Guardian Watchmen programs are nation-driven stewardship initiatives to monitor and study the health of their resources within a nation's territory. Often, the Guardians are on the land, sea, and rivers to serve as the eyes and ears of the nation. Guardians record data related to various disciplines, learning many different methods to track and better understand local ecologies, species' health, erosion, impacts of industry (e.g., logging and fishing), rehabilitation strategies, and heritage through archaeology. I've been working with Guardian programs through the Nanwakolas Council for over nine years. See "Ha-ma-yas Stewarship Network" at https://nanwakolas.com/ha-ma-yas-stewardship-network and "Nanwakolas Guardians Story Final" at https://vimeo.com/761207269.

11 The Archaeology Branch's policy is to stay out of issues around Aboriginal Rights and Title and land claims. My colleague Chelsey G. Armstrong argues that such

a position is naïve, at best, and is rooted in a delusion about history (personal communication, March 16, 2021).
12 On this subject, see Atalay (2006a, 2006b, 2012); Atalay et al. (2014); Colwell-Chanthaphonh and Ferguson (2008); Croes (2010); Dowdall and Parrish (2003); Gonzalez (2016); Gonzalez et al. (2018); Kew (1993); Klassen (2013); Langford (1983); Lewis and Rose (1985); Little and Shackel (2007); Lyons (2013, 2104); Lyons, Hoffmann, et al. (2018); McGuire (2008, 2014); McNiven and Russell (2005); Nicholas (2010); Nicholas and Andrews (1997a); Sabloff (2008); Schaepe (2007); Schaepe et al. (2017); C. Smith and Wobst (2005); L. Smith (2012); Steeves (2015); Swidler et al. (1997); Supernant et al. (2020); Two Bears (2008); Watkins (2001); Zimmerman (1989); Zorzin (2015).

Chapter 1: Birth of an Anthropologist

1 This useful definition was offered by Professor Ken Sassaman, who always said in class that we needed a "back pocket definition of culture" when describing the term to audiences.
2 *Enculturation* is a process in which an individual learns an identity through their parents/family, friends, media, government, and other social forces.
3 See https://americananthro.org/membership/member-testimonials.
4 Anthropology and archaeology, as disciplines, still have to confront many challenges. Issues include addressing abuse of power/status over junior colleagues, equity for women in positions of power and influence, lifting up voices of Indigenous scholars and people of colour (through representation and by reading and citing their work and engaging in the discussion), and providing opportunities for junior scholars to acquire legitimate academic positions (as opposed to exploiting the labour of sessionals/adjuncts). Anthropologists also discuss the ethics related to their methods and the dissemination of their work, which can at times be co-produced in the field with Indigenous communities.
5 My PhD supervisor, David Burley, created what he called the "Pacific Moka": basically, you pour boiling water into a cup containing equal parts Nescafé and Milo (a chocolate malt beverage). He thinks he invented the greatest drink ever (I admit that it is good).
6 An interesting cross-cultural misunderstanding that arises from questions is the idea that, as a foreign "researcher," you are wealthy. In some ways, this is true, but it is also relative. At twenty-three, I owed rent, had bills, and bought only basic food in order to exist on a student budget. Someone in Tubou on Lakeba Island once said to me that the only *palagi* who visit the islands are either rich or intelligent. I responded that I was neither of those, but it led me to think more on the privilege I carry and how I am perceived by the village. The remark brought home the reality that tourists with money to spend at restaurants, hotels, and exclusive resorts on beautiful beaches demonstrate what the locals consider opulent wealth.

In the South Pacific, one's relationships in the village may encourage local friends or colleagues to ask for money for school fees, boat motors, or other needs. There are times when you can accommodate them and other times when this is more difficult. Social media has made it easier to ask for such things, and it has also created a medium for easier communication.

7 I use these terms only in a geographic sense, as opposed to as a racial categorization. There are inherent problems with terms like *Micronesia*, *Melanesia*, and *Polynesia*, which are based on settler colonialism and notions of race and origins in the Pacific.

8 NAGPRA came into law in 1990. It's a set of regulations and procedures for federal agencies, and institutions that receive federal funding, to care for Native American cultural belongings and return them to the lineal descendants. Cultural belongings may include human (ancestral) remains, funerary objects, sacred objects, and objects passed down through family lines.

9 A "federally recognized tribe" is an American Indian or Alaska Native tribal entity that is recognized as having a government-to-government relationship with the United States. Historically, the US government conferred this recognition on Indigenous communities through treaties. Today, there are three mechanisms for recognition: by act of Congress, administrative procedures through law, or US court decision. Through this designation comes responsibilities, powers, limitations, and obligations, as well as eligibility for funding and services from the Bureau of Indian Affairs. Federally recognized tribes also possess certain inherent rights of self-government (i.e., tribal sovereignty) and are entitled to receive certain federal benefits, services, and protections through their relationship with the United States. Currently, there are 574 federally recognized tribes in the United States.

10 Andrew Jackson was the seventh president of the United States, in office from 1829 to 1837. Prior to that, he was involved in many wars against Native American tribes. As president, he is perhaps most known for the Trail of Tears, the route taken by many Native American communities displaced from their ancestral lands by the Indian Removal Act of 1830.

Chapter 2: Working in CRM, a Cautionary Tale

1 I did improve my shovel test form. It's critical that shovel tests are uniform and excavated (i.e., shovel tested) in a controlled and deliberate manner. In British Columbia, shovel tests must measure at least 35 cm by 35 cm and maintain this form from top to bottom.

2 PNG Liquefied Natural Gas (LNG) Project, Hydrocarbons Technology, https://www.hydrocarbons-technology.com/projects/pnglng/.

3 ExxonMobil, 2018 Summary Annual Report (PDF), https://corporate.exxonmobil.com/-/media/Global/Files/annual-report/2018-Financial-and-Operating-Review.pdf.

Notes to pages 38–46   193

4   Food and Agriculture Organization of the United Nations, Family Farming Knowledge Platform, http://www.fao.org/family-farming/countries/png/en/.
5   These issues are by no means limited to Papau New Guinea. See, for example, Scott MacEachern's (2010) article on the archaeological program under an ExxonMobil resource extraction venture in Chad, Africa.
6   An odd rule enforced by ExxonMobil was prohibiting the chewing of *buai*, both in the office and out in the field. Across Papua New Guinea, *buai* is widely chewed – it is a cultural practice. For field crews who were picked up early, chewing betel nut helped stave off hunger and acted as a stimulant similar to nicotine. However, it is also a carcinogen and can be addictive. I tried it with my crew, who taught me how to consume it properly. Doing so required a jar of *kambang* (lime powder), which was always available at our site, a bean-like green fern called *daka* (mustard), and green *buai*. My colleagues Teto, Iava, Lahui, and Nick watched over me one morning as I plunged my *daka* into the jar of crushed lime. I had already taken half of the betel nut and was sucking on it in the side of my mouth to get it moist and juicy. I inserted the bean with lime into my mouth, mixed it with the betel nut, and began chewing. A high like no other took over, like a hundred espressos all at once. I became dizzy and had to sit on our wooden field bench. Later, I came to do it in secret in the field as my crew would survey the land for safety officers.
7   Myself and my team at Tanamu 1, which included Tedy (Teto) Tolana, Iava Homoka, Lahui Morea, Pune Vagi, Dr. Nick Araho, and various UPNG students, such as Kim Sambua and Evanee Kove, were the first to clearly identify Lapita ceramics within mainland PNG. We showed these belongings to Professor Ian McNiven and pointed out the similarity to Tongan motifs on my wedding ring.
8   Overview section in Coffey Natural Systems Appendix O in 1284 HSS PNG LNG Travel Plan (2009), on file with author.
9   This sort of thinking goes back to the mid-1800s and earlier notions of unilinear cultural evolution and the "noble savage." To continue to perceive Indigenous people this way is misinformed and misguided, and ignores their knowledge, skill, and agency.
10 UNDRIP comprises forty-six articles, which function as an international instrument encouraging nation-states to address injustice, prejudice, and violence against Indigenous peoples.
11 Although two-way communication is offered in theory, this was hardly the case in practice in PNG. Not only did the corporations issue directives that all archaeologists and local workers follow stringent safety protocols, but when alternative views regarding our safety were expressed, they usually met with minimal attention from safety facilitators.
12 PNG LNG Project SSHE Induction – PowerPoint Presentation conducted in August 2009 (on file with the author).

13　The "eye for eye" compensation common in certain parts of Papua New Guinea means that if you kill a person in a car, you may well be killed soon after by relatives. It would be interesting to ask locals from the highlands what they think of Exxon's rule of "don't stop, keep driving."

14　I also recall issues with local villagers' pay: another party was hired to pay them, but the villagers had to open bank accounts to receive payment. This inconvenienced the villagers, who also had to travel all the way to Port Moresby to use an ATM. To make it to bank on time, the field crews had to leave the site earlier than normal, and they were not compensated for the work time they lost.

15　Minimum wage in 2018 in Papua New Guinea was only 3.50 kina. See https://www.rnz.co.nz/international/pacific-news/365820/png-to-review-minimum-wage.

16　See Ilya Gridneff, "Four shot dead at PNG LNG site," *Sydney Herald*, February 1, 2010, https://www.smh.com.au/world/four-shot-dead-at-png-lng-site-20100201-n80t.html.

17　It is revealing that the archaeological team heard the news before our employers did. Our friendships, built in the field and forged through trust, honesty, and the ability to listen, created a space for the transmission of sensitive information. Sharing an excavation breaks down perceived barriers and lets in humanity. It's a space where honest conversations take place and vulnerabilities are exposed, a place of respite from the outside world.

18　Leahy was a white national in Papua New Guinea, with family ties going back to the mid-1930s.

19　I had tried, with some of my archaeological colleagues, to arrange an overnight visit in the villages with our friends with whom we worked in the field. They had been asking us to visit them in their homes. This was something I had done across the South Pacific, as I often lived and worked in Indigenous villages. In PNG, I had to negotiate this visit with Coffey and ExxonMobil representatives, who wanted waivers, signed pieces of paper from local big men that no alcohol would be in the village, and complete control over the visit. In the end, when it seemed we had jumped through all possible hoops, ExxonMobil denied our application to visit the villages.

Chapter 3: Industrial Archaeology

1　Archaeologists have also campaigned for changes, as reflected in the talks currently going on around the Heritage Conservation Act Transformation Project in British Columbia – which aims to reform the HCA and align with the UNDRIP articles.

2　See https://www.rcaanc-cirnac.gc.ca/eng/1297278586814/1542811130481.

3　The Section 4 Agreement that Stó:lō Nation has been working on since 2012 has been approved by Cabinet and received the Order in Council in mid-July 2022. At the time of writing, it was before the minister for final sign-off. It will apply to forty-five sites, with four defined site types of Stó:lō Indigenous Heritage Landscape Features (landmarks, belongings, places, and cemeteries).

4 Technically, the Crown has a legal duty to consult (even if that requirement is not included in the HCA). Given this duty, the province must refer HCA permits to First Nations during the "formal comments period," but this doesn't necessarily constitute meaningful consultation. The province determines the duration of consultation and whether to take notice of comments from First Nations. Consultation must take place for any proposed archaeological assessment, under HCA permit, so that any perceived impacts to heritage do not impact Aboriginal Rights and Title.

5 Moving the Archaeology Branch to the MoF further aligns archaeology with logging, industry, and development capitalism. According to the MoF's Service Plan (2024/25–2026/27), the MoF "supports resiliency of the province's land-base and economy by providing collaborative management of forest, range and archaeological resources, and leading the Province's wildfire response and mitigation." The Ministry is "continually pursuing ways to strengthen partnerships, collaboration, and engagement with Indigenous Peoples." See https://www.bcbudget.gov.bc.ca/2024/sp/pdf/ministry/for.pdf.

6 Academics who are not able to hold provincial permits may apply for a research-only Section 12.2 permit, which differs from the development-focused Section 12.2 application, as it is not tied to a development project.

7 The only exceptions to post-1846 sites that are protected are rock art (e.g., pictographs and petroglyphs) sites and burial sites.

8 There are now a lot of much smaller firms, and many CRM outfits housed within First Nations government structures, but I feel this statement is still accurate.

9 What about the universities, you may ask. The academic world needs to do a better job preparing students for a life outside academia, as most of them will end up in the private sector. So, students need to be taught to question the CRM world that they are spat into, the one where they will practise archaeology daily. While the academy needs to be accountable, it is clear that, given the bulk of work done by archaeological consultants, these three "teachers" contribute the most to the miseducation of archaeologists after they leave university.

10 See also the World Archaeological Congress First Code of Ethics, which I personally prefer, as it is more progressive relative to Indigenous communities. For example, see Point 4: "To acknowledge that the important relationship between Indigenous peoples and their cultural heritage exists irrespective of legal ownership." See https://worldarchaeologicalcongress.com/code-of-ethics.

11 By all accounts from professional archaeologists, First Nations, and the Archaeology Branch, the influx of requests for permits, projects, and participation were at an all-time high – during a pandemic!

Chapter 4: Indigenous Rights

1 For UNDRIP, as well as background on the declaration, see the United Nations Declaration on the Rights of Indigenous Peoples, https://www.un.org/development/desa/indigenouspeoples/declaration-on-the-rights-of-indigenous-peoples.html.
2 First Nations in the lower mainland of Vancouver with a permitting system include xʷməθkʷəy̓əm (Musqueam Indian Band), Katzie Nation, Skwxwú7mesh Úxwumixw (Squamish Nation), Stó:lō Nation, and səlilwətaɫ (Tsleil-Waututh Nation).
3 Connaughton and Sellers (Inlailawatash 2020a) recorded in-the-field discussions with natural resource officers (NROs) who are responsible for enforcing the HCA and making sure that citizens and corporations are in compliance with it. We made clear that the conversations were going to be documented throughout the week for a report (as evinced by photographs of note taking with NROs). The NROs said that, despite legislation updates, they consider the HCA to be a weak piece of legislation that is difficult to enforce, both in relation to resource extraction development and individual impacts. The province asked us to remove the direct quotes around "weakness" in the report. We honoured this request, although it did not seem right to do so. The lead NRO officer said, "If the authors were genuine in their intentions in the field, they would have let the officers know their words and comments would be used as officially authorizing." As noted above, we *did* make our intentions clear right from the beginning of their week-long field meeting. What this comment really means is, if the NROs had understood the implications of their being recorded, they would have been less honest.
4 A point made by Maura Finkelstein (2019, 33) in another context in her book *The Archive of Loss: Lively Ruination in Mill Land Mumbai*: "From the space of the factory floor, I consider how Dhanraj workers understand their lived, ongoing experience at the mill, even as larger narratives of history, media accounts, and urban infrastructure challenge their existence: they are not *misrecognized* (as I initially thought) but *nonrecognized*. Similarly, they are not invisible: they are *unvisible*. I reframe these passive terms as active words: there is work being done in the mill lands of Mumbai; this way of not recognizing and not seeing is far from accidental."
5 Catherine Bell provides a wonderful discussion in "Indigenous Cultural Heritage: Issues of Canadian Law," January 8, 2015, https://www.youtube.com/watch?v=z_1hB0jYevg.

Chapter 5: A Matter of Values

1 Although generally true, this is not always the case, and depends on the specifics of a project and/or the needs of a community. First Nations are obviously not monolithic. Nations possess diversity of ideas and interests, and many have economic development programs to provide security for their community. Some nations possess limited internal capacity to properly manage heritage or conduct

environmental assessments: for some of the reasons for this, see Hanson (2018).
2 See Max Liboiron's *Pollution Is Colonialism* (2021), including the discussion of L/l (land) relations and how capitalism and colonialism require access to Indigenous land. This is a wonderful book!
3 See also Julie Cruikshank's *Do Glaciers Listen? Local Knowledge, Colonial Encounters, and Social Imagination* (2006), which explores Indigenous oral histories and competing views arising from Indigenous knowledge and European natural science knowledge in relation to the idea that glaciers are sentient, animate, and can respond to human language, behaviour, and action. The book illuminates how two people can experience glaciers differently, in ways that reflect different values and social relations.
4 See, for example, Deloria (1969); Liboiron (2021); Lippert (2006); Watkins (2001); E. White (2006); Yellowhorn (2002, 2006).
5 Proponents often think only of themselves and their projects, not the unceded Indigenous lands on which they operate and wish to impact through development capitalism. The burden is on the Indigenous nations to engage in the consultation process, regardless of whether they possess the infrastructure, personnel, labour, time, and/or money to do so. First Nations referrals offices are inundated with requests and projects related to their territory. First Nations themselves are typically not proactively driving large-scale projects within their territory to meet their community needs.
6 These were ancestral remains discovered in 1974 about 760 kilometres west of Sydney along the shore of Lake Mungo. The remains are about 42,000 years old. On their repatriation see Sewell (2017).
7 Dugongs are medium-size marine mammals similar to manatees.
8 See, for example, Atalay, Clauss, et al. (2014); Colwell-Chanthaphonh and Ferguson (2008); Denzin et al. (2008); McNiven and Russell (2005); Nicholas (2010); Nicholas and Andrews (1997); Rizvi and Lydon (2010); C. Smith and Wobst (2005); L. Smith (1994); Swidler et al. (1997); Watkins (2001); Zorzin (2014).
9 The British Columbia Association of Professional Archaeologists (BCAPA) is a professional group whose members engage in archaeological research and the archaeological resource management process in British Columbia. The Archaeological Society of British Columbia (ASBC) is a public society for both professional archaeologists and amateur enthusiasts. It encourages the identification and protection of archaeological sites and materials in British Columbia and provides lectures and publications on archaeology, including the journal *The Midden*. The Council of Elrond is a tongue-in-cheek name for a working group that started up online (due to the pandemic) in 2021 and consists of individuals representing First Nations archaeologists and heritage managers, professionals in CRM, and academics. They meet to discuss current heritage issues within British Columbia and work toward developing strategies to engender change.
10 See the 2023 Amnesty International report at https://amnesty.ca/wp-content/uploads/2023/12/wetsuweten-report.pdf.

Chapter 6: Reimagining Archaeology

1 For discussion of the importance of control over heritage, see, for example, Angelbeck and Jones (2019); Budhwa (2005); Gonzalez et al. (2018); Hammond (2009); Irlbacher-Fox (2009); Klassen (2013); Lyons (2013, 2014); Lyons, Dawson, et al. (2010); Lyons and Marshall (2014); McNiven and Russell (2005); and Spice (2018).
2 Even today, due to the lack of understanding colonialism and legislation, many settlers hold beliefs that may include a misunderstanding that Indigenous people do not pay taxes, that they all receive free postsecondary education (this is not true, as it is competitive within each Nation), and they receive huge government cheques extracted from settler taxes to spend frivolously.
3 For every field project where First Nations representatives are on site, one should ask whether their voices are having an impact on the work or whether they are being ignored, stifled, or silenced.
4 I used Indigenous texts and authors in my "Transforming CRM in British Columbia" course that I designed and taught at Kwantlen Polytechnic University. I also try to reassess my syllabi for other courses each term to ensure Indigenous voices are present, but, still, I'm a white male professor teaching the courses.
5 Archaeology for profit does not make sense in my academic brain, nor is it compatible with how my own experiences have taught me to practise archaeology (although I understand how academic archaeology too can extract social/cultural status value from knowledge production). I ultimately feel that archaeology for profit compels many practitioners to make choices that favour the bottom line and not the Indigenous heritage of descendant communities. Myself, I figure I do the archaeology for free but get paid for the bullshit.
6 Open Letter to the Archaeology Branch of the BC Ministry of Forests, Lands and Natural Resource Operations engaging in direct dialogue on behalf of Unist'ot'en: Heal the People, Heal the Land, n.d., https://unistoten.camp/open-letter-to-the-archaeology-branch-of-the-bc-ministry-of-forests-lands-and-natural-resource-operations/.
7 See, for example, Colwell and Ferguson (2014); Deloria (1969); Jones and Jenkins (2008); Hunter (2008); Million (2005); Two Bears (2008); Watkins (2001, 2005); and Yellowhorn (2006).
8 A horizon plan refers to a goal that can be seen on the horizon, but is at a distance far too great to ever be reached. When governments announce a horizon plan, the public often think of it as reachable. This benefits the government because it doesn't actually have to do any work toward the goal, which is, in reality, not obtainable.

Conclusion

1 Curtin (1990) and Howe (1995) have documented, recorded, and made recommendations regarding impacts to this site on Berry Island. These recommendations have been ignored by the province.

2 The province began this process with the Heritage Conservation Act Transformation Project (HCATP), which was a series of engagement sessions held in summer–fall 2022. Co-chairs of the Joint Working Group on First Nations Heritage Conservation (JWG), Matt Austin and Judith Sayers, sent a letter to First Nations in British Columbia about opportunities to engage on the Heritage Conservation Act and its administration as part of the HCATP. Currently there are seven sessions scheduled. Still waiting to see what comes of this project.
3 This perspective reflects a line in a report published by Inlailawatash for a client First Nation, based on a pilot project conducted in the Broughton Archipelago by an Indigenous council and the province. The reporter was on a week-long joint patrol with members from the Archaeology Branch, the Compliance and Enforcement Office (C&E), and two First Nations Guardian teams whose territory was within the pilot project area. The sentence was originally "It is not yet certain whether C&E will be the ally needed to implement changes in policy." In its review of the report, the province responded, "Remove loaded statements like this; opinion of the author ... So disappointing to see inflammatory comments like this in a collaborative effort by all. The author seems to have a negative bias to government and may not be the best choice for this project." The province insisted that the sentence be removed before it would accept the report.

References

Alfred, T. 2004. Warrior scholarship: Seeing the university as a ground of contention. In D.A. Mihesua and A.C. Wilson (Eds.), *Indigenizing the academy: Transforming scholarship and empowering communities* (pp. 88–99). University of Nebraska Press.

–. 2008. Opening words. In L.B. Simpson (Eds.), *Lighting the eighth fire: The liberation, resurgence, and protection of Indigenous nations* (pp. 9–11). Arbeiter Ring Publishing.

Angelbeck, B., and C. Grier. 2014. From paradigms to practices: Pursuing horizontal and long-term relationships with Indigenous peoples for archaeological heritage management. *Canadian Journal of Archaeology, 38*: 519–40.

Angelbeck, B., and J. Jones. 2019. Direct actions and archaeology. *Journal of Contemporary Archaeology, 5*(2): 219–29. https://doi.org/10.1558/jca.33578.

Apland, B. 1993. The roles of the provincial government in British Columbia archaeology. *BC Studies, 99*: 7–24.

Archaeological and Historical Sites Protection Act, British Columbia. RSBC 1960, c. 15.

Archaeology Branch. 2018. *British Columbia archaeological resource management handbook*. Province of British Columbia, Archaeology Branch, Ministry of Forests, Lands, Natural Resource Operations and Rural Development.

–. 2020. Heritage Conservation Act permitting process policy guide. Updated April 20, 2020. https://www2.gov.bc.ca/assets/gov/farming-natural-resources-and-industry/natural-resource-use/archaeology/forms-publications/hca_permitting_process_policy_guide.pdf.

Armstrong, C., J. Miller, A.C. McAlvay, P.M. Ritchie, and D. Lepofsky. 2021.

Historical Indigenous land-use explains plant functional trait diversity. *Ecology and Society,* 26(2): 6. https://doi.org/10.5751/ES-12322-260206.

Armstrong, C., A. Spice, M. Ridsdale, and J. Welch. 2023. Liberating trails and travel routes in Gitxsan and Wet'suwet'en territories from the tyrannies of heritage resource management regimes. *American Anthropologist* 125(2): 361–76.

Atalay, S. 2006a. Decolonizing archaeology. *American Indian Quarterly, 30*(3–4): 269–79.

–. 2006b. Indigenous archaeology as decolonizing practice. *American Indian Quarterly, 30*(3–4): 280–310.

–. 2008. Pedagogy of decolonization: Advancing archaeological practice through education. In S.W. Silliman (Ed.), *Collaborating at the trowel's edge: Teaching and learning in Indigenous archaeology* (pp. 123–44). University of Arizona Press.

–. 2012. *Community-based archaeology: Research with, by, and for Indigenous and local communities.* University of California Press.

Atalay, S., L.R. Clauss, R.H. McGuire, and J.R. Welch (Eds.). 2014. *Transforming archaeology: Activist practices and prospects.* Left Coast Press.

Atlas, W.I., N.C. Ban, J.W. Moore, A.M. Tuohy, S. Greening, A.J. Reid, N. Morven, E. White, W.G. Housty, J.A. Housty, C.N. Service, L. Greba, S. Harrison, C. Sharpe, K.I.R. Butts, W.M. Shepert, E. Sweeney-Bergen, D. Macintyre, M.R. Sloat, and K. Connors. 2021. Indigenous systems of management for culturally and ecologically resilient Pacific salmon (*Oncorhynchus* spp.) fisheries. *BioScience,* 71(2): 186–204. https://doi.org/10.1093/biosci/biaa144.

Atlas, W.I., W.G. Housty, A. Béliveau, D. DeRoy, G. Callegari, M. Reid, and J.W. Moore. 2017. Ancient fish weir technology for modern stewardship: Lessons from community-based salmon monitoring. *Ecosystem Health and Sustainability,* 3.

Atleo, C. 2021. Between a rock and a hard place: Canada's carbon economy and Indigenous ambivalence. In W.K. Carroll (Ed.), *Regime of obstruction: How corporate power blocks energy democracy* (pp. 355–73). Athabasca University Press.

Atleo, E.R. 2004. *Tsawalk: A Nuu-chah-nulth worldview.* UBC Press.

Baker, J.M., and C.N. Westman. 2018. Extracting knowledge: Social science, environmental impact assessment, and indigenous consultation in the oil sands of Alberta, Canada. *Extractive Industries and Society,* 5(1): 144–53.

Baldwin, J. 1993 [1962]. *The fire next time.* Vintage International.

Balter, M. 2010. Anthropologist brings worlds together. *Science, 329*(5993): 743–45. DOI: 10.1126/science.329.5993.743

Behar, R. 1996. *The vulnerable observer: Anthropology that breaks your heart.* Beacon Press.

Bell, D. 2014. What is liberalism? *Political Theory,* 42(6): 682–715.

Belshaw, C.S. 1959. The identification of values in anthropology. *American Journal of Sociology,* 64(6): 555–62.

Berreman, G.D. 1968. Is anthropology alive? Social responsibility in social anthropology. *Current Anthropology,* 9(5): 391–96.

Binney, J. 1986. Reviewed work: Islands of history by M. Sahlins. *Journal of the Polynesian Society, 95*(4): 527–30.

Black, S.L., and K. Jolly. 2003. *Archaeology by design: Archaeologists' toolkit* (Vol. 1). AltaMira Press.

Blackburn, C. 2005. Searching for guarantees in the midst of uncertainty: Negotiating Aboriginal Rights and Title in British Columbia. *American Anthropologist, 107*(4): 586–96.

Bracken, A. 2020, January 14. "They are erasing our history": Indigenous sites buried under Coastal GasLink pipeline infrastructure. The Narwhal.

British Columbia. 2022. Declaration on the rights of Indigenous Peoples Act action plan. Victoria. https://www2.gov.bc.ca/assets/gov/government/ministries-organizations/ministries/indigenous-relations-reconciliation/declaration_act_action_plan.pdf.

British Columbia Association of Professional Archaeologists. 2005. Constitution. https://www.bcapa.ca/wp-content/uploads/BylawsforWebsiteOct2005.pdf.

Brown, A.M. 2017. *Emergent strategy: Shaping change, changing worlds.* AK Press.

Budhwa, R. 2005. An alternative model for First Nations involvement in resource management archaeology. *Canadian Journal of Archaeology, 29*(1): 20–45.

Burley, D.V. 1994. A never ending story: Historical developments in Canadian archaeology and the quest for federal heritage legislation. *Canadian Journal of Archaeology, 18*: 77–98.

Canadian Archaeological Association. 2024. Ethics. https://canadianarchaeology.com/caa/about/ethics/principles-ethical-conduct.

Carman, J. 2015. *Archaeological resource management: An international perspective.* Cambridge University Press.

Carr-Locke, S. 2015. *Indigenous heritage and public museums: Exploring collaboration and exhibition in Canada and the United States.* Unpublished PhD dissertation, Simon Fraser University.

CBC News. 2019, March 7. *B.C. strengthens protections of heritage, archaeological sites with updated law.* https://www.cbc.ca/news/canada/british-columbia/b-c-strengthens-protections-of-heritage-archeological-sites-with-updated-law-1.5046365.

Coffey Natural Systems. 2009. 1284 HSS PNG LNG travel plan, Appendix O. In PNG LNG project HSS plan, Esso Highlands Limited. On file with the author.

Colwell, C., and T.J. Ferguson. 2014. The snow-capped mountain and the uranium mine: Zuni heritage and the landscape scale in cultural resource management. *Advances in Archaeological Practice, 2*(4): 234–51. doi: 10.7183/2326-3768.2.4.234.

Colwell-Chanthaphonh, C., and T.J. Ferguson. 2004. Virtue ethics and the practice of history: Native Americans and archaeologists along the San Pedro valley of Arizona. *Journal of Social Archaeology, 4*(1): 5–27.

Colwell-Chanthaphonh, C., and T.J. Ferguson (Eds.). 2008a. *Collaboration in archaeological practice: Engaging descendant communities.* AltaMira Press.

–. 2008b. Introduction: The collaborative continuum. In C. Colwell-Chanthaphonh and T.J. Ferguson (Eds.), *Collaboration in archaeological practice: Engaging descendant communities* (pp. 1–34). AltaMira Press.

Colwell-Chanthaphonh, C., T.J. Ferguson, D. Lippert, R.H. McGuire, G.P. Nicholas, J.E. Watkins, and L.J. Zimmerman. 2010. The premise and promise of Indigenous archaeology. *American Antiquity*, 75(2): 228–38.

Connaughton, S.P. 2015. *Emergence and development of ancestral Polynesian society in Tonga*. Archaeopress.

Connaughton, S.P., and J. Herbert. 2017. Engagement within: An anthropological exploration of First Nations engagement and consulting archaeology within a transnational corporation. *Archaeologies: Journal of the World Archaeological Congress*, 13(2): 306–43.

Connaughton, S.P., G. Hill, J. Morin, C. Frank, N. Greene, and D. McGee. 2022. Tidal belongings: First Nations driven archaeology to preserve a large wooden fish trap panel recovered from the Comox Harbour Intertidal Fish Trap Complex in British Columbia. *Canadian Journal of Archaeology*, 46: 16–51.

Connaughton, S.P., M. Leon, and J. Herbert. 2014. Collaboration, partnerships, and relationships within a corporate world. *Canadian Journal of Archaeology*, 38: 541–62.

Connaughton, S.P., K. Tache, and D.V. Burley. 2010. Taupita: A 3000-year-old shell game in the Lapita cultural complex of Tonga. *Journal of Social Archaeology*, 10(1): 118–37.

Coulthard, G.S. 2014. *Red skin, white masks: Rejecting the colonial politics of recognition*. University of Minnesota Press.

Croes, D. 2010. Courage and thoughtful scholarship = Indigenous archaeology partnerships *American Antiquity*, 75(2): 211–16.

Cruikshank, J. 2006. *Do glaciers listen? Local knowledge, colonial encounters, and social imagination*. UBC Press.

Curtin, J.A. 1990. *The Berry Island burial site (EdSp-75): An assessment*. Consultant's report on file with Ministry of Lands, Forests and Natural Operations, Victoria, BC. HCA Permit 1989-0034.

David, B., B. Duncan, J. Ash, R. Skelly, and N. Araho. 2009. *Cultural heritage at the LNG facility site at Portion 2456, Papua New Guinea: Review of the ethnography and archaeology and new findings*. Programme for Australian Indigenous Archaeology, School of Geography and Environmental Science, Monash University.

David, B., I.J. McNiven, and T. Richards. 2009. *Cultural heritage site surveys and salvage excavation procedures and protocols: Portfolio*. Programme for Australian Indigenous Archaeology, School of Geography and Environmental Science, Monash University.

David, B., I.J. McNiven, T. Richards, S.P. Connaughton, M. Leavesley, B. Barker, and C. Rowe. 2011. Lapita sites in the central province of Mainland Papua New Guinea. *World Archaeology*, 43(4): 576–93.

David, B., T. Richards, I.J. McNiven, K. Aplin, F. Petchey, K. Szabo, J. Mialanes, C. Rowe, B. Barker, S.P. Connaughton, M. Leavesley, H. Mandui, and C. Jennings. 2022. Tanamu 1: A 5000 year sequence from Caution Bay. In B. David, K. Szabo, M. Leavesley, I.J. McNiven, J. Ash, and T. Richards (Eds.), *The archaeology of Tanamu 1: A pre-Lapita to post-Lapita site from Caution Bay, South Coast of Mainland Papua New Guinea* (pp. 13–54). Archaeopress.

Davis, W. 2009. *The wayfinders: Why ancient wisdom matters in the modern world.* CBC Massey Lectures. Anansi Press.

Declaration on the Rights of Indigenous Peoples Act. RSBC 2019, c. 44.

Declaration on the safeguarding of Indigenous ancestral burial grounds as sacred sites and cultural landscapes. 2014, December 10. Intellectual property issues in cultural heritage: Theory, practice, policy, ethics (IPinCH). http://www.sfu.ca/ipinch/resources/declarations/ancestral-burial-grounds/.

Delgamuukw v. British Columbia. [1997] 3 S.C.R. 1010.

Delisle, A., M.K. Kim, N. Stoeckl, F.W. Lui, and H. Marsh. 2018. The socio-cultural benefits and costs of the traditional hunting of dugongs (*Dugong dugon*) and green turtles (*Chelonia mydas*) in Torres Strait, Australia. *Oryx*, 52(2): 250–61.

Deloria, V., Jr. 1969. *Custer died for your sins: An Indian manifesto.* Macmillan.

–. 1992. Indians, archaeologists, and the future. *American Antiquity*, 57(4): 595–98.

Dent, J. 2016. *Accounts of engagement: Conditions and capitals of Indigenous participation in Canadian commercial archaeology.* Unpublished PhD dissertation, University of Western Ontario.

–. 2017. Tailors-made: Heritage governance customization in late modern Canada. *Archaeologies: Journal of the World Archaeological Congress*, 13(1): 136–52.

Denzin, N.K., Y.S. Lincoln, and L.T. Smith (Eds.). 2008. *Handbook of critical and Indigenous methodologies.* SAGE Publications.

De Paoli, M.L. 1999. *Beyond tokenism: Aboriginal involvement in archaeological resource management in British Columbia.* Unpublished master's thesis, University of British Columbia.

Desmond, M. 2023. *Poverty, by America.* Crown.

Dowdall, K.M., and O.O. Parrish. 2003. A meaningful disturbance of the earth. *Journal of Social Archaeology*, 3(1): 99–133.

Duffield, S., J. Walkus, E. White, I. McKechnie, Q. Mackie, and D. McLaren. 2022. Documenting 6,000 years of Indigenous fisheries and settlement as seen through vibracore sampling on the central coast of British Columbia, Canada. *American Antiquity*, 87(1): 168–83.

Duke, P., and D. Saitta. 1998. An emancipatory archaeology for the working class. *Assemblage* 4. https://archaeologydataservice.ac.uk/archives/view/assemblage/html/4/4duk_sai.html.

Everson, C. 2021a. *Tlik'sala: research report and guidebook.* Final deliverable for new relationship trust – Indigenous law and resource management research project. On file with the author.

–. 2021b. *Tłik'sala "showing the right way to live": A guidebook to show how to respectfully implement Indigenous law in the modern context*. On file with the author.

ExxonMobil. 2002. http://www.mobil.com.au/pdf/news/article_CCR_2002.pdf.

–. 2009. PNG LNG project SSHE induction, PowerPoint presentation, August.

–. 2015. *Corporate citizenship report*. https://corporate.exxonmobil.com/en/~/media/Global/Files/sustainability-report/publication/2015-ccr-full-digital.pdf.

–. 2018a. *2018 Summary annual report*. https://corporate.exxonmobil.com/-/media/Global/Files/investor-relations/annual-meeting-materials/annual-report-summaries/2018-Summary-Annual-Report.pdf.

–. 2018b. *PNG LNG environmental and social report: Annual 2018*. https://pnglng.com/media/PNG-LNG-Media/Files/Environment/Environment%20and%20Social%20reports/2018-Annual-ES-Report-FINAL_FULL_300419-(ENG-WEB).pdf.

Ferris, N. 2003. Between colonial and Indigenous archaeologies: Legal and extra-legal ownership of the archaeological past in North America. *Canadian Journal of Archaeology*, 27(2): 154–90.

Finkelstein, M. 2019. *The archives of loss: Lively rumination in mill land Mumbai*. Duke University Press.

First Peoples' Cultural Council. 2020. *Recommendations for decolonizing British Columbia's heritage-related processes and legislation*. Prepared by D.M. Schaepe, G. Nicholas, and K. Dolata.

Fisher, M. 2009. *Capitalist realism: Is there no alternative?* Zero Books.

Franklin, M., J.P. Dunnavant, A.O. Flewellen, and A. Odewale. 2020. The future is now: Archaeology and the eradication of anti-Blackness. *International Journal of Historical Archaeology*, 24: 753–66.

Freeden, M. 2005. *Liberal languages*. Princeton University Press.

Goldstein, D.M. 2016. *Tools for dismantling the master's house*. Savage minds: Notes and queries in anthropology. https://savageminds.org/2016/06/14/tools-for-dismantling-the-masters-house/.

Gonzalez, S.L. 2016. Indigenous values and methods in archaeological practice: Low-impact archaeology through the Kashaya Pomo Interpretive Trail Project. *American Antiquity*, 81: 533–49.

Gonzalez, S.L., I. Kretzler, and B. Edwards. 2018. Imagining Indigenous and archaeological futures: Building capacity with the Confederated Tribes of Grand Ronde. *Archaeologies: Journal of the World Archaeological Congress*, 14(1): 85–114.

Graeber, D. 2001. *Toward an anthropological theory of value: The false coin of our own dreams*. Palgrave.

–. 2013. It is value that brings universes into being. *HAU: Journal of Ethnographic Theory*, 3(2): 219–43.

Grey, S., and R. Kuokkanen. 2020. Indigenous governance of cultural heritage: Searching for alternatives to co-management. *International Journal of Heritage Studies*, 26: 919–41.

Gupta, N., S. Blair, and R. Nicholas. 2020. What we see, what we don't see: Data governance, archaeological spatial databases and the rights of Indigenous peoples in an age of big data. *Journal of Field Archaeology, 45*: suppl. 1, S39–S50. DOI: 10.1080/00934690.2020.171396.

Gupta, N., A. Martindale, K. Supernant, and M. Elvidge. 2023. The CARE principles and the reuse, sharing, and curation of Indigenous data in Canadian archaeology. *Advances in Archaeological Practice, 11*(1): 76–89.

Hagihara, R., C. Cleguer, S. Preston, S. Sobtzick, M. Hamann, T. Shimada, and H. Marsh. 2016. *Improving the estimates of abundance of dugongs and large immature and adult-sized green turtles in Western and Central Torres Strait*. Report to the National Environmental Science Programme. Reef and Rainforest Research Centre Limited.

Hall, R.L. 1997. *An archaeology of the soul: North American Indian belief and ritual*. University of Illinois Press.

Hamilakis, Y. 2007. From ethics to politics. In Y. Hamilakis and P. Duke (Eds.), *Archaeology and capitalism: From ethics to politics* (pp. 15–40). Left Coast Press.

Hamilakis, Y., and P. Duke (Eds.). 2007. *Archaeology and capitalism: From ethics to politics*. Left Coast Press.

Hammond, J. 2009. *Archaeology without reserve: Indigenous heritage stewardship in British Columbia*. Unpublished MA thesis, Simon Fraser University.

Hanna, M.G. 1997. We can go a long way together, hand-in-hand. In G.P. Nicholas and T.D. Andrews (Eds.), *At a crossroads: Archaeology and First Peoples in Canada* (pp. 69–84). Simon Fraser University Archaeology Press.

Hanson, E.M. 2018. *Coast Salish law and jurisdiction over natural resources: A case study with the Tsleil-Waututh Nation*. Unpublished MA thesis, University of British Columbia.

Harris, H. 2005. Indigenous worldviews and ways of knowing as theoretical and methodological foundations for archaeological research. In C. Smith and H.M. Wobst (Eds.), *Indigenous archaeologies: Decolonising theory and practice* (pp. 33–41). Routledge.

Harvey, D. 2005. *A brief history of neoliberalism*. Oxford University Press.

–. 2018, November 15. The contradictions of neo-liberalism. [Podcast episode]. In *David Harvey's anti-capitalist chronicles*.

Herbert, J., and S.P. Connaughton. 2015, April 15–19. *Minding the ideological gap in consulting archaeology* [Paper presentation]. Society for American Archaeology Conference, 80th Annual Meeting, San Francisco, CA.

–. 2017, March 29–April 2. *Exploring helicopter archaeology* [Paper presentation]. Society for American Archaeology Conference, 82nd Annual Meeting, Vancouver, BC.

Herbert, J., S.P. Connaughton, and M. Leon. 2014, April 23–27. *Collaboration and corporations: An internalist dialogue* [Paper presentation]. Society for American Archaeology Conference, 79th Annual Meeting, Austin, Texas.

Heritage Conservation Act. RSBC 1996, c. 187.

Historical Resources Act. RSA 2000, c. H-9.

Hocart, A.M. 1929. *Lau Islands, Fiji*. B.P. Bishop Museum Bulletin 62.

Hodgetts, L., K. Supernant, N. Lyons, and J.R. Welch. 2020. Broadening #MeToo: Tracking dynamics in Canadian archaeology through a survey on experiences within the discipline. *Canadian Journal of Archaeology, 44*: 20–47.

Hoffmann, T., N. Lyons, D. Miller, A. Diaz, A. Homan, S. Huddlestan, and R. Leon. 2016. Engineered feature used to enhance gardening at a 3800-year-old site on the Pacific Northwest Coast. *Science Advances*, 2: e1601282.

Hogg, E.A., J. Welch, and N. Ferris. 2017. Full spectrum archaeology. *Archaeologies: Journal of the World Archaeological Congress, 13*(1): 175–200.

Howe, D.G. 1995. *Berry Island archaeological inventory and impact assessment, Broughton Archipelago*. B.C. Ministry of Lands, Forests and Natural Operations. HCA Permit 1995-0021.

Hunter, A.A. 2008. A critical change in pedagogy: Indigenous cultural resource management. In S.W. Silliman (Ed.), *Collaborating at the trowel's edge: Teaching and learning in Indigenous archaeology* (pp. 165–87). Amerind Studies in Archaeology. University of Arizona Press.

Hurston, Z.N. 1978 [1935]. *Mules and Men*. Indiana University Press.

Hutchings, R.M., and J. Dent. 2017. Archaeology and the late modern state: Introduction to the special issue. *Archaeologies: Journal of the World Archaeological Congress, 13*(1): 1–25.

Inlailawatash Limited Partnership. 2017. *Field program summary for North Vancouver Island Phase 2 – Field verification* (authored by S.P. Connaughton and M. Ritchie). Submitted to Nanwakolas Council, Campbell River.

–. 2018. *Nanwakolas Council Guardians North Vancouver Island cultural heritage 2017 field program* (authored by S.P. Connaughton). Submitted to Nanwakolas Council, Campbell River.

–. 2019a. *Nanwakolas Council Guardians North Vancouver Island cultural heritage 2018 field program* (authored by S.P. Connaughton). Submitted to Nanwakolas Council, Campbell River.

–. 2019b. *Nanwakolas Guardians post-harvest cultural heritage assessments* (authored by S.P. Connaughton, I. Sellers, and J. Benner). Submitted to Nanwakolas Council, Campbell River.

–. 2020a. *Joint patrol archaeological, heritage, and cultural area management pilot project* (authored by S.P. Connaughton and I. Sellers). Submitted to Nanwakolas Council, Campbell River.

–. 2020b. *Nanwakolas Council Guardians North Vancouver Island cultural heritage 2019 field program* (authored by S.P. Connaughton). Submitted to Nanwakolas Council, Campbell River.

–. 2021. *Nanwakolas Guardians North Vancouver Island cultural heritage 2020 field program* (authored by S.P. Connaughton). Submitted to Nanwakolas Council, Campbell River.

–. 2023. *Protecting the ancestors on Berry Island. EdSp-75, site alteration final report* (authored by S.P. Connaughton and Anisa Côté). Report on file with the Archaeology Branch, Victoria. SAP 2023-0008.

Intellectual Property Issues in Cultural Heritage (IPinCH). 2014. Declaration on the safeguarding of Indigenous ancestral burial grounds as sacred sites and cultural landscapes. December 10. Vancouver, BC. https://www.sfu.ca/ipinch/sites/default/files/resources/declarations/declaration_safeguarding_indigenous_ancestral_burial_grounds.pdf.

Irlbacher-Fox, S. 2009. *Finding dahshaa: Self-government, social suffering, and Aboriginal policy in Canada*. UBC Press.

Jackson, G., and C. Smith. 2005. Living and learning on Aboriginal lands: Decolonizing archaeology in practice. In C. Smith and H.M. Wobst (Eds.), *Indigenous archaeologies: Decolonising theory and practice* (pp. 328–51). Routledge.

Jansen, R.J. 2010. *Yukon heritage conservation districts: Case studies and strategies for success*. Unpublished MSc thesis, University of Oregon.

Jones, A., with K. Jenkins. 2008. Rethinking collaboration: Working the Indigene-colonizer hyphen. In N.K. Denzin, Y.S. Lincoln, and L.T. Smith, *Handbook of critical and Indigenous methodologies* (pp. 471–86). Sage.

Jones, S. 2009. *Food and gender in Fiji: Ethnoarchaeological explorations*. Lexington Books.

–. 2015. Eating identity: An exploration of Fijian foodways in the archaeological past. *Journal of Indo-Pacific Archaeology*, 37: 64–71.

Kew, M. 1993. Anthropology and First Nations in British Columbia. *BC Studies*, 93–94(100): 78–105.

Kewibu, V. 2010. Archaeology and perceptions of the past in Papua New Guinea. In G.P. Nicholas (Ed.), *Being and becoming Indigenous archaeologists* (pp. 156–66). Left Coast Press.

Kirch, P.V. 2015. *Unearthing the past: Explorations and adventures of an island archaeologist*. University of Hawai'i Press.

Kirch, P.V., and R.C. Green. 2001. *Hawaiki, ancestral Polynesia: An essay in historical anthropology*. Cambridge University Press.

Klassen, M.A. 2008. First Nations, the Heritage Conservation Act, and the ethics of heritage stewardship. *The Midden*, 40(4): 8–17.

–. 2013. *Indigenous heritage stewardship and the transformation of archaeological practice: Two case studies from the mid-Fraser region of British Columbia*. Unpublished PhD dissertation, Simon Fraser University.

Klassen, M.A., R. Budwa, and R. Reimer/Yumks. 2009. First Nations, forestry, and the transformation of archaeological practice in British Columbia, Canada. *Heritage Management*, 2(2): 199–238.

Kluckhohn, C.K. 1951. Values and value orientations in the theory of action. In T. Parsons and E.A. Shils (Eds.), *Toward a general theory of action*. Harvard University Press.

Knauft, B.M. 1996. *Genealogies for the present in cultural anthropology*. Routledge.

Kohn, E. 2013. *How forests think: Toward an anthropology beyond the human*. University of California Press.

Ladner, K.L. 2001. Negotiated inferiority: The Royal Commission on Aboriginal People's vision of a renewed relationship. *American Review of Canadian Studies*, 21(1/2): 241–64.

Laluk, N.C., L.M. Montgomery, R. Tsosie, C. McCleave, R. Miron, S.R. Carroll, J. Aguilar, A. Big Wolf Thompson, P. Nelson, J. Sunseri, I. Trujillo, G.M. DeAntoni, G. Castro, and T.D. Schneider. 2022. Archaeology and social justice in Native America. *American Antiquity*, 87: 659–82.

Langford, R.F. 1983. Our heritage, your playground. *Australian Archaeology*, 16: 2–6.

La Salle, M., and R. Hutchings. 2012. Commercial archaeology in British Columbia. *The Midden*, 44(2): 8–16.

Leavesley, M.G., B. Minol, H. Kop, and V.H. Kewibu. 2005. Cross-cultural concepts of archaeology: Kastom, community, education and cultural heritage management in Papua New Guinea. *Public Archaeology*, 4(1): 3–13.

Lepofsky, D., C.G. Armstrong, D. Mathews, and S. Greening. 2020. Understanding the past for the future: Archaeology, plants, and First Nations' land use and rights. In N.J. Turner (Ed.), *Plants, people, and places: The roles of ethnobotany and ethnoecology in Indigenous peoples' land rights in Canada and beyond* (pp. 86–106). McGill-Queen's University Press.

Lewis, D., and D.B. Rose. 1985. Some ethical issues in archaeology: A methodology of consultation in northern Australia. *Australian Aboriginal Studies*, 1: 37–44.

Liboiron, M. 2021. *Pollution is colonialism*. Duke University Press.

Lilley, I. 2000. *Native title and the transformation of archaeology in the postcolonial world*. University of Sydney.

Lippert, D. 2006. Building a bridge to cross a thousand years. *American Indian Quarterly*, 30 (3/4): 431–40.

Little, B.J., and P.A. Shackel (Eds.). 2007. *Archaeology as a tool of civic engagement*. AltaMira Press.

Locke, J. 1727. *The second treatise on Government: The Works of John Locke* (Vol. 2). London.

–. 1764. *Two treatises of government* (Thomas Hollis, Ed.). A. Millar.

Low, S.M., and D. Lawrence-Zúñiga (Eds.). 2003. *The anthropology of space and place*. Blackwell Publishing.

Lydon, J., and U.Z. Rizvi (Eds.). 2010. *Handbook of postcolonial archaeology*. Routledge.

Lyons, N. 2013. *Where the winds blow us: Practicing critical community archaeology in the Canadian North*. University of Arizona Press.

–. 2014. Localized critical theory as an expression of community archaeology practice: With a case study from Inuvialuit Elders of the Canadian Western Arctic. *American Antiquity*, 79(2): 183–203.

Lyons, N., P. Dawson, M. Walls, D. Uluadluak, L. Angalik, M. Kalluak, P. Kigusiutuak, L. Kiniksi, J. Karetak, and L. Suluk. 2010. Person, place, memory, thing: How Inuit elders are informing archaeological practice in the Canadian North. *Canadian Journal of Archaeology*, 34: 1–31.

Lyons, N., T. Hoffmann, D. Miller, S. Huddlestan, R. Leon, and K. Squires. 2018. Katzie and the Wapato: An archaeological love story. *Archaeologies: Journal of the World Archaeological Congress*, 14(1): 7–29.

Lyons, N., R. Leon, J. Peone, S. Hazell, D. Miller, J. Dent, and T. Hoffman. 2022. Decolonizing archaeology: Decolonizing CRM is about the power to decide. *SAA Archaeological Record*: 14–17.

Lyons, N., and Y. Marshall. 2014. Memory, practice, telling community. *Canadian Journal of Archaeology*, 38: 496–518.

MacEachern, S. 2010. Seeing like an oil company's CHM programme. *Journal of Social Archaeology*, 10(3): 347–66.

Mackey, E. 2014. Unsettling expectations: (Un)certainty, settler states of feeling, law, and decolonization. *Canadian Journal of Law and Society*, 29(2), *Law and Decolonization*: 235–52. DOI: https://doi.org/10.1017/cls.2014.10.

Main, M. 2017, March 8. *Papua New Guinea gets a dose of the resource curse as ExxonMobil's natural gas project foments unrest. The Conversation.* http://theconversation.com/papua-new-guinea-gets-a-dose-of-the-resource-curse-as-exxonmobils-natural-gas-project-foments-unrest-70780.

Marsh, H., and M. Hamann. 2016, December 5. *Traditional hunting gets headlines, but is not the big threat to turtles and dugongs.* The Conversation. https://theconversation.com/traditional-hunting-gets-headlines-but-is-not-the-big-threat-to-turtles-and-dugongs-69038.

Marsh H., A.N.M. Harris, and I.R. Lawler. 1997. The sustainability of the Indigenous dugong fishery in Torres Strait, Australia/Papua New Guinea. *Conservation Biology*, 11: 1375–86.

Marsh, H., T.J. O'Shea, and J.E. Reynolds III. 2011. *The ecology and conservation of Sirenia: Dugongs and manatees*. Cambridge University Press.

Marsh, H. and S. Sobtzick. 2015. Dugong dugon. *The IUCN red list of threatened species 2015*: e.T6909A43792211. http://dx.doi.org/10.2305/IUCN.UK.2015-4.RLTS.T6909A43792211.en.

Martindale, A., and C.G. Armstrong. 2019. The vulnerability of archaeological logic in Aboriginal rights and title cases in Canada: Theoretical and empirical implications. *Collaborative Anthropologies*, 11(2): 55–91.

McGuire, R.H. 2008. *Archaeology as political action*. University of California Press.

–. 2014. Working class archaeology. In S. Atalay, L.R. Clauss, R.H. McGuire, and J.R. Welch (Eds.), *Transforming archaeology: Activist practices and prospects* (pp. 115–31). Left Coast Press.

McGuire, R.H., M. O'Donovan, and L. Wurst. 2005. Probing praxis in archaeology: The last eighty years. *Rethinking Marxism*, 17(3): 355–72.

McMillan, A.D., and E. Yellowhorn. 2004. *First Peoples in Canada*. Douglas and McIntyre.

McNiven, I.J. 2010. Navigating the human-animal divide: Marine mammal hunters and rituals of sensory allurement. *World Archaeology, 42*(2): 215–30.

–. 2016. Theoretical challenges of Indigenous archaeology: Setting an agenda. *American Antiquity, 81*(1): 27–41.

–. 2023. Dugong and turtle as kin: Relational ontologies and archaeological perspectives on ritualised hunting by coastal Indigenous Australians. In I.J. McNiven and B. David (Eds.), *Oxford handbook of the archaeology of Indigenous Australia and New Guinea* (993–1022). Oxford University Press.

McNiven, I.J., and A.C. Bedingfield. 2008. Past and present marine mammal hunting rates and abundances: Dugong (*Dugong dugon*) evidence from Dabangai Bone Mound, Torres Strait. *Journal of Archaeological Science, 35*: 505–15.

McNiven, I.J., and S.P. Connaughton. 2019. Cultural heritage management and the colonial culture. In Claire Smith (Ed.), *Encyclopedia of global archaeology* (pp. 1–9). Springer. https://doi.org/10.1007/978-3- 319-51726-1_1222-3.

McNiven, I.J., B. David, T. Richards, K. Aplin, B. Asmussen, J. Mialanes, M. Leavesley, P. Faulkner, and S. Ulm. 2011. New direction in human colonisation of the Pacific: Lapita settlement of south coast New Guinea. *Australian Archaeology, 72*: 1–6.

McNiven, I.J., B. David, T. Richards, C. Rowe, M. Leavesley, J. Mialanes, S.P. Connaughton, B. Barker, K. Aplin, B. Asmussen, P. Faulkner, and S. Ulm. 2012. Lapita on the south coast of Papua New Guinea: Challenging new horizons in Pacific archaeology. *Australian Archaeology, 75*: 16–22.

McNiven, I.J., and L. Russell. 2005. *Appropriated pasts: Indigenous peoples and the colonial culture of archaeology*. AltaMira Press.

Meskell, L. 2005. Archaeological ethnography: Conversations around Kruger National Park. *Archaeologies: Journal of the World Archaeological Congress, 1*(1): 81–100.

Meskell, L., and P. Pels (Eds.). 2005. *Embedding ethics: Shifting boundaries of the anthropological profession*. Berg.

Mickel, A. 2021. *Why those who shovel are silent: A history of local archaeological knowledge and labor*. University Press of Colorado.

Million, T. 2005. Developing an Aboriginal archaeology: Receiving gifts from White Buffalo Calf Woman. In C. Smith and H. Martin Wobst (Eds.), *Indigenous archaeologies: Decolonizing theory and practice* (pp. 43–55). Routledge.

Mohs, G. 1994. Sto:lo sacred ground. In D.L. Carmichael, J. Hubert, and B. Reeves (Eds.), *Sacred sites, sacred places* (pp. 184–208). Routledge.

Morin, J., T.C.A. Royle, H. Zhang, C. Speller, M. Alcaide, R. Morin, M. Ritchie, A. Cannon, Mic. George, Mi. George, and D. Yang. 2021. Indigenous sex-selective salmon harvesting demonstrates pre-contact marine resource management in Burrard Inlet, British Columbia, Canada. *Scientific Reports, 11*: 21160. https://doi.org/10.1038/s41598-021-00154-4.

Morton, H. 1996. *Becoming Tongan: An ethnography of childhood*. University of Hawai'i Press.

Napoleon, V. 2013. Thinking about Indigenous legal orders. In R. Provost and C. Sheppard (Eds.), *Dialogues on human rights and legal pluralism* (pp. 229–45). Springer.

Native American Graves Protection and Repatriation Act (NAGPRA 1990). Pub. L. 101-601, 25 USC 3001 et seq., 104 Stat. 3048.

Nicholas, G.P. 1997. Education and empowerment: Archaeology with, for, and by the Shuswap Nation, British Columbia. In G.P. Nicholas and T.D. Andrews (Eds.), *At a crossroads: Archaeology and First Peoples in Canada* (pp. 85–104). Simon Fraser University Archaeology Press.

–. 2006. Decolonizing the Archaeological landscape: The practice and politics of archaeology in British Columbia. *American Indian Quarterly*, 30(3): 350–80.

–. 2007. Editor's notes: On archaeology and the "burden" of responsibility. *Canadian Journal of Archaeology*, 31(2): iii–vi.

–. (Ed). 2010. *Being and becoming Indigenous archaeologists*. Left Coast Press.

–. 2014. Reconciling inequalities in archaeological practice and heritage research. In S. Atalay, L.R. Clauss, R.H. McGuire, and J.R. Welch (Eds.), *Transforming archaeology: Activist practices and prospects* (pp. 133–58). Left Coast Press.

–. 2017a. Culture, rights, indigeneity and intervention: Addressing inequality in Indigenous heritage protection and control. In C. Hillerdal, A. Karlström, and C.G. Ojala (Eds.), *Archaeologies of "us" and "them": Debating history, heritage, and Indigeneity* (pp. 199–216). Routledge.

–. 2017b. Touching the intangible: Reconsidering material culture in the realm of Indigenous cultural property research. In J. Anderson and H. Geismar (Eds.), *The Routledge companion to cultural property* (pp. 212–31). Routledge.

–. 2018a, February 14. *It's taken thousands of years, but Western science is finally catching up to Traditional Knowledge*. The Conversation. http://theconversation.com/its-taken-thousands-of-years-but-western-science-is-finally-catching-up-to-traditional-knowledge-90291.

–. 2018b, September 9. *Protecting heritage is a human right*. The Conversation. https://theconversation.com/protecting-heritage-is-a-human-right-99501.

Nicholas, G.P., and T.D. Andrews (Eds.). 1997a. *At a crossroads: Archaeology and First Peoples in Canada*. Simon Fraser University Archaeology Press.

–. 1997b. Indigenous archaeology in the postmodern world. In G.P. Nicholas and T.D. Andrews (Eds.), *At a crossroads: Archaeology and First Peoples in Canada* (pp. 1–18). Simon Fraser University Archaeology Press.

Nicholas, G.P., B. Egan, K. Bannister, and E. Benson. 2015. Intervention as a strategy in protecting Indigenous cultural heritage. *SAA Archaeological Record*, 15(4): 41–47.

Nicholas, G.P., J.R. Welch, and E.C. Yellowhorn. 2008. Collaborative encounters. In C. Colwell-Chanthaphonh and T.J. Ferguson (Eds.), *Collaboration in archaeo-*

logical practice: Engaging descendant communities (pp. 273–98). AltaMira Press.

Noble, B. 2016. *Learning to listen: Snapshots of Aboriginal participation in environmental assessments*. Macdonald-Laurier Institute.

O'Day, S.J. 2004. *The socioeconomics of rank in late prehistoric and contemporary Fiji: An exploration of ethnographic and archaeological indicators*. Unpublished PhD dissertation, University of Florida.

Orwell, G. 1949. *Nineteen eighty-four*. Secker and Warburg.

Otto, T., and R. Willerslev. 2013. Prologue. Value as theory: Value, action, and critique. *HAU: Journal of Ethnographic Theory, 3*(2): 1–10.

Rex [Alex Golub]. 2010, June 3. *Indigenes or citizens in Papua New Guinea*. Savage minds: Note and queries in anthropology. http://savageminds.org/2010/06/03/indigenes-or-citizens-in-papua-new-guinea.

Richards, T., B. David, K. Aplin, and I.J. McNiven (Eds.). 2016. *Archaeological research at Caution Bay, Papua New Guinea: Cultural, linguistic, and environmental setting*. Archaeopress.

Rizvi, U., and J. Lydon. 2010. *Handbook on postcolonialism and archaeology*. Left Coast Press.

Robbins, B. 2017. *The beneficiary*. Duke University Press.

Robinson, M.P. 1996. Shampoo archaeology: Towards a participatory action research approach in civil society. *Canadian Journal of Native Studies, 16*(1): 125–38.

Royal Commission on Aboriginal Peoples. 1996. Volume 3, *Gathering strength*. Ottawa.

Royal Commission on Aboriginal Peoples. 1996. Volume 5, *Renewal: A twenty-year commitment*. Ottawa.

Sabloff, J. 2008. *Archaeology matters: Action archaeology in the modern world*. Left Coast Press.

Sahlins, M. 1985. *Islands of history*. University of Chicago Press.

Sassaman, K.E. 1993. *Early pottery in the Southeast: Tradition and innovation in cooking technology*. University of Alabama Press.

–. 2006. *People of the shoals: Stallings culture of the Savannah River Valley*. University Press of Florida.

Schaepe, D.M. 2007. Stó:lo identity and the cultural landscape of S'ólh Téméxw. In Bruce Granville Miller (Ed.), *Be of good mind: Essays on the Coast Salish* (pp. 234–59). UBC Press.

–. 2018, January 11. Public heritage as transformative experience: The co-occupation of place and decision-making. In A.M. Labrador and N.A. Silberman (Eds.), *The Oxford handbook of public heritage theory and practice*. Oxford Academic. DOI: 10.1093/oxfordhb/9780190676315.013.28.

Schaepe, D.M., B. Angelbeck, D. Snook, and J.R. Welch. 2017. Archaeology as therapy connecting belongings, knowledge, time, place, and well-being. *Current Anthropology, 58*(4): 502–33.

Schmidt, P.R. 2010. Social memory and trauma in northwestern Tanzania: Organic, spontaneous community collaboration. *Journal of Social Archaeology*, 10: 255–79.

Sewell, D. 2017, November 19. Mungo man: The final journey of our 40,000-year-old ancestor. *Guardian*. https://www.theguardian.com/australia-news/2017/nov/19/mungo-man-the-final-journey-of-our-40000-year-old-ancestor.

Shanks, M., and R. McGuire. 1996. The craft of archaeology. *American Antiquity*, 61(1): 75–88.

Shaver, J.H., and R. Sosis. 2014. How does male ritual behavior vary across the lifespan? An examination of Fijian kava ceremonies. *Human Nature*, 25: 136–60. DOI: 10.1007/s12110-014-9191-6.

Silliman, S.W. (Ed.). 2008. *Collaborating at the trowel's edge: Teaching and learning in Indigenous archaeology*. University of Arizona Press.

Simpson, A. 2014. *Mohawk interruptus: Political life across the borders of settler states*. Duke University Press.

Simpson, L.B. 2017. *As we have always done: Indigenous freedom through radical resistance*. University of Minnesota Press.

Sissons, J. 2005. *First Peoples: Indigenous cultures and their futures*. Reaktion Books.

Smith, C., and H.M. Wobst (Eds.). 2005. *Indigenous archaeologies: Decolonising theory and practice*. Routledge.

Smith, L. 1994. Heritage management as postprocessual archaeology. *Antiquity*, 68: 300–9.

–. 2004. *Archaeological theory and the politics of cultural heritage*. Routledge.

Smith, L.T. 2005. On tricky ground: Researching the Native in the age of uncertainty. In N.K. Denzin and Y.S. Lincoln (Eds.), *The Sage handbook of qualitative research* (pp. 85–107). Sage Publications.

–. 2012. *Decolonizing methodologies: Research and Indigenous peoples*. (2nd ed.). Zed Books.

Smith, L.T., E. Tuck, and K.W. Yang (Eds.). 2019. *Indigenous and decolonizing studies in education: Mapping the long view*. Routledge.

Spice, A. 2016, December 22. *Interrupting industrial and academic extraction on Native land*. Society for Cultural Anthropology. https://culanth.org/fieldsights/interrupting-industrial-and-academic-extraction-on-native-land.

–. 2018. Fighting invasive infrastructures: Indigenous relations against pipelines. *Environment and Society*, 9: 40–56.

Spurling, B.E. 1986. *Archaeological resource management in Western Canada: A policy sciences approach*. Unpublished Ph.D. dissertation, Simon Fraser University.

Steeves, P. 2015. Academia, archaeology, CRM, and tribal historic preservation. *Archaeologies: Journal of the World Archaeological Congress*, 11(1): 121–41.

–. 2017. Unpacking neoliberal archaeological control of ancient Indigenous heritage. *Archaeologies: Journal of the World Archaeological Congress*, 13(1): 48–65.

–. 2021. *The Indigenous palaeolithic of the Western hemisphere*. Nebraska University Press.

Stryd, A.H., and M. Eldridge. 1993. CMT archaeology in British Columbia: The Meares Island Studies. *BC Studies*, 99: 184–234.

Supernant, K. 2020. Grand challenge no. 1: Truth and reconciliation archaeological pedagogy, Indigenous histories, and reconciliation in Canada. *Journal of Archaeology and Education*, 4(3). https://digitalcommons.library.umaine.edu/jae/vol4/iss3/2.

Supernant, K., J.E. Baxter, N. Lyons, and S. Atalay (Eds.). 2020. *Archaeologies of the heart*. Springer International Publishing.

Sutton, D. 2004. Anthropology's value(s). *Anthropological Theory*, 4(3): 372–78.

Swidler, N., K. Dongoske, and A. Downer. 1997. *Native Americans and archaeologists: Stepping stones to common ground*. AltaMira Press.

Tabar, L., and C. Desai 2017. Decolonization is a global project: From Palestine to the Americas. *Decolonization: Indigeneity, Education Society*, 6(1): i–xix.

Tax, S. 1975. Action anthropology. *Current Anthropology*, 16(4): 514–17.

Thomas, K.R. 2019. *The toolstone formerly known as green andesite: A geochemical characterization of fine-grained lithic materials from the Burrard Inlet area, Vancouver, B.C. Canada*. Unpublished MA thesis, University of British Columbia.

Thompson, L. 1940. *Southern Lau, Fiji: An ethnography*. B.P. Bishop Museum Bulletin 162.

Trigger, B.G. 1980. Archaeology and the image of the American Indian. *American Antiquity*, 45(4): 662–76.

–. 2000. *A history of archaeological thought*. Cambridge University Press.

Truth and Reconciliation Commission of Canada. 2015. *Truth and Reconciliation Commission of Canada: Calls to action*. http://www.trc.ca/websites/trcinstitution/File/2015/Findings/Calls_to_Action_English2.pdf.

Tsilhqot'in Nation v. British Columbia. 2014 SCC 44 (June 26, 2014).

Tsing, A.L. 2015. *The mushroom at the end of the world: On the possibility of life in capitalist ruins*. Princeton University Press.

Tuck, E., and K.W. Yang. 2012. Decolonization is not a metaphor. *Decolonization: Indigeneity, Education & Society*, 1(1): 1–40.

Turner, N.J., C.G. Armstrong, and D. Lepofsky. 2021. Adopting a root: Documenting ecological and cultural signatures of plant translocations in northwestern North America. *American Anthropologist*, 124(4): 1–19.

Two Bears, D.R. 2008. 'Íhoosh'aah, learning by doing: The Navajo Nation Archaeology Department Student Training Program. In S.W. Silliman (Ed.), *Collaborating at the trowel's edge: Teaching and learning in Indigenous archaeology* (pp. 188–207). University of Arizona Press.

United Nations (General Assembly). 2007. Declaration on the rights of Indigenous People.

Urwin, C., I.J. McNiven, S. Clarke, L. Macquarie, and T. Whap. 2016. Hearing the evidence: Using archaeological data to analyse the long-term impacts of dugong (Dugong dogon) hunting on Mabuyag, Torres Strait, over the past 1000 years. *Australian Archaeology*, 82(3): 201–17.

Voss, B.L. 2012. Curation as research: A case study in orphaned and underreported archaeological collections. *Archaeological Dialogues*, 19(2): 145–69.

Watkins, J. 2001. *Indigenous archaeology: American Indian values and scientific practice*. AltaMira Press.

–. 2003. Beyond the margins. *American Antiquity*, 68(2): 273–85.

–. 2005. Through wary eyes: Indigenous perspectives on archaeology. *Annual Review of Anthropology*, 34: 429–49.

Weil, M.E. 1978. A Canadian perspective on legislation and the role of the private sector in archaeology. *Historical Archaeology*, 12: 51–57.

Weiner, J.L. 1991, December Colonial engagement in Third World oil extraction: Some examples from Papua New Guinea. *World Energy Council Journal*: 69–74.

Welch, J.R., and N. Ferris. 2014. "We have met the enemy and it is us": Transforming archaeology through sustainable design. In S. Atalay, L.R. Clauss, R.H. McGuire, and J.R. Welch (Eds.), *Transforming archaeology: Activist practices and prospects* (pp. 91–114). Left Coast Press.

West, P. 2016. *Dispossession and the environment: Rhetoric and inequality in Papua New Guinea*. Columbia University Press.

White, E. (Xanius). 2006. *Heiltsuk stone fish traps: Products of my ancestors' labour*. Unpublished MA thesis, Simon Fraser University.

White, S. 2021, June 1. *No longer "the disappeared": Mourning the 215 children found in graves at Kamloops Indian Residential School*. The Conversation. https://theconversation.com/no-longer-the-disappeared-mourning-the-215-children-found-in-graves-at-kamloops-indian-residential-school-161782.

Wickwire, W. 1992. Ethnology and archaeology as ideology: The case of the Stein River Valley. *BC Studies*, 91–92: 51–78.

Willey, G.R., and P. Phillips. 1958. *Method and theory in American archaeology*. University of Chicago Press.

Wilson, A.C. 2004. Reclaiming our humanity: Decolonization and the recovery of Indigenous knowledge. In D.A. Mihesuah and A.C. Wilson (Eds.), *Indigenizing the academy: Transforming scholarship and empowering communities* (pp. 69–87). University of Nebraska Press.

Wilson, H.A. 1996. *European thought from Locke to Lenin*. (2nd ed.). McGraw-Hill.

Wilson, J. 2016. "Belongings" in "c̓əsnaʔəm: the city before the city." IPinCH intellectual property issues in cultural heritage: Theory, practice, policy, ethics. Blog entry, January 27, 2016, https://www.sfu.ca/ipinch/outputs/blog/citybeforecitybelongings/, accessed June 23, 2022.

Wilson, S. 2008. *Research is ceremony: Indigenous research methods*. Fernwood Publishing.

Wolfe, P. 2006. Settler colonialism and the elimination of the native. *Journal of Genocide Research*, 8(4): 387–409.

–. 2016. *Traces of history: Elementary structures of race*. Verso.

World Bank. 2024. https://www.worldbank.org/en/home.

Wylie, A. 2003. On ethics. In Larry J. Zimmerman, Karen D. Vitelli, and Julie Hollowell-Zimmer (Eds.), *Ethical Issues in Archaeology* (pp. 3–16). AltaMira Press.

–. 2015. A plurality of pluralisms: Collaborative practice in archaeology. In F. Padovani, A. Richardson, and J.Y. Tsou (Eds.), *Objectivity in science: New perspectives from science and technology studies* (pp. 189–210). Springer.

Yellowhorn, E. 2002. *Awakening internalist archaeology in the Aboriginal world.* Unpublished PhD dissertation, McGill University.

–. 2006. The awakening of internalist archaeology in the Aboriginal world. In R. Williamson (Ed.), *Archaeology of Bruce Trigger: Theoretical empiricism* (pp. 194–209). McGill-Queen's University Press.

–. 2012. Brave new digs: Archaeology and Aboriginal people in British Columbia, Canada. *Canadian Journal of Native Studies, 32*: 87–99.

Yukon Historic Resources Act. RSY 2002, c.109.

Zimmerman, L.J. 1989. Made radical by my own: An archaeologist learns to understand reburial. In R. Layton (Ed.), *Conflict in the archaeology of living traditions* (pp. 60–67). Unwin Hyman.

Zimmerman, L.J., K.D. Vitelli, and J. Hollowell-Zimmer (Eds.). 2003. *Ethical issues in archaeology*. AltaMira Press.

Zorzin, N. 2014. Heritage management and Aboriginal Australians: Relations in a global, neoliberal economy – A contemporary case study from Victoria. *Archaeologies: Journal of the World Archaeological Congress, 10*(2): 132–67.

–. 2015. Archaeology and capitalism: Successful relationship or economic and ethical alienation? In C. Gnecco and D. Lippert (Eds.), *Ethics and archaeological praxis* (Vol. 1) (pp. 115–39). Springer.

Index

Note: "(f)" after a page number indicates a figure.

Aboriginal Rights and Title, 4, 11–12, 73, 91, 111, 189*n*2, 190*n*11, 195*n*4
accountability, 93, 95, 106, 126, 176(f); and colonialism, 181–82; relational, 124–27, 139, 163–64
Adams, Clyde, 139
Aiwa Lailai, 23
Aiwa Levu, 23, 30(f)
anthropology, 9, 14, 18–19, 20–21, 27, 135, 150–51, 188, 191*n*4; anthropological archaeologist, 18–20, 28, 117; blog Anthro[dendum], 44; four-field, 32–33
anticolonial approaches, 111, 123, 134, 136, 183–84
Arabo, Nick, 51–52, 55, 193*n*6, 193*n*7
Archaeological and Historic Sites Protection Act, 63
archaeology: community-based, 27, 123, 160, 163; "do the archaeology for free," 198*n*5; ethnoarchaeology, 21; facilitating, 14–15; internalist, 146–49; post-processual, 20; processual, 20–21; reimagining of, 14, 101, 143, 160, 163, 175; tasks associated with, 9. *See also* anthropology; compassionate archaeology
Archaeology Branch, 10, 64, 66–67, 68(f), 69–73, 75–76, 77(f), 78, 83, 96, 107, 110–11, 120, 134–35, 153, 155–56, 165, 168–70, 175, 177, 182, 185, 187, 190*n*5, 190*n*11, 195*n*5, 195*n*11, 198*n*6, 199*n*3
Atalay, Sonya, 89, 112, 123, 133, 144, 160–61
Atleo, Cliff, 119–20
Atleo, E.R., 112
axiology. *See* accountability

Baldwin, James, 183
betel nut (also *buai*), 193*n*6; ExxonMobil policies on, 39

Bill 41. *See* Declaration on the Rights of Indigenous Peoples (DRIPA)
Brown, Adrienne Maree, 113–14

Call to Actions (of Truth and Reconciliation Commission), 90, 94, 96, 102, 113, 142, 153, 174, 186
capitalism, 8, 14–15, 38, 41, 59, 62, 68(f), 95, 101, 103, 113, 118–22, 136–37, 140, 142, 160, 170, 173, 177–79; development capitalism, 14, 59, 77(f), 95, 101, 103, 160, 195n5, 197n5
closeness, 59, 124, 188
Coffey Natural Systems, 36–40, 46, 54–58, 193n8, 194n19
community-based participatory research (CBPR), 160–61, 168
compassionate archaeology, 15, 20, 113–14, 116, 125, 134, 137, 143–44, 166, 176(f), 177, 188
Coulthard, Glen Sean, 13
COVID-19, 82–83
cultural resource management (CRM): definition of, 4; firms, 5–6; Indigenous representation within, 79–80, 83–84, 105, 113, 168, 176(f), 198n4; origins of, 6–9, 61; process of, 10, 15, 21, 60, 62, 65, 67, 68(f), 74, 124–26, 149–51, 179–80, 188, 189n4; safety within, 45; "teachers," 76, 77(f), 78, 195n9, 88; working in, 5–7, 14, 58, 132
cultural shell deposits, 3–4, 25; creation of in Fiji, 32
culture, definition of, 19, 191n1

David, Bruno, 37
Davis, Wade, 122
Declaration on the Rights of Indigenous Peoples Act (DRIPA), 64, 96, 102, 142, 146, 154–55, 157, 162, 177, 185, 187; BC Provincial DRIPA Action Plan 4.35, 103, 177; Section 3 of, 156–57; Section 7 of, 142, 155–56, 186
decolonization, 15, 93, 96, 110–11, 123, 160; as a metaphor, 14, 136; uncertainty around, 90, 110–12, 136, 155–56
Delgamuukw v. British Columbia, 146
Deloria, Jr., Vine, 20, 144–46
Dickinson, Martin F., 35
direct historical approach, 28, 147
dispossession, 12–13, 72, 170, 179; in Papua New Guinea, 40, 44
Doctrine of Discovery, 110
dugong, 129–31

Elliot, Dan, 25
enculturation, 19, 94
ethnography, 18, 31–32, 183
Everson, Charlene, 161–62
ExxonMobil, 36, 38–40, 42, 54–60; observations from the field, 39; safety culture and rules, 44–47, 193n6; wages, 49–50

Finkelstein, Maura, 109
free, prior, and informed consent (FPIC), 10, 42–43, 73, 81, 102–3, 105, 157, 175, 176(f)

Glendale, Jr., Harold, 128, 131–32, 133(f)
Glendale, Nolan Puglas, 128, 131–32
Goodyear, Al, 25
Grace Islet, 71–73
Graeber, David, 115–17
Green, Roger, 32

Hall, Robert, L., 147–48
Heritage Conservation Act (HCA), 3, 6–7, 9, 14, 64–65, 67–73, 76–77, 82,

103, 111, 155, 161–62, 182, 194*n*1, 195*n*4, 199*n*2; compliance with, 6; overhaul of, 157, 177, 185–87; overview of the act, 4–5, 62, 155; permits under, 69–70, 109; power of, 65, 106, 196*n*3; Section 4 of, 65, 141–42, 156, 186
Historical Resources Act (HRA), 63
Homoka, Iava, 48, 49(f), 53–55, 193*n*6, 193*n*7
Hurston, Zora Neale, 18

Indian Act (1876), 11, 140, 182
Indian Removal Act (1830), 192*n*10
Indigenous lands, unceded, ix, 5, 10–12, 60, 73, 76, 81, 89, 102, 120, 134, 153, 167, 170, 174–75, 197*n*5
Indigenous law, 12, 14, 73, 129, 152–53, 162, 184
Inlailawatash, 172–75
intangible heritage, 5, 70, 79, 97, 107, 130, 135, 147, 157–58, 164, 169, 172, 177, 187
Irlbacher-Fox, Stephanie, 89–90

Jackson, Andrew, 26, 192*n*10
Jennings, Chris, 56–57
Jones, Sharyn, 21–22, 24–25, 27–29, 32–33

kava, 23–24, 30
Kewibu, Vincent, 50–51
Kirch, Patrick, 32
Klassen, Michael, 7, 65
Knauft, Bruce, 43
Kove, Evanee, 193*n*7
Kunst'aa guu – Kunst'aayah Reconciliation Protocol, 158

Lakeba Island, 22
Lau Group, 17, 25; Southern Lau Group, 28

Leavesley, Matthew, 51
liberalism, 117–18
Liboiron, Max, 136, 170

Mandui, Herman, 51
Matararaba, Sepeti (Mata), 22–23, 30(f)
McNiven, Ian, 37, 51, 56–57, 103, 123, 160
Melanesia, 17
Melbourne, FL, 18, 19(f)
Menson, Menson, 49(f)
Ministry of Forests (MoF), BC, 64, 66, 71, 198*n*6, 195*n*5
Monash University, 36
Morea, Lahui, 48, 49(f), 53–54, 193*n*6, 193*n*7

Native American Graves Protection and Repatriation Act (NAGPRA), 26, 150
Nayau Island, 23, 27, 28, 29; Namasimasi, 29, 31
neoliberalism, 118–21

O'Day, Patrick, 22, 24–25, 29, 32–33
Orwell, George, 89

Paul, Dennis, 139
permits, site alteration, 7
place-based learning, xii, 12, 31, 59, 85–86, 166
PNG LNG Project, 36–37, 51
Point, Terry, 139–40
Polynesia, 17
Provincial Archaeological Inventory Database, 66–67, 107
Provincial Archaeological Resource Library (PARL), 67

Ratu Mara, 23
relationality, 121–22, 124–25, 163–64

Remote Access to Archaeological Data (RADD). *See* Provincial Archaeological Inventory Database
Richards, Tom, 37
Rowe, Cassandra, 53
Russell, Lynette, 103, 123, 160

Sambua, Kim, 193*n*7
Sassaman, Ken, 24, 25, 26
sevusevu, 23–24
Shaw, Ben, 56–57
Simon Fraser University, 21
Simonsen, Bjorn, 66
Simpson, Audra, 13
Smith, Linda Tuhiwai, 160
Stallings Island, 25, 26
Stanford, Dennis, 25
Starke, FL, 18, 19(f)
Steeves, Paulette, 123, 144, 148–53, 160
Stó:lō Research and Resource Management Centre (SRRMC), 108, 172

Tai Kabara, 17
tangible heritage, 8–9, 70, 95, 97–101, 157, 169
terra nullius, 110
Tolana, Tedy, 48, 49(f), 53–55, 193*n*6, 193*n*7

Torres Strait, 130–31
Trail of Tears, 26
Tribal Historic Preservation (THP) programs, 150–51
Tsilhqot'in Nation v. British Columbia, 111
Tubou, 22

United Nations Declaration on the Rights of Indigenous Peoples (UNDRIP), 42–43, 64, 95–96, 153, 174
University of Florida, 21, 24, 26, 32, 35
University of Papua New Guinea (UPNG), 37, 39, 50–52

Vagi, Pune, 55, 193*n*7
Voss, Barbara, 109

Wayne, Lucy B., 35
West, Paige, 42
Williams, Tia, 139
Wilson, Harold, 118
Wilson, Jordan, 139
Wilson, Shawn, 123–25, 134, 160
Wylie, Alison, 126

Yellowhorn, Eldon, 144, 146–48
Yukon Historic Resources Act, 63

Printed and bound in Canada

Set in Sabon and Myriad by Julie Cochrane

Copy editor: Barbara Tessman

Cover designer: Alexa Love

Authorized Representative:
Easy Access System Europe
Mustamäe tee 50, 10621 Tallinn, Estonia
gpsr.requests@easproject.com